P9-CLX-538

POPE'S *EPISTLE TO BATHURST*

POPE'S
EPISTLE TO BATHURST

A Critical Reading
with
An Edition of the Manuscripts

by Earl R. Wasserman

The Johns Hopkins Press: Baltimore

Distributed in Great Britain by Oxford University Press, London

Printed in the United States of America

Library of Congress Catalog Card Number: 60–12741

This book has been brought to publication with the assistance of a grant from The Ford Foundation.

Table of Contents

Epistle to Bathurst: The Text

EPISTLE

TO ALLEN LORD BATHURST

OF THE USE OF RICHES *

Who shall decide, when Doctors disagree,
And soundest Casuists doubt, like you and me?
You hold the word, from Jove to Momus giv'n,
That Man was made the standing jest of Heav'n;
5 And Gold but sent to keep the fools in play,
For some to heap, and some to throw away.
But I, who think more highly of our kind,
(And surely, Heav'n and I are of a mind)
Opine, that Nature, as in duty bound,
10 Deep hid the shining mischief under ground:
But when by Man's audacious labour won,
Flam'd forth this rival to, its Sire, the Sun,
Then careful Heav'n supply'd two sorts of Men,
To squander these, and those to hide agen.
15 Like Doctors thus, when much dispute has past,
We find our tenets just the same at last.
Both fairly owning, Riches in effect
No grace of Heav'n or token of th' Elect;
Giv'n to the Fool, the Mad, the Vain, the Evil,
20 To Ward, to Waters, Chartres, and the Devil.
What Nature wants, commodious Gold bestows,
'Tis thus we eat the bread another sows:
But how unequal it bestows, observe,

* This text, which is the basis of the following analysis of the poem, is the one that appears in F. W. Bateson's edition in the Twickenham Pope. It represents the readings of the "death-bed" text of 1744, but without those omissions, additions, and alterations for which Warburton no doubt was responsible. Mr. Bateson's reasons for claiming that his text represents Pope's last version of the poem seem entirely valid. His version of the text is here modified slightly by collation with the "death-bed" edition.

Pope's extensive notes to the poem are also available in Bateson's edition and have not been reproduced here. Nor has any attempt been made in this study to repeat information about the poem collected in Bateson's own annotations.

The first edition of the *Epistle*, dated 1732, is reproduced at the end of this volume.

'Tis thus we riot, while who sow it, starve.
25 What Nature wants (a phrase I much distrust)
Extends to Luxury, extends to Lust:
And if we count among the Needs of life
Another's Toil, why not another's Wife?
Useful, I grant, it serves what life requires,
30 But dreadful too, the dark Assassin hires:
Trade it may help, Society extend;
But lures the Pyrate, and corrupts the Friend:
It raises Armies in a Nation's aid,
But bribes a Senate, and the Land's betray'd.
35 Oh! that such bulky Bribes as all might see,
Still, as of old, incumber'd Villainy!
In vain may Heroes fight, and Patriots rave;
If secret Gold saps on from knave to knave.
Could France or Rome divert our brave designs,
40 With all their brandies or with all their wines?
What could they more than Knights and Squires confound,
Or water all the Quorum ten miles round?
A Statesman's slumbers how this speech would spoil!
" Sir, Spain has sent a thousand jars of oil;
45 " Huge bales of British cloth blockade the door;
" A hundred oxen at your levee roar."
Poor Avarice one torment more would find;
Nor could Profusion squander all in kind.
Astride his cheese Sir Morgan might we meet,
50 And Worldly crying coals from street to street,
(Whom with a wig so wild, and mien so maz'd,
Pity mistakes for some poor tradesman craz'd).
Had Colepepper's whole wealth been hops and hogs,
Could he himself have sent it to the dogs?
55 His Grace will game: to White's a Bull be led,
With spurning heels and with a butting head.
To White's be carried, as to ancient games,
Fair Coursers, Vases, and alluring Dames.
Shall then Uxorio, if the stakes he sweep,
60 Bear home six Whores, and make his Lady weep?
Or soft Adonis, so perfum'd and fine,
Drive to St. James's a whole herd of swine?
Oh filthy check on all industrious skill,
To spoil the nation's last great trade, Quadrille!
65 Once, we confess, beneath the Patriot's cloak,
From the crack'd bag the dropping Guinea spoke,
And gingling down the backstairs, told the crew,
" Old Cato is as great a Rogue as you."
Blest paper-credit! last and best supply!
70 That lends Corruption lighter wings to fly!
Gold imp'd by thee, can compass hardest things,

Can pocket States, can fetch or carry Kings;
A single leaf shall waft an Army o'er,
Or ship off Senates to a distant Shore;
75 A leaf, like Sibyl's, scatter to and fro
Our fates and fortunes, as the winds shall blow:
Pregnant with thousands flits the Scrap unseen,
And silent sells a King, or buys a Queen.
Since then, my Lord, on such a World we fall,
80 What say you? "Say? Why take it, Gold and all."
What Riches give us let us then enquire,
Meat, Fire, and Cloaths. What more? Meat, Cloaths, and Fire.
Is this too little? would you more than live?
Alas! 'tis more than Turner finds they give.
85 Alas! 'tis more than (all his Visions past)
Unhappy Wharton, waking, found at last!
What can they give? to dying Hopkins Heirs;
To Chartres, Vigour; Japhet, Nose and Ears?
Can they, in gems bid pallid Hippia glow,
90 In Fulvia's buckle ease the throbs below,
Or heal, old Narses, thy obscener ail,
With all th'embroid'ry plaister'd at thy tail?
They might (were Harpax not too wise to spend)
Give Harpax self the blessing of a Friend;
95 Or find some Doctor that would save the life
Of wretched Shylock, spite of Shylock's Wife:
But thousands die, without or this or that,
Die, and endow a College, or a Cat:
To some, indeed, Heaven grants the happier fate,
100 T'enrich a Bastard, or a Son they hate.
Perhaps you think the Poor might have their part?
Bond damns the Poor, and hates them from his heart:
The grave Sir Gilbert holds it for a rule,
That "every man in want is knave or fool:"
105 "God cannot love (says Blunt, with tearless eyes)
"The wretch he starves"—and piously denies:
But the good Bishop, with a meeker air,
Admits, and leaves them, Providence's care.
Yet, to be just to these poor men of pelf,
110 Each does but hate his Neighbour as himself:
Damn'd to the Mines, an equal fate betides
The Slave that digs it, and the Slave that hides.
Who suffer thus, mere Charity should own,
Must act on motives pow'rful, tho' unknown:
115 Some War, some Plague, or Famine they foresee,
Some Revelation hid from you and me.
Why Shylock wants a meal, the cause is found,
He thinks a Loaf will rise to fifty pound.
What made Directors cheat in South-sea year?

120 To live on Ven'son when it sold so dear.
Ask you why Phryne the whole Auction buys?
Phryne foresees a general Excise.
Why she and Sappho raise that monstrous sum?
Alas! they fear a man will cost a plum.
125 Wise Peter sees the World's respect for Gold,
And therefore hopes this Nation may be sold:
Glorious Ambition! Peter, swell thy store,
And be what Rome's great Didius was before.
The Crown of Poland, venal twice an age,
130 To just three millions stinted modest Gage.
But nobler scenes Maria's dreams unfold,
Hereditary Realms, and worlds of Gold.
Congenial souls! whose life one Av'rice joins
And one fate buries in th' Asturian Mines.
135 Much injur'd Blunt! why bears he Britain's hate?
A wizard told him in these words our fate:
" At length Corruption, like a gen'ral flood,
" (So long by watchful Ministers withstood)
" Shall deluge all; and Av'rice creeping on,
140 " Spread like a low-born mist, and blot the Sun;
" Statesman and Patriot ply alike the stocks,
" Peeress and Butler share alike the Box,
" And Judges job, and Bishops bite the town,
" And mighty Dukes pack cards for half a crown.
145 " See Britain sunk in lucre's sordid charms,
" And France reveng'd of ANNE's and EDWARD's arms! "
'Twas no Court-badge, great Scriv'ner! fir'd thy brain,
Nor lordly Luxury, nor City Gain:
No, 'twas thy righteous end, asham'd to see
150 Senates degen'rate, Patriots disagree,
And nobly wishing Party-rage to cease,
To buy both sides, and give thy Country peace.
" All this is madness," cries a sober sage:
But who, my friend, has reason in his rage?
155 " The ruling Passion, be it what it will,
" The ruling Passion conquers Reason still."
Less mad the wildest whimsey we can frame,
Than ev'n that Passion, if it has no Aim;
For tho' such motives Folly you may call,
160 The Folly's greater to have none at all.
Hear then the truth: " 'Tis Heav'n each Passion sends,
" And diff'rent men directs to diff'rent ends.
" Extremes in Nature equal good produce,
" Extremes in Man concur to gen'ral use."
165 Ask we what makes one keep, and one bestow?
That POW'R who bids the Ocean ebb and flow,
Bids seed-time, harvest, equal course maintain,

Thro' reconcil'd extremes of drought and rain,
Builds Life on Death, on Change Duration founds,
170 And gives th' eternal wheels to know their rounds.
Riches, like insects, when conceal'd they lie,
Wait but for wings, and in their season, fly.
Who sees pale Mammon pine amidst his store,
Sees but a backward steward for the Poor;
175 This year a Reservoir, to keep and spare,
The next a Fountain, spouting thro' his Heir,
In lavish streams to quench a Country's thirst,
And men and dogs shall drink him 'till they burst.
Old Cotta sham'd his fortune and his birth,
180 Yet was not Cotta void of wit or worth:
What tho' (the use of barb'rous spits forgot)
His kitchen vy'd in coolness with his grot?
His court with nettles, moats with cresses stor'd,
With soups unbought and sallads blest his board.
185 If Cotta liv'd on pulse, it was no more
Than Bramins, Saints, and Sages did before;
To cram the Rich was prodigal expence,
And who would take the Poor from Providence:
Like some lone Chartreux stands the good old Hall,
190 Silence without, and Fasts within the wall;
No rafter'd roofs with dance and tabor sound,
No noontide-bell invites the country round;
Tenants with sighs the smoakless tow'rs survey,
And turn th' unwilling steeds another way:
195 Benighted wanderers, the forest o'er,
Curse the sav'd candle, and unop'ning door;
While the gaunt mastiff growling at the gate,
Affrights the beggar whom he longs to eat.
Not so his Son, he mark'd this oversight,
200 And then mistook reverse of wrong for right.
(For what to shun will no great knowledge need,
But what to follow, is a task indeed.)
What slaughter'd hecatombs, what floods of wine,
Fill the capacious Squire, and deep Divine!
205 Yet no mean motive this profusion draws,
His oxen perish in his country's cause;
'Tis GEORGE and LIBERTY that crowns the cup,
And Zeal for that great House which eats him up.
The Woods recede around the naked seat,
210 The Sylvans groan—no matter—for the Fleet:
Next goes his Wool—to clothe our valiant bands,
Last, for his Country's love, he sells his Lands.
To town he comes, completes the nation's hope,
And heads the bold Train-bands, and burns a Pope.
215 And shall not Britain now reward his toils,

Britain, that pays her Patriots with her Spoils?
In vain at Court the Bankrupt pleads his cause,
His thankless Country leaves him to her Laws.
The Sense to value Riches, with the Art
220 T'enjoy them, and the Virtue to impart,
Not meanly, nor ambitiously pursu'd,
Not sunk by sloth, nor rais'd by servitude;
To balance Fortune by a just expence,
Join with Œconomy, Magnificence;
225 With Splendour, Charity; with Plenty, Health;
Oh teach us, BATHURST! yet unspoil'd by wealth!
That secret rare, between th' extremes to move
Of mad Good-nature, and of mean Self-love.
To Worth or Want well-weigh'd, be Bounty giv'n,
230 And ease, or emulate, the care of Heav'n.
Whose measure full o'erflows on human race,
Mend Fortune's fault, and justify her grace.
Wealth in the gross is death, but life diffus'd;
As Poison heals, in just proportion us'd:
235 In heaps, like Ambergrise, a stink it lies,
But well-dispers'd, is Incense to the Skies.
Who starves by Nobles, or with Nobles eats?
The Wretch that trusts them, and the Rogue that cheats.
Is there a Lord, who knows a cheerful noon
240 Without a Fiddler, Flatt'rer, or Buffoon?
Whose table, Wit or modest Merit share,
Un-elbow'd by a Gamester, Pimp, or Play'r?
Who copies Your's, or OXFORD's better part,
To ease th' oppress'd, and raise the sinking heart?
245 Where-e'er he shines, oh Fortune, gild the scene,
And Angels guard him in the golden Mean!
There, English Bounty yet a-while may stand,
And Honour linger ere it leaves the land.
But all our praises why should Lords engross?
250 Rise, honest Muse! and sing the MAN of ROSS:
Pleas'd Vaga echoes thro' her winding bounds,
And rapid Severn hoarse applause resounds.
Who hung with woods yon mountain's sultry brow?
From the dry rock who bade the waters flow?
255 Not to the skies in useless columns tost,
Or in proud falls magnificently lost,
But clear and artless, pouring thro' the plain
Health to the sick, and solace to the swain.
Whose Cause-way parts the vale with shady rows?
260 Whose Seats the weary Traveller repose?
Who taught that heav'n-directed spire to rise?
The MAN of ROSS, each lisping babe replies.
Behold the Market-place with poor o'erspread!

The MAN of Ross divides the weekly bread:
265 He feeds yon Alms-house, neat, but void of state,
Where Age and Want sit smiling at the gate:
Him portion'd maids, apprentic'd orphans blest,
The young who labour, and the old who rest.
Is any sick? the MAN of Ross relieves,
270 Prescribes, attends, the med'cine makes, and gives.
Is there a variance? enter but his door,
Balk'd are the Courts, and contest is no more.
Despairing Quacks with curses fled the place,
And vile Attornies, now an useless race.
275 "Thrice happy man! enabled to pursue
"What all so wish, but want the pow'r to do!
"Oh say, what sums that gen'rous hand supply?
"What mines, to swell that boundless charity?"
Of Debts, and Taxes, Wife and Children clear,
280 This man possest—five hundred pounds a year.
Blush, Grandeur, blush! proud Courts, withdraw your blaze!
Ye little Stars! hide your diminish'd rays.
"And what? no monument, inscription, stone?
"His race, his form, his name almost unknown?"
285 Who builds a Church to God, and not to Fame,
Will never mark the marble with his Name:
Go, search it there, where to be born and die,
Of rich and poor makes all the history;
Enough, that Virtue fill'd the space between;
290 Prov'd, by the ends of being, to have been.
When Hopkins dies, a thousand lights attend
The wretch, who living sav'd a candle's end:
Should'ring God's altar a vile image stands,
Belies his features, nay extends his hands;
295 That live-long wig which Gorgon's self might own,
Eternal buckle takes in Parian stone.
Behold what blessings Wealth to life can lend!
And see, what comfort it affords our end.
In the worst inn's worst room, with mat half-hung,
300 The floors of plaister, and the walls of dung,
On once a flock-bed, but repair'd with straw,
With tape-ty'd curtains, never meant to draw,
The George and Garter dangling from that bed
Where tawdry yellow strove with dirty red,
305 Great Villers lies—alas! how chang'd from him,
That life of pleasure, and that soul of whim!
Gallant and gay, in Cliveden's proud alcove,
The bow'r of wanton Shrewsbury and love;
Or just as gay, at Council, in a ring
310 Of mimick'd Statesmen, and their merry King.
No Wit to flatter, left of all his store!

No Fool to laugh at, which he valu'd more.
There, Victor of his health, of fortune, friends,
And fame; this lord of useless thousands ends.
315 His Grace's fate sage Cutler could foresee,
And well (he thought) advis'd him, " Live like me."
As well his Grace reply'd, " Like you, Sir John?
" That I can do, when all I have is gone."
Resolve me, Reason, which of these is worse,
320 Want with a full, or with an empty purse?
Thy life more wretched, Cutler, was confess'd,
Arise, and tell me, was thy death more bless'd?
Cutler saw tenants break, and houses fall,
For very want; he could not build a wall.
325 His only daughter in a stranger's pow'r,
For very want; he could not pay a dow'r.
A few grey hairs his rev'rend temples crown'd,
'Twas very want that sold them for two pound.
What ev'n deny'd a cordial at his end,
330 Banish'd the doctor, and expell'd the friend?
What but a want, which you perhaps think mad,
Yet numbers feel, the want of what he had.
Cutler and Brutus, dying both exclaim,
" Virtue! and Wealth! what are ye but a name! "
335 Say, for such worth are other worlds prepar'd?
Or are they both, in this their own reward?
A knotty point! to which we now proceed.
But you are tir'd—I'll tell a tale. " Agreed."
Where London's column, pointing at the skies
340 Like a tall bully, lifts the head, and lyes;
There dwelt a Citizen of sober fame,
A plain good man, and Balaam was his name;
Religious, punctual, frugal, and so forth;
His word would pass for more than he was worth.
345 One solid dish his week-day meal affords,
An added pudding solemniz'd the Lord's:
Constant at Church, and Change; his gains were sure,
His givings rare, save farthings to the poor.
The Dev'l was piqu'd such saintship to behold,
350 And long'd to tempt him like good Job of old:
But Satan now is wiser than of yore,
And tempts by making rich, not making poor.
Rouz'd by the Prince of Air, the whirlwinds sweep
The surge, and plunge his Father in the deep;
355 Then full against his Cornish lands they roar,
And two rich ship-wrecks bless the lucky shore.
Sir Balaam now, he lives like other folks,
He takes his chirping pint, and cracks his jokes:
" Live like yourself," was soon my Lady's word;

360 And lo! two puddings smoak'd upon the board.
Asleep and naked as an Indian lay,
An honest factor stole a Gem away:
He pledg'd it to the knight; the knight had wit,
So kept the Diamond, and the rogue was bit.
365 Some scruple rose, but thus he eas'd his thought,
" I'll now give six-pence where I gave a groat,
" Where once I went to church, I'll now go twice—
" And am so clear too of all other vice."
The Tempter saw his time; the work he ply'd;
370 Stocks and Subscriptions pour on ev'ry side,
'Till all the Dæmon makes his full descent,
In one abundant show'r of Cent. per Cent.,
Sinks deep within him, and possesses whole,
Then dubs Director, and secures his soul.
375 Behold Sir Balaam, now a man of spirit,
Ascribes his gettings to his parts and merit,
What late he call'd a Blessing, now was Wit,
And God's good Providence, a lucky Hit.
Things change their titles, as our manners turn:
380 His Compting-house employ'd the Sunday-morn;
Seldom at Church ('twas such a busy life)
But duly sent his family and wife.
There (so the Dev'l ordain'd) one Christmas-tide
My good old Lady catch'd a cold, and dy'd.
385 A Nymph of Quality admires our Knight;
He marries, bows at Court, and grows polite:
Leaves the dull Cits, and joins (to please the fair)
The well-bred cuckolds in St. James's air:
First, for his Son a gay Commission buys,
390 Who drinks, whores, fights, and in a duel dies:
His daughter flaunts a Viscount's tawdry wife;
She bears a Coronet and P–x for life.
In Britain's Senate he a seat obtains,
And one more Pensioner St. Stephen gains.
395 My Lady falls to play; so bad her chance,
He must repair it; takes a bribe from France;
The House impeach him; Coningsby harangues;
The Court forsake him, and Sir Balaam hangs:
Wife, son, and daughter, Satan, are thy own,
400 His wealth, yet dearer, forfeit to the Crown:
The Devil and the King divide the prize,
And sad Sir Balaam curses God and dies.

ABBREVIATIONS

Bateson = Alexander Pope, *Epistles to Several Persons* (*Moral Essays*), ed. F. W. Bateson. London, 1951. (The Twickenham Edition)

Elwin-Courthope = *The Works of Alexander Pope,* ed. Whitwell Elwin and W. J. Courthope, 10 vols. London, 1871–1889.

Sherburn = *The Correspondence of Alexander Pope,* ed. George Sherburn, 5 vols. Oxford, 1956.

A Critical Reading

1

For the most subtle feature of Pope's art there probably is no canonical term; the best that comes to mind is " climate of attitudes," or perhaps " tone of voice." His characteristic poem tends to draw its vitality from a set of complexly acting and interacting attitudes which usually are so deeply and yet allusively incorporated that they can be overlooked by us, in our remoteness from his culture and its values, with unfortunate ease. Neglect of this " climate of attitudes " permits only a limited reading, if not a distorted one; recognition can excite the intricate artistry and intention of the poem, just as the earth's atmosphere makes possible to us our variegated world.

What recovery we have made of Pope's poetry is largely due to recovery of this feature. The ambiguous comic-seriousness of *The Rape of the Lock,* for example, has become available through realization that its mock-epic attitude is not merely one-dimensional; for, while it mockingly contrasts current conduct with heroic behavior, it also seriously urges society to transprose epic standards into its own diminished idiom and abide by the results as a nevertheless purposeful way of life. We have recognized that the *Epistle to Dr. Arbuthnot* is not a flat autobiographical self-justification, but a work that artfully creates the personality of the orator and conditions our attitude toward that creation in the very act of his presenting his oration of self-defense. And, just as we have discerned the Grub Street projector who writes *A Tale of a Tub,* we have learned to detect the fine Roman aristocrat who stands behind the *Epistle to Burlington* and is responsible for the values governing it. This tone of voice —implied by a dramatic stance, or point of view, or the personality of the implied speaker—is perhaps the most carefully controlled and most energizing feature of Pope's art; for most of his satires are essentially dramatic, and, like Swift, he usually speaks in them through personae. This artfully insinuated tone of voice is the atmosphere in which the act of the poem occurs, and by which that act is modified to form the poem's unique significance.

Nowhere, I believe, did Pope manage the technique more skillfully than in his control of the satiric and Christian tones in the *Epistle to Bathurst,* the artistic complexity and perfection of which he intimated when he wrote, " I never took more care in my life of any [other] poem." [1] In the epistle to Burlington, the companion piece on riches, he examined the ethics of magnificent expenditure in terms of aesthetics and social deportment in order to persuade us that the vice of lavishness is also bad taste and that Timon's prodigality violates not only good sense but also the decorum of human relations:

> Treated, caress'd, and tir'd, I take my leave,
> Sick of his civil Pride from Morn to Eve.

The role of the speaker, therefore, is not notably complex, and his voice is largely Horatian, as befits an aristocratic sensibility recoiling from offenses against *magnificentia.* But the *Epistle to Bathurst* is on a grander scale, and its largeness of purpose imposed on Pope an especially delicate posture. For here the subject of his satire is not the limited one of the tastelessness and social indelicacy of conspicuous consumption, but the whole corruptness of the new moneyed society he sees mushrooming about him and invading his values.

Loosely, the *Epistle to Bathurst* is of the rhetorical order of the Horatian epistolary satire.

[1] Pope to Swift, 16 February 1732/3 (Sherburn, III. 348).

As in, say, Horace's satire on frugality (*Satires,* II. ii), we are to imagine the speaker and his friend engaged in easy, intimate conversation on some warmly familiar occasion. With impressive rhetorical skill the speaker persuades his companion to some ethical position, the satire of vices being one of the more significant means to that end. And the epistolary satire gains its final end not only by the reader's identifying himself with the speaker's friendly antagonist and being carried along by the current of suasion, but also by his observing impartially the dramatic interchange of views and being impressed that so worthy an antagonist has capitulated. To this extent Pope's poem is a highly artful adaptation of an established and effective rhetorical mode. Its distinctiveness, however, lies in the source from which its ethics derives its sanctions and by means of which the Horatian *sermo* is assimilated into a more inclusive rhetorical mode.

More than almost any other of Pope's poems, this one is splendid with theological and scriptural references: providence, charity, grace, election, revelation, alms, God, Devil, demon, Balaam, Job—to cite only a few. But the list is impressive enough to suggest that because of the dimensions of his moral theme Pope elected to measure the corrupting power of misused money, not with the standards of human taste, but with the all-inclusive and eternal demands of revealed religion. The improper use of wealth, the general tone intimates, is a form of sacrilege, and the offense here is not against decorum and sensibility but against God.

Yet, to describe the poet's position this simply is to attenuate the complexities of the voice. For example, clearly something more than a merely pious tone is suggested when the speaker, having solemnly reached a difficult theological crux, abruptly decides not to pursue the " knotty point": " But you are tir'd—I'll tell a tale " (337–38)—a tale that turns out to be a devastating satire and yet a parable. Although the persistent Christian resonances in the poem identify his religious commitment, the main speaker concedes, as a rhetorician should, to adapt his discourse to the character of his immediate audience, the worldly, cynical nonbeliever—the persona here named " Bathurst." We would be closer to the " voice " of the poem, then, if we recognize the speaker as a lay theologian, or lay apostle, gently leading his friend toward a conversion of beliefs and, to that end, incorporating and transforming his satiric bias. Simultaneously the poem is a Horatian *sermo*, intimate and satiric, and a Christian sermon, religiously earnest; and we could more precisely define the mode of the poem if we could discover the true relation in it of these two genres.

Ponderous and intrusive though Warburton was, he did recognize to a degree the special complexity of voice in this epistle. Of the opening exchange between the fictive Bathurst and Pope's speaker, he wrote:

> As much as to say, " You, my Lord, hold the subject we are upon, as fit only for SATIRE; I, on the contrary, esteem it amongst the high points of Philosophy, and profound ETHICS: But as we both agree in the main *Principle* . . . let us compromise the matter, and consider the subject both under your idea and mine conjointly, i. e. *Satirically* and *Philosophically*."—And this, in fact, we shall find to be the true character of this poem; which is of a *Species* peculiar to itself; partaking equally of the nature of his *Ethic Epistles* and of his Satires. . . .

Warburton is off the mark, but not by far. Perhaps he felt it improper, in view of his office in the Church, to speak of one of the points of view as Christian; and " ethical " or " philosophical " provided him with a way out of his uneasiness. But at least he was sensitive to the unique tone of this satiric homily, which, while it lacerates men as fools and knaves in their vicious practices, seeks at the same time, in all Christian charity, to show them the salvation that lies in their fulfilling their moral and religious duties. Pope himself named rather better the components of the complex voice when, five years before the publication of the poem, he wrote to Lord Bathurst on the very topic that was to be the theme of the poetic epistle addressed to him:

> As much as you give into Philosophy, I incline to the side of Religion: It was ever so, your Lordship well remembers. Yet I am glad to find among the topicks of your Lordships own Panegyrick, One, that I can refer rather to the latter than the former; I mean Charity to the Poor, which the Philosophers ascribe to a meaner principle namely our compliance [with] Human weakness & Compassion on seeing the miseries of another, (and which the Stoicks held rather a Frailty than a Virtue) whereas . . . Christian authors call it a Christmas virtue, and give you some hopes at this time of the year to get Heaven by it.[2]

" Philosophic " and " religious " more closely approximate the dispositions of the two speakers if one adds Pope's qualification that mere philosophy can cynically and erroneously denigrate man and hence is the source of Bathurst's initial misanthropic attitude in the poem.[3]

During the years given to composing the *Essay on Man* and the *Epistle to Bathurst,* Pope frequently thought of himself as a kind of lay theologian. Unquestionably this conception faithfully reflects the degree to which he was religiously committed and confirms the sincerity of his hope " to contribute to some honest and moral purposes in writing on human life and manners, not exclusive of religious regards." [4] For although we tend to think of him only as a secular moralist, Pope, holding " the Christian doctrine, as the perfection of all moral," [5] was disposed to see the moral virtues in the perspective of the theological virtues. Alluding to the still incomplete *Essay on Man,* Bolingbroke described its author as " our divine Pope "; [6] when Pope found himself writing Oxford in millennial language, he jestingly feared that, were he of the clergy, he might be held suspect by his fellow clergymen; [7] and he was delighted to learn that the *Essay on Man* was being attributed (" I think with some reason ") to a divine.[8]

But the persuasive means to his religious ends were, for Pope, a compound of the homiletic and the satiric. Speaking of the forthcoming *Epistle to Bathurst,* he described his literary works as " directed to a good end, the advancement of moral and religious virtue," which he treats " with the utmost seriousness and respect," and " the discouragement of vicious and corrupt hearts," for which " any means are fair and any method equal, whether preaching or laughing, whatever will do best." [9] Preaching and satire, religious exhortation and scornful laughter, are not incompatible for his purposes. Perhaps, however, the most telling clue to the nature of the *Epistle to Bathurst* appears in a letter written shortly after its publication:

> You [Caryll] live daily in my thoughts, and sometimes in my prayers, if you will let a poet talk of prayers. Yet at least I have some title to *sermons,* which are next of kin to prayers. I find the last I made [i. e., the *Epistle to Bathurst*] had some good effect, and yet the preacher less railed at than usually those are who will be declaiming against popular or national vices.[10]

The denominations " sermon " and " preacher " are in accord with the similar references to Pope's religious purposes, and the passage suggests that if a poem is necessarily less religious than a prayer, it may nevertheless be a Christian sermon. But of course the *Epistle to Bathurst* is a sermon in the more obvious sense that it is in the manner of the satiric *sermones* of Horace. " Sermon " is a nicely poised term, since it embraces both Pope's Horatian model and the Christian sermon, and the poem belongs simultaneously and indiscriminately to both categories. For, as Pope manages the forms, the Christian sermon is what Horace, who proposed the teaching of wisdom as the end of poetry,

[2] December, 1728 (Sherburn, II. 531).

[3] What Pope thought of the moral efficacy of philosophy one can judge from his description of Bathurst as " Philosopher and Rake " (*Sober Advice from Horace,* 158).

[4] Pope to Caryll, 6 December 1730 (Sherburn, III. 155).

[5] Pope to Caryll, 23 October 1733 (Sherburn, III. 390).

[6] Bolingbroke and Pope to Swift, 20 March 1731 (Sherburn, III. 183). The 1741 edition of Pope's letters reads, " Pope, our Divine."

[7] Pope to Oxford, 28 April 1732 (Sherburn, III. 280).

[8] Pope to Caryll, 8 March 1733 (Sherburn, III. 354).

[9] Pope to Caryll, 27 September 1732 (Sherburn, III. 316).

[10] Pope to Caryll, 31 January 1733 (Sherburn, III. 345). For another instance of Pope's conflating the idea of the Horatian *sermo* and of the Christian sermon, see his *Imitations of Horace,* Satire II. ii. 9.

would have written had he known the divine word; and the Horatian *sermo* is a sermon without benefit of revelation. Horace's moral satire is to Pope's Christian sermon as natural theology is to supernatural—not distinct from it, but understood in it. On these grounds the *Epistle to Bathurst* finds the artistic justification for its two areas of reference: cynical and urbane Bathurst and the theologically earnest speaker; contemporary satire and Christian doctrine; the classical and the scriptural. Just as Pope has integrated the Horatian *sermo* into the Christian sermon, the function of much of the poem is to assimilate the first of each of these pairs to the second. Consequently, the presence of Bathurst, cast as a follower of Momus, makes especially appropriate the Horatian nature of the poem: its polished, witty chat; the subtle modulation between seemingly casual bits of ethical doctrine and satire; the slightly outlined portraits in the first half of the poem; and the use of two major contrasting portraits in the last half. But the presence of the lay theologian transmutes the Horatian controls by causing the ethical doctrines to fan out into a coherent system of Christian principles and by interfusing the looseness of the Horatian structure with a strict ordonnance of argument that derives from Christian theology and the organization of Christian homiletic literature. This artistic elevation of the Classical to the Christian is strikingly characteristic of Pope and perfectly defines his Christian humanism and much of his poetic mission—witness especially his transformation of Hadrian's "Animula vagula, blandula" into "The Dying Christian to his Soul," his translation of Virgil's "Pollio" into the terms of Isaiah, and his integration of the Orpheus legend with that of St. Cecilia in order to relate secular to divine music.

2

Since its religious content, unlike its Horatian manner, is not the face that the epistle immediately presents to the reader, it would be well first to recognize to some degree, through a few random examples, that its basic texture and inner form are of a piece with the traditional Christian homilies on the subject of riches. For the ideal contemporary reader, confronting the poem as Horatian satire, would have felt a strangely dislocating but rich familiarity with its core through his experience with sermons and moral writings on that theme. Most of the scriptural echoes, although frequently given a satiric turn, are still fairly obvious to us, such as "'Tis thus we eat the bread another sows" (22)[11] and "Riches, like insects, . . . / Wait but for wings, and in their season, fly" (171–72).[12] The protest that riches can give us only "Meat, Cloaths, and Fire" (81–82) reflects "And having food and raiment let us be therewith content" (1 Timothy 6: 8),[13] just as "Bids seed-time, harvest, equal course maintain, / Thro' reconcil'd extremes of drought and rain" (167–68) evokes "While the earth remaineth, seedtime and harvest, and cold and heat, and summer and winter, and day and night shall not cease" (Genesis 7: 22).

The ideal contemporary would also have recognized, as we in general do not, the rich composition and adaptation of commonplaces that derive from the characteristic moral and pious literature on covetousness and that therefore draw into Pope's poem the whole tradition of their customary contexts. Pale Mammon pining amidst his store (173), for example, is a familiar homiletic figure, usually presented as the rich miser starving, like Midas—or thirsting, like Tantalus—in the midst of his plenty.[14] But

[11] Cp. Isaiah 65: 22, and Job 31: 8.

[12] Proverbs 21: 5.

[13] George Gascoigne commented on this text in an attack on covetousness: "If we have (sayth the Appostle) meat, drynck, and cloth, let us there with be contented" (*View of Worldly Vanities*, in *Works*, ed. J. W. Cunliffe [Cambridge, 1910], II. 241). Cp. Ecclesiasticus 29: 21: "The chief thing for life is water, and bread, and a garment, and a house to cover shame."

William Law's words, "meat, and drink, and clothing are the only things necessary in life" (*Serious Call*, chap. XI), which Leslie Stephen thought to be Pope's source (*History of English Thought in the Eighteenth Century*, II. 399), merely share with Pope's in the tradition of the glosses on 1 Timothy 6: 8. See, e. g., Sir George Mackenzie, *The Moral History of Frugality* (1691), p. 6.

(Unless otherwise indicated, London is to be understood as the place of publication.)

[14] E. g., Shakespeare, *Rape of Lucrece*, 96–98; Gerard de Malynes, *Saint George for England* (1601), p. 19; Thomas

we can more fully sense the great tide of rhetorical and moral tradition flowing into Pope's sermon by examining the significance of the phrase "want of what he had" (332), with which Cutler's portrait is brought to a close. Perhaps nothing is more recurrent in both classical and Christian moral writing than the distinguishing of the miser from all others in need by the fact that he thirsts not only for his lack, but even for his possessions and therefore is, according to the fixed metaphor, like the hydropic in his insatiable thirst. Since, ran the witty reasoning, poverty is to be defined as the lack of something wanted, the miser alone is truly poor, for he alone can never have sufficient.

> Wishes proceed from want: The Richest then,
> Most wishing, want most, and are poorest men:
> If he be poore, that wanteth much, how poore
> Is he that hath too much, and yet wants more? [15]

Such a person, said Horace, is "magnas inter opes inops"; [16] and in another context Ovid left us the tag, "inopem me copia fecit." [17] But the English word "want" permits the easy play on both "desire" and "lack," and Pope's words, "the want of what he had," repeat the endlessly recurrent phrasing of the aphorism. The covetous man, wrote Thomas Goddard, among countless others, "alwaies wants what he hath." [18] By adopting these particular words to define Cutler, Pope has aligned his poem with the whole corpus of moral treatises and cast over it the authoritative air of their established moral rightness.

However, in the stationing of his phrase Pope has also brought another tradition to bear. It will be noticed that there is an especially moving rhythm that runs through the portrait of Cutler and carries it to a climax. Having established at the beginning the ambiguous nature of the word "want" ("Want with a full, or with an empty purse" [320]), the poet then thrice uses the word as a mocking refrain in a series of alternate lines to explain Cutler's miserliness, varying his phrase lest it become too obtrusive: "For very want" (324, 326), "'Twas very want" (328). Delayed during an entire couplet, the refrain now becomes massive and ominous when it recurs—"What but a want" (331). And finally it explodes into the full satiric significance of the punning aphorism when, in the immediately following line, it emerges from its muted, minor position as a first hemistich and, gathering together all its accumulated insistence, brings both the couplet and the portrait to an abrupt conclusion: "the want of what he had" (332).

Now, the earliest known ancestor of Pope's final phrase appears in the *Sententiae* of Publius Syrus: "Tam deest avaro, quod habet, quam quod non habet"; and that apothegm had the good fortune to be borrowed by Quintilian as one of his major examples of the rhetorical use of *sententiae*.[19] Such luminous phrasings of

Adams, *Workes* (1630), p. 200; Alexander Ross, *Mystagogus Poeticus* (third ed., 1653), pp. 290, 291, 397; and A. Alciati, *Emblemata* (Patavii, 1661), pp. 370–72. Cp. also Garth, *The Dispensary*, VI. 149–50: "But, like a Miser, in Excess she's poor;/And pines for Thirst amidst her wat'ry Store."

Pallor is a traditional iconic feature of the miser: see Cesare Ripa, *Iconologia* (Venice, 1669), pp. 51–69.

[15] Francis Quarles, *Job Militant*, in *Complete Works*, ed. A. B. Grosart (1880), II. 74.

[16] *Odes*, III. xvi. 28.

[17] *Met.*, III. 466. Cp. Spenser's description of Avarice:

> Most wretched wight, whom nothing might suffise,
> Whose greedy lust did lacke in greatest store,
> Whose need had end, but no end couetise,
> Whose wealth was want, whose plenty made him pore.
> (*F. Q.*, I. iv. 29)

Thomas Pierce, *The Sinner Impleaded in his own Count* (third ed., 1670), p. 24: "The unhappy fruit of whose Avarice is, to be possessingly in want, and to famish in the midst of plenty." W. M., *The Man in the Moon* (1609; Percy Society, XXIX. 28): the miser "will always want, for he uses nothing."

[18] *Miscellanea* (1661), p. 52. George Gascoigne, *View of Worldly Vanities*, in *Works*, ed. Cunliffe, II. 242: "Tantalus is thirsty in ye myddest of his welth. Unto whom asmuch avayleth yt which he hath not, as yt which he hath." *The Treasury of Ancient and Modern Times* (1619), quoted in William Crouch, *The Enormous Sin of Covetousness Detected* (1708), p. 37: "St. Jerome saith, 'The Covetous Man is so needy of that which he hath as if he had it not at all.'" John Gaule, *Distractions, or the Holy Madnesse* (1629), pp. 372, 400, 458. Thomas Fuller, *Church History*, bk. X, cent. 17: "Here lies his Grace in cold clay clad, / Who dy'd for want of what he had." Jeremy Collier, *Essays upon Several Moral Subjects* (sixth ed., 1709), pt. II, p. 147: "And he that dares not Enjoy, wants that which he has, as well as that which he has not." Wycherley, "Upon Avarice": "So you, Vain Miser! are extravagant, / In wanting what you have, for Fear of Want."

[19] *Institutio oratoria*, VIII. v. Obviously derived from Quintilian, one of the examples of *sententiae* listed in Henry Peacham's *Garden of Eloquence* (1593), p. 190, reads, "The covetous man wanteth as well that which he hath, as that which he hath not."

moral insights as this, Quintilian added, are especially appropriate as means of bringing a rhetorical period to a close.[20] Pope not only has regulated the tempo of his paragraph so as to apply Quintilian's rhetorical doctrine of the *sententia* with powerful dramatic effect and so to fulfill the trained rhetorical anticipations of his audience, but has done so with one of the very illustrations Quintilian offered. Yet, by his phrasing of the maxim, he has also brought to bear on the paragraph the familiar homiletic tradition in English. Here the Roman orator, the Roman moralist, and the English homilist are one.

Pope's more characteristic technique, however, is to echo the commonplace, together with its traditional context, at the same time that he transforms it in order to integrate it with his special artistic purposes. One persistent moral metaphor in the literature on avarice likens wealth to muck or dung, " which while it lyeth upon an heap doth no good, but dispersed and cast abroad, maketh fields fruitful." [21] By substituting ambergris for muck, Pope both evokes the tradition and exalts the humble moral proverb into a devotional ritual, making charity both a human good and an act of obeisance to God. To this transformation he adds the other customary metaphor of poison in order to consider charity in its two phases, first as an act of corporal mercy and then as an act of spiritual mercy:

> Wealth in the gross is death, but life diffus'd,
> As Poison heals, in just proportion us'd:
> In heaps, like Ambergrise, a stink it lies,
> But well-dispers'd, is Incense to the Skies.
> (233–36)

" And yet if Riches be sanctified," Thomas Goddard wrote, " they are great blessings, and singular advantages to honour God, and to do good withall to others, if not curses; being like poison, if corrected, physick, if not, death: and like muck, if not spread abroad, good for nothing." [22] Indeed, by replacing muck with ambergris, the " Incense to the Skies," Pope has Christianized the moral metaphor, for his lines now echo St. Paul's description of alms as " an odour of a sweet smell, a sacrifice acceptable, well-pleasing to God " (Philippians 4: 18) .[23]

Similarly, in introducing miserly Cotta and his prodigal son, Pope was, at one level of significance, giving flesh to the *topos* that avaricious men are inclined to nurture spendthrifts, a *topos* that will be recognized as the governing principle of many comic dramas. Of such fathers and sons Richard Brathwaite wrote aphoristically, ". . . a Fathers injudicious doing, becomes oftimes his Heires undoing; the Fathers raising, the Sonnes ruine." [24] According to John Gaule, " Tis true, and just; both said, and found: ' After a great Getter, there commonly comes a Spender. Goods ill gotten, are ill spent '. . . ." [25] Whether

In addition to this rhetorical tradition, the maxim was perpetuated in the moral literature. Publius' sentence was borrowed by Seneca (*Controversiae*, VII. 3.8) and by Jerome (*Epistolae*, LIII) ; it was incorporated in accounts of the miser in such moral works as Cesare Ripa's *Iconologia* (see there also, under " Avaritia," the poem by Urban VIII) and Alciati's *Emblemata* (Patavii, 1661) , pp. 371, 372. The *Sentences* persisted as a basic schoolbook in scores of editions.

[20] " Sed consuetudo iam tenuit, ut mente concepta sensus vocaremus, lumina autem praecipueque in clausulis posita sententias." In the section on the *sententia* in his *De copia*, Erasmus also used the maxim from Publius Syrus as an example and discussed the special power of the *sententia* " in clausula."

[21] Henry Peacham, *The Worth of a Penny* (1641) , in Arber's *English Garner*, VI. 251. Also Bacon, *Essays*, no. 15; Samuel Butler, *Characters*, ed. A. R. Waller (Cambridge, 1908) , p. 146; George Leyburn, *Holy Characters* (Doway, 1662) , I. 286.

[22] *Miscellanea* (1661) , p. 48.

[23] The commentators gloss " odour of a sweet smell ": " alludit enim ad vetera sacrificia, quae ad Deum per ignem et fumum ascendebant. . . . Eleemosyna vestia quasi thus, vel thymiama suavissimi odoris. . . ." (Cornelius a Lapide, *Commentaria in Vetus et Novum Testamentum*) . Bishop Fleetwood (*Complete Collection of Sermons* [1737], p. 1) calls Paul's words the " ritual and pontific Terms " for alms.

The original reading in Pope's manuscript " Earth & Skies," probably reflects his intention to show both the moral and religious value of alms. Undoubtedly it also suggests that something of the anterior metaphor of dung lingers in his thoughts. See below, pp. 94, 124.

The metaphoric possibilities of ambergris had attracted Pope earlier: " For Praise is like Ambergrize; a little unexpected Whiff of it . . . is the most agreeable thing in the world; but when a whole lump of it is thrust to your nose, it is a Stink, and strikes you down " (Pope to Swift, 14 December 1725 [Sherburn, II. 349]) . Pope thought well of this and repeated it in his " Thoughts on Various Subjects " (Elwin-Courthope, X. 560) .

[24] *A Survey of History* (1638) , p. 330.

[25] *Distractions, or the Holy Madnesse* (1629) , pp. 437–38. See also Thomas Adams, *Workes* (1630) , p. 200; Sir George Mackenzie, *The Moral History of Frugality* (1691) , p. 42;

or not the belief is statistically or psychologically sound, the important fact is that a long moral tradition said it was; and with the Cottas, Pope is carefully depositing his poem in that rich moral tradition. Along with this tradition of misers and their prodigal sons went a metaphor comparing them to cistern and conduit. Probably the metaphor had its origin in Plutarch's essay on riches; [26] but subsequently the metaphor took a variety of forms. For John Gaule, the father is "the Conduit-Pipe," the son "the Cesterne"; [27] and Geoffrey Fenton admonished the covetous man that although "[you] adventure your honour to fyll but one Jarre or Pitcher wyth Water: . . . it will not quench your appetite, so in the ende you will be dryven to dye of Thirst, and the Potte which wyth so great payne you have fylled in your lyfe, shall after your death be broken against the walles of a prodigall heire, who will laugh to see it runne as a ryver, and reioyce to water the streates wyth the Ryches. . . ." [28] But in adapting this conventional metaphor of the moral treatises, Pope, tongue in cheek, accepts it as literally true and thereby converts it into a description of a grotesque landscape:

> This year a Reservoir, to keep and spare,
> The next a Fountain, spouting thro' his Heir,
> In lavish streams to quench a Country's thirst,
> And men and dogs shall drink him 'till they burst. (175–78)

By combining the metaphor with the tradition that the avaricious man is hydropic, he has dehumanized such fathers and sons by freezing them ludicrously into features of a formal garden, just as, later in the poem, inhuman Hopkins will transform himself into a statue. Denying their status as man, they have reduced themselves to ornamental waterworks, a shocking mockery of man, grotesquerie of the sort that Pope ridiculed in his *Guardian* essay on topiary: "A Queen *Elizabeth* in Phylyraea, a little inclining to the Green Sickness, but of full growth." [29]

Finally, the ideal contemporary would have heard in the *Epistle* from point to point thematic echoes of the doctrinal and moral works on riches. For example, by spending, Harpax might gain "the blessing of a Friend" (94) because by alms "we reap the benefit of the poors prayers to God for us." [30] Unlike the Man of Ross, who provides seats for the weary traveller,

A Trip from St. James's, in *Tricks of the Town*, ed. Ralph Straus (1927), pp. 230–31.

[26] "But to what end, I pray, would [misers] leave such a deal of Money and a great Estate to their Children and Heirs? That they forsooth may preserve it also for others, and those others in like manner should hand it down to their Children (just like those Earthen Pipes the Potters make for a Water-course, which retain none of the Water themselves, but one Pipe only conveighs it to the next) till some informing false Accuser or Tyrant appears, who cuts off this Keeper in Trust, and when his Breath is stopped, derives and diverts the course of Wealth into another Chanel: or as they say, till some one that is the most wicked of the Race, devours and consumes all, that those who went before him had preserved. For not only as Euripides says,

> Children from Slaves deriv'd, and baser Blood,
> Prove Prodigal and lewd, none come to good,

but it's as true of the Children of the Parsimonious." (*Plutarch's Morals*, trans. from the Greek by Several Hands [1704], II. 301–302.)

[27] *Op. cit.*, p. 434.

[28] *Golden Epistles* (1575), pp. 142–43. For the same metaphor, see also Peter de la Primaudaye, *The French Academy* (1614), p. 419; Jeremy Taylor, *Rule and Exercise of Holy Living* (1650), IV. viii. 6–7; [Richard Allestree], *The Gentleman's Calling* (1674), p. 53; Thomas Clutterbuck, *Spittle-Sermon* (1687), p. 12. Because of their similarity to Pope's lines, Thomas May's deserve to be quoted in full:

> Some men were made to be
> The conduit pipes of an estate, or rather
> The sieves of Fortune, through whose leaking holes
> She means to scatter a large flood of wealth,
> Besprinkling many with refreshing showers.
> So usurers, so dying aldermen,
> Pour out at once upon their sieve-like heirs
> Whole gusts of envied wealth, which they together
> Through many holes let out again in showers,
> And with their ruin water a whole country.
> (*Old Couple*, III. i)

[29] The younger Cotta's making "The woods recede" and "The Sylvans groan" (209–10) is a similar use of personification to comment on his failure as man. Cutler also will damn himself by his inhumanity, for he understands the falling of a house ("Cutler saw tenants break, and houses fall" [323]) to be a material event depending on the building of a wall, rather than what it really is, the dissolution of a human household. Consequently, he sees the breaking of tenants, not as the bankruptcy of human beings, but as the fracture of things, on the same order as the falling of houses. And the "capacious Squire, and deep Divine" (204) who are to be filled with wine substitute spatial dimensions for human intelligence. (Cp. the "soft Dean" who, like a cushion, invites to rest [*Epistle to Burlington*, 149].)

That the proper study of mankind is man can hardly be expounded better than by this satiric confusion of human nature with things. Cp. also the metamorphoses of the belles into grotesques as teapots, bottles, etc., in *The Rape of the Lock* (IV. 47–54).

[30] Samuel Clarke, *Medulla theologia* (1659), p. 242. Cp. 2 Corinthians 9: 14.

the elder Cotta violates hospitality, one of the important moral purposes of riches: " Benighted wanderers, the forest o'er, / Curse the sav'd candle, and unop'ning door " (195–96). The line " To Worth or Want well-weigh'd, be Bounty giv'n " (229) recalls the entire Aristotelian-Christian thesis that " the Works of Charity are . . . acceptable both to God and Man, when exercis'd on those that *only want*. . . . But when both Want and Merit meet, the Practice of this Grace is . . . more agreeable to God and Man. . . ." [31] And the principle that to give alms to the poor is to " ease, or emulate, the care of Heav'n " (230) is deeply rooted in all Christian thought: " If any thing deserves our Emulation, great and generous Charities do, which are a Resemblance and Imitation of the Divine Goodness, than which nothing can more endear us to God or Man." [32] Charity, added Bishop Fleetwood, is

> mending the Works of God, and bettering the Creation: For he, in his all-wise Disposal of Affairs, has ordered Matters so, that there should seem to be a great many Defects in Nature, a great deal of Partiality in the Distribution of the Things of this World, and Inequality in the Gifts of Fortune: and hath submitted all the World to the Dominion of what we call Chance and Accident. . . . And therefore he that best repairs these Breaches, supplies these Defects, makes up these Inequalities . . . best accomplishes the Works of God and the Designs of Providence.[33]

3

By such evocative means as these, Pope has adjusted his " sermon " to the firmly established Christian doctrines and traditions of the use of riches, and by lending it all the familiarity and authority of those traditions, he has endowed his speaker with a Christian *ethos*.[34] With this fact in hand we are in a position to understand the subtle rhetorical maneuver with which the poem begins.

The tone of the speaker's opening words seems to be one of warm familiarity and eagerness to make concessions: " Who shall decide, when Doctors disagree,/ And soundest Casuists doubt, like you and me." Superficially, his address seems to amount to no more than this: Although you and I, Bathurst, differ on the origin of misers and spendthrifts and the consequent worth of man, the difference is inconsequential and we can pass it by. But the phrase " Doctors disagree " had once signaled the beginning of serious theological dispute. Since the Schoolmen (" Doctors ") are in disagreement, there is no undeniable church tradition or authority, and so the casuist, beset by " doubt," —the theological *dubium* with which the Scholastic thesis customarily began—may undertake to resolve the problem. However, by Pope's post-Reformation date, the differences among the Schoolmen having been notorious (such phrases as " alii dicunt " and " magna controversia est inter doctores, an . . ." speckle the pages of the casuists), the tag " Doctors disagree " had lost its value as a point of departure for serious disputation and had become a standing joke to give a mock-serious air to any difference of opinion. " Well," says Wycherley's Freeman on the subject of candor, " doctors differ.

[31] William Fleetwood, *Compleat Collection of Sermons* (1737), pp. 3–4.

[32] William Sherlock, *Sermons Preach'd upon Several Occasions* (third ed., 1719), I. 228–29. Thomas Whincop, *A Sermon . . . December 3, 1695*, p. 27: ". . . Charity to the Necessitous . . . makes us resemble God himself, . . . whose Excellency consists in being, and doing Good."

[33] *Op. cit.*, p. 2. Cp. Pope's letter to Caryll, 18 June 1711 (Sherburn, I. 119): " To relieve the injured (if you will pardon a poetic expression in prose) is no less to take the work of God off his hands, and an easing Providence of its care: 'Tis the noblest act that human nature is capable of. . . ." Pope must have cherished this thought, for he repeated it in his " Thoughts on Various Subjects " (Elwin-Courthope, X. 552).

[34] Precisely how saturated the poem is with moral and religious doctrine could be grasped only by an extensive survey of the didactic and pious works. But something of the degree may be sensed by comparing the works of the Man of Ross with Thomas Fuller's catalogue of the " seven kinds of corporal Alms ": feed the hungry; give drink to the thirsty; clothe the naked; entertain strangers; bury the dead. Among the twelve corporal alms he adds to these are: give physic to the sick; mend highways and bridges; reduce or guide wandering travellers; deliver the poor from their oppressors; and pay maidens' dowries (*The Rule and Exercise of Holy Living* [Oxford, 1868], p. 299).

You are for plain-dealing, I find; but against your particular notions, I have the practice of the whole world." [35] The contemporary connotation of this formulaic opening—especially in view of the obvious inappropriateness of identifying admittedly pagan Bathurst with Schoolmen and casuists—confirms the concession that the difference between the two speakers is a negligible quibble. Yet, if the phrase is a jesting exaggeration that establishes friendly accord despite disagreement, it also is a token of the theological perspective in which the speaker is inclined to consider the subject; and he has covertly won from Bathurst acquiescence to a Christian frame of thought even in the act of disclaiming any intent against Bathurst's pagan beliefs.

Unlike the Christian speaker, Bathurst the persona appears as avowedly a kind of Roman satirist of Plautine caste who, with aristocratic fatalism, mocks the baseness of man; and the speaker, while dissenting, outwardly concedes Bathurst's right, Momus-like, to hold man in contempt. The god of satire who ridiculed the creator-gods for their careless, inadequate handiwork—and whom Warburton, in one of his better phrases, once explained as " the complaining against Providence " [36]—has brought Bathurst the revelation that man was created to be an entertaining spectacle for the gods. Both misers and spendthrifts are needed for the game played with gold that amuses the spectator deities, and the capitalistic organization of man is only the fulfillment of his inherent foolishness. Yet, in conceding to his antagonist the right to hold this view, the speaker ingeniously shapes his expression of pagan misanthropy into a recognizably Christian pattern. By substituting the pagan gods in a sentence that otherwise would describe the divine transmission of the Pentateuch, the theologian attributes to his friend the acceptance of " the word " handed down—not from Jehovah to Moses—but " from Jove to Momus " (3). [37] If the speaker is willing for the moment to permit his opponent his pagan cynicism, he insists on putting it in a form that allows, and demands, a Christian evaluation: this worldly Roman can tolerate his conception of human triviality only by subscribing to the Books of Momus. Moreover, Bathurst's opinion that man is " the standing jest of Heav'n " contains in its verbal formulation the evidence of its falseness, even as the speaker brushes the opinion aside as unimportant. For behind its surface meaning (i. e., a permanent jest of the gods) the phrase alludes to the theme that man is *homo erectus*. Originating in Plato's etymology of *anthropos*, spreading throughout classical literature, and then incorporated into Christian symbolism, the doctrine taught that man's upright form distinguishes him from the brutes and, by allowing him to look up to the heavens, is a sign of his spiritual origin and destiny. God gave man " an erected and upright Body . . . to mount up his understanding, and elevate his eyes unto the Heavens, his originall, to contemplate there Divine occasions and permanent, leaving the Terrestriall as vaine." [38]

[35] *Plain-Dealer*, I. i. Cp. Dryden, " The Cock and the Fox," 507; and *Hind and the Panther*, 687. For the traditional status of the phrase, see *Notes and Queries*, ser. 6, vol. 7 (1883), 186; and *Gentleman's Magazine* (1813), pt. 1, p. 627: " I shall stand protected by the rhyming adage: 'When Doctors disagree, Disciples then are free.' " Prior entitled his epigram on a dispute between Bentley and the Bishop of Gloucester, " Doctors Differ."

Pope again used the word " Doctors " in the sense of " Schoolmen " in *Imitations of Horace*, Epistle I. i. 23–24: " But ask not, to what Doctors I apply?/Sworn to no Master, of no Sect am I."

[36] Spence, *Anecdotes*, ed. S. W Singer (1820), p. 310.

[37] It was common among the scholars to hold that " Jehovah " and " Jove " are etymologically the same; e. g., Theophilus Gale, *The Court of Gentiles* (Oxford, 1672), bk. II, pp. 11–12; Solomon Glassius, *Philologia sacra* (Lipsiae, 1705; first ed., 1645), p. 1278. Lilius Gyraldus refers to those who pronounce the Tetragrammaton " Jova " and thence " *Jovis* nomen volunt esse derivatum " (*Opera omnia* [Lugduni, 1696], I. 3).

[38] Thomas Milles, *The Treasurie of Auncient and Moderne Times* (1613), p. 19. For the classical and Christian history of this commonplace, see Theodore Spencer, *Shakespeare and the Nature of Man* (New York, 1942), pp. 4–5; Douglas Bush, " Notes on Milton's Classical Mythology," *SP*, 28 (1931), 269–70; and C. A. Patrides, " Renaissance Ideas on Man's Upright Form," *JHI*, 19 (1958), 256–58. For Pope's use of the *topos* in *Windsor Forest*, see Earl R. Wasserman, *The Subtler Language* (Baltimore, 1959), pp. 148–51.

Compare Pope's use of the same pun in *Essay on Man*, III. 77–78: " Great standing miracle! that Heav'n assign'd / Its only thinking thing this turn of mind." The pun is not only on " standing " but also on " turn of mind," alluding to man's unique ability to look up to heaven.

That Pope intended the phrase " standing jest " to define man by calling upon an attribute distinguishing him from all other creatures is testified by the manuscript, which here

Bathurst may have his misanthropy for the moment, but if he should assent to the speaker's terms for it, he is in danger of finding he may have agreed, not to the triviality of man, but to his spiritual greatness.

In opposition to Bathurst's cynical Genesis of economic man, the speaker offers a more charitable one: only when man uncovered gold did Heaven then divide mankind into spendthrift and miser to restore harmony by economic balance. Although he disclaims any desire to impose his view on his companion, he has given it a form familiar and congenial to Bathurst the classicist and calculated therefore to gain from him at least sympathetic attention. For the speaker has cast his Christian belief into the design of Ovid's account of the Iron Age, the last stage in man's decline. Although the many classical descriptions of the Four Ages are essentially alike and belong to a common tradition, Ovid's is the best known and most influential; and that the *Metamorphoses* is Pope's reference is attested by his adaptation of Ovid's "quasque recondiderat Stygiisque admoverat umbris / effodiuntur opes, irritamenta malorum": "Nature, as in duty bound, / Deep hid the shining mischief under ground" (9–10). Like Ovid, the speaker assumes that the economic potentialities for evil were originally present but were concealed by a benevolent Nature, and that economic evil arose only when men, disobeying Nature's laws, disemboweled the earth of gold.

But of all classical works that seemed consonant with Christianity the *Metamorphoses*, especially its first book, was, for obvious reasons, the most prominent. The fourteenth-century author of the *Ovide moralisé* and subsequent Renaissance commentators such as Petrus Lavinius had recognized the parallel with the Book of Genesis, and on this basis had elaborately Christianized the poem.[39] Therefore, in adapting Ovid on the subject of man's decline from the Golden Age to that of Iron, the speaker is at the same time rendering into a history of economics the scriptural story of man's expulsion from the Garden of Eden, the Christian Golden Age; and the unearthing of the gold concealed by Nature, God's second cause, is equatable with the eating of the fruit forbidden by God. Some additional pressure toward this Christian rendering of the speaker's words is exerted by his attributing the discovery of gold to "Man's audacious labour" (11), an audacity which is the classical equivalent of the Christian Pride responsible for the violation of God's injunction and the introduction of sin.[40] Moreover, the poet has added to Ovid's story a picture of gold's dramatic entry into the world as a result of man's "audacious" labor: "Flam'd forth this rival to, its Sire, the Sun" (12). The basis of the metaphor, to be sure, is the sun's golden color and the ancient belief that gold is generated by the sun's rays. But this is only the ground for Pope's expansion of the metaphor into a function of his theme. Although the myth is suppressed and folded in, the line recreates the legend of Phaëthon, whose name means "shining," or "radiant." To prove he was the son of Apollo, Phaëthon insisted upon driving his father's sun-chariot, and this rashness would have destroyed the universe had Jupiter not intervened.[41] Since the myth is alluded to at the end of the first book of Ovid's poem and is told in full at the opening of the second, the speaker has been consistently Ovidian for Bathurst's benefit. On the other hand, in the *Ovide moralisé* Phaëthon's ambitious attempt to usurp his father's place was Christianized as Lucifer's revolt against God. The analogy is an obvious one, and almost all other commentators read the myth as an allegory on audacity, pride, and unnatural ambition.[42] That

reads: "Is not the Thing that laughs but is laughed at" (below, p. 72). Like his upright form, man's ability to laugh was held as an index to his having a status above that of all other animals.

[39] Matthew Prior gives evidence that the Christian reading of Ovid persisted: see his *Literary Works*, ed. H. B. Wright and M. K. Spears (Oxford, 1959), I. 663–73.

[40] In the *Metamorphoses* Ovid seems to attribute the uncovering of gold to deceit, treachery, force, and avarice, but not to pride. However, in his very similar account of the Iron Age in the *Amores* (III. viii. 35–56) he implied something like the Christian idea of Pride. Undoubtedly both this passage and the one from the *Metamorphoses* are conflated in Pope's lines.

[41] With Pope's lines cp. Dryden's translation of *Metamorphoses*, I. 247–48: Phaëthon "claims and boasts his sire the Sun."

[42] For example, Golding in the preliminary epistle to his translation of Ovid: "In Phaetons fable unto sight the Poet

this classical-Christian allusion to Phaëthon immediately succeeds the line on man's audacious labor in uncovering gold tends to support this reading of the implied myth: man's unnatural ambition has released Pride itself into the world and violated the paradisiacal pre-economic state. Through his unnatural sin man has subverted the plan required of Nature as God's second cause and let loose the evil of gold. Only by organizing the new economic man into spendthrift and miser could Heaven, in its loving care for creation, reconstitute an order in this postlapsarian world.

The adaptation of Ovid's Iron Age, however, has an even more intimate bearing on the speaker's Christian purpose. For Pope did not merely take rhetorical advantage of the traditional parallelism of Ovid's narrative and the scriptural story of the Fall, and then ingeniously bend the Christianized myth into a Genesis of *homo pecuniarius.* Insofar as the *Epistle to Bathurst* is a sermon, it is primarily a sermon against avarice; and a long Christian tradition which considered avarice rather than pride the chief of the Deadly Sins [43] esteemed Ovid's words as an especially appropriate introduction to this theme. The vices introduced by the Iron Age were, according to Ovid, not only avarice (" amor sceleratus habendi "), but also deceit, knavery, treachery, and violence; but in the Christian adaptations all of these, probably on the basis that " radix omnium malorum est cupiditas," were collapsed into the one term, avarice. Lavinius, for example, in converting Ovid's first book into a Christian text, fastened upon only the one vice: " effodiuntur opes, irritamenta malorum." And at this point his commentary on Ovid erupts into a lengthy sermon on avarice: " O pestem truculentissimam. O avaritiam virtutum praeclarissimarum ruinam. . . . O malorum omnium radix. . . ." [44] Similarly, Boethius supplemented a prose lament on the vanity of worldly riches with verses [45] (later adapted by Chaucer as " The Former Age ") that were generally accepted as largely, if not entirely, derived from Ovid's lines on the Iron Age.[46] At the same time, then, that he is countering Bathurst's pagan philosophy with another classical philosophy, the speaker is consistent with his own theological position in finding in Ovid's explanation of the Fall of Man the appropriate point of departure for a Christian sermon on avarice. Indeed, it is quite likely that when, a few lines later (26–34), he outlines the crimes against mankind that riches permit—lust for another's wife, hired assassination, piracy, the corruption of friends, the betrayal of one's country—he is continuing to adapt Ovid's catalogue of the vices introduced with the Iron Age.[47]

The opening of the poem therefore is an elaborate, ingenious rhetorical gambit, a refinement of the classical figure of epitrope, or concession. John Ward, summarizing the rhetorical tradition, defined *epitrope* as the figure which " grants one thing to obtain another more advantageous. It is either real or feigned. And either the whole of a thing, or a part only is granted. . . . Nothing more confounds an adversary, than to grant him his whole argument, and at the same time either to shew that it is nothing to the purpose, or to offer something else, which may invalidate it." [48] Pope's speaker seemingly

doth express / The natures of ambition blind, and youthful wilfulness." Natalis Comes, *Mythologiae* (1616), lists Phaëthon under " Audaces." See also Alexander Ross, *Mystagogus Poeticus* (1647); Thomas Hall, *Phaeton's Folly; or the Downfall of Pride* (1655). For other references to this persistent interpretation, see Erwin Panofsky, *Studies in Iconology* (New York, 1939), pp. 218–21; and D. T. Starnes and E. W. Talbert, *Classical Myth and Legend in Renaissance Dictionaries* (Chapel Hill, 1955), pp. 117–20.

[43] Morton W. Bloomfield, *The Seven Deadly Sins* (East Lansing, 1952).

[44] Ovid, *Metamorphoses* (Venice, 1536), p. 10.

[45] *De consolatione*, II, metrum v.

[46] See, e. g., Pierre Cally's notes in his edition of Boethius (Paris, 1680); and George Hakewill, *An Apologie or Declaration* (Oxford, 1630), pp. 323 ff.

Juan de Pineda also illustrates the homiletic tendency to draw from Ovid's passage to inveigh against avarice. Annotating the scriptural lines on Job's riches, he declaims against riches for their own sake and easily slips into recollections of Ovid's Iron Age: ". . . quando itaque nullus erat auri splendor, nullusque usus aureum erat saeculum: cum vero 'effossae sunt opes irritamenta malorum,' ferrea aetas. . . ." And then he quotes Ovid's succeeding lines in full. (*Commentarium in Job* [Venice, 1736; first ed., 1608], I. 20.)

See Harald Hagendahl, *Latin Fathers and the Classics*, Acta Universitatis Gothoburgensis, vol. 64, pt. 2 (Goteborg, 1958), for evidence that Arnobius and Lactantius also had drawn on Ovid for their attacks on avarice. For further use of Ovid's lines for this purpose, see Vincent of Beauvais, *Bibliotheca mundi* (Duaci, 1624), II. 384.

[47] *Metamorphoses*, I. 144–48.

[48] *A System of Oratory* (1759), II. 73.

has granted his friend's beliefs, at least to the extent of declining to impose his own contrary position, in order to suspend Bathurst's misanthropy as irrelevant and thus to find the common ground of agreement in their rejection of the Calvinist explanation for the distribution of riches: " Both fairly owning, Riches in effect / No grace of Heav'n or token of th'Elect " (17–18). But the speaker's modes of expression that we have examined indicate that the concession is merely feigned and leads the opponent to assent unknowingly to more and other than he intends. For Bathurst's misanthropy is put in terms that contain in themselves a possible Christian refutation, and the speaker's Ovidian formulation of his own view is implicitly that of orthodox Christianity. Even in outwardly refusing to press his doctrine the speaker parenthetically shifts the weight heavily to his own side: " surely, Heav'n and I are of a mind " (8).

Only with a calculating irony, then, can the speaker call the problem a casuistic disagreement of the Doctors. Although his phrasing of the matter serves simultaneously to laugh the disagreement into a quibble and yet to draw Bathurst into the frame of Christian theology, the Christian speaker cannot truly mean that the divine purpose of organizing mankind into misers and spendthrifts is a question admitting indeterminate dispute. Nor can he be sincere in calling his companion a sound casuist. In the sense of " sophist " the term is part of the machinery of the epitrope, and in the sense of " a resolver of cases of conscience " it is disarming flattery and points generally to the fact that the ensuing poem will deal with a major aspect of moral conduct. But since casuistry, strictly speaking, is the moral application of religious principles to the peculiarities of human events, the speaker, who believes in a " careful Heav'n " (13) and the moral dignity of man, cannot be accepting as one of the " soundest Casuists " a man who, like Momus, believes that the gods are careless and their creations are fools. Even Milton's Satan knew, as pagan Bathurst does not, that " out of our evil " Providence seeks " to bring forth good." The obvious inappropriateness of the speaker's terms and their inconsistency with his explicit position call out for clarification. The Renaissance dictionary of Ambrosius Calepinus, quoting the fifth-century Rufinus, defines " epitrope " as the figure by which we permit one to hold his beliefs while we do not truly assent to them at all; and the figure, added Abraham Fraunce, is especially delightful " when we grant that which hurteth him to whom it is granted." [49] But what Pope's speaker has already gained by the rhetorical success of his opening gambit warrants his resting the point until a more auspicious moment in his argument.

4

Satire, especially in the form of the satiric *exemplum*, is an established feature of the Christian sermon, and therefore, even if we suppress the Horatian nature of this poem, we might readily expect Pope's preacher to employ it. But the special personae Pope has created endow the satire with peculiarly apt and complex rhetorical functions. Since Bathurst is a disciple of Momus, his orientation is professedly worldly and satiric, and the rhetorically skillful speaker can profitably adapt his companion's private bias to his own religious ends. For since Bathurst holds that all men were created to be fools, the preacher's satire of vices is consistent with both his own role and his antagonist's disposition. And yet, paradoxically, in the process of his satire the preacher's purpose in part is to use the instrument to undermine the satiric doctrine of Momus and to persuade his misanthropic companion that, not by nature, but only insofar as men sin against their moral obligations and fall below their God-given moral dignity are they fools and the proper objects of satire.

As a result of having thus interwoven into a single fabric the divine and the worldly, the Christian and Roman, the preceptive and satiric, Pope has released the opportunity for significant dramatic modulations of voice that evoke his reader's satiric smile and transform it into not merely moral indignation, but moral embarrass-

[49] *The Arcadian Rhetorike* (1588), ed. Ethel Seaton (Oxford, 1950), p. 105.

ment. The neoclassic satirist frequently pondered the artistic problem of how to promote into self-involved resentment the detached superiority usually attendant upon reading satire. In a "*City* Pulpit," said Swift, you may be "as fierce as you please, against Avarice. . . . 'Tis but a *Ball* bandied to and fro, and every Man carries a *Racket* about Him to strike it from himself among the rest of the Company." For, he added, "Satyr is a sort of Glass, wherein Beholders do generally discover every body's Face but their Own: which is the chief Reason for that kind Reception it meets in the World, and that so very few are offended with it." As poetic rhetorician, Pope repeatedly confronted himself with the same problem, as the *Epilogue to the Satires*, among other poems, testifies.

> To attack Vices in the abstract, without touching Persons, may be safe fighting indeed, but it is fighting with Shadows. General propositions are obscure, misty, and uncertain, compar'd with plain, full, and home examples: Precepts only apply to our Reason, which in most men is but weak: Examples are pictures, and strike the Senses, nay raise the Passions, and call in those (the strongest and most general of all motives) to the aid of reformation. Every vicious man makes the case his own; and that is the only way by which such men can be affected, much less deterr'd.
>
> (Pope to Arbuthnot, 26 July 1734; Sherburn, III. 419)

The two-edged engine fashioned by the creation of the two personae is an ingenious instrument designed precisely to perform this task of implicating the reader morally, not despite, but as an outcome of the satire; and much of the poem proceeds by a series of transitions between the speaker's satiric and preceptive voices as he draws cynical Bathurst to successive moral positions. In small, the rhetorical technique can be examined in a single couplet. Bathurst and the speaker having agreed to reject the Calvinist principle of the London merchants that wealth is a sign of election, the speaker adds, as evidence, that riches are

> Giv'n to the Fool, the Mad, the Vain, the Evil,
> To Ward, to Waters, Chartres, and the Devil.
> (19–20) [50]

The couplet includes both areas of the poem: the first line is a moral generality, the second a particularized personal attack. But the two areas do not seem to play upon each other. It is the personal satirist who names Ward, Waters, and Chartres, all notorious money-merchants who have bilked the populace and justify Bathurst's satiric contempt. The reader, however, holds himself detached from this personal assault because he, of course, belongs to another and unaffected order of men; and the generalized morality of the first line is "fighting with Shadows." But although the word "Devil" at first seems merely to complete the four names that correspond to the four general categories in the first line and to specify "Evil," it is given the grammatical form of one of the categories, "the Devil"; and thereby it dissolves the abstractions and the specific names into each other so that the attack becomes simultaneously particular and general, satiric and preceptive.

Moreover, the word "Devil" is clearly spoken by the religious voice that has alluded to casuists and the disagreement of the Doctors, has just spoken of election, grace, and religious tenets, and will sprinkle the lines with scriptural allusions. In such a religious context, the Devil is clearly the reader's concern, as the general types and the specific criminals need not be. The named individuals are now only specific instances of the Devil, for although some riches have been given them, possession of all the gold in the earth has been granted by God to the master of Hell, the Christian successor to the Pluto whom classical Bathurst would recognize as the underworld god of wealth. Alone, the personal satire earns only the smile that recognizes, but tolerates, the vices of others; without the personal satire, the attack "in the abstract" and the religious note at the end earn only a Sunday reverence. But taken together, the specific crimi-

[50] Cp. the entry signed "D. A." in Pope's "Thoughts on Various Subjects" (Elwin-Courthope, X. 559): "We may see the small value God has for riches, by the people he gives them to."

nals in society are assimilated into every man's personal enemy, the Devil; and the Devil goes to and fro in the earth in the forms of Ward, Waters, and Chartres.

The paragraphs succeeding this couplet employ the same rhetorical strategy with wider scope. Beginning with the quasi-scriptural line, "'Tis thus we eat the bread another sows," the speaker examines with considerable gravity and without a hint of satire the equal capacity of riches for good and evil.[51] The paragraph (21–34) has the neatly systematic organization that has always characterized the sermon form, progressing from the individual to society to the nation: riches may preserve life or hire the assassin, help trade or lure the pirate, extend society or corrupt a friend, raise an army or betray the nation.

However, the paragraphs that follow this solemnity are among the most lightly bantering and Momus-like in the poem, as the scoffing satiric voice of the preacher now assumes control. If gold is a too-convenient instrument for perfidy, would it not be well to revert to the premonetary Golden Age? To answer, the speaker preposterously imagines the sophisticated, bewigged aristocracy of the Age of George translated to the barter culture of the heroic era. The vision is in the tradition of—if it is not directly influenced by—Prudentius' witty satire on the *laudator temporis acti* who argues that since the times are degenerate, man should return to the primitive life. Granted, says Prudentius ironically; then

> let us roll all time back on its tracks right up to the beginning, and decide to condemn step by step all that successive experience has found out in later ages. . . . What are ploughs good for, or the useless labor of the barrow? Better to sate the belly with acorns from the oak trees. The first men used to split their timber with wedges; let our axes be reduced in the furnace from a hot moulding into a lump of metal, the iron dripping back again into its own ore. Slaughtered oxen used to provide clothing, and a chilly cave a little home; so let us go back to the caverns and put on shaggy wraps of unsewn skins. . . . Let the very race of Romulus weave huts of fragile straw . . . , spread their royal couches with hay, or wear on their hairy bodies a cloak made of an African bearskin.[52]

In the same manner, Pope's speaker, pointedly paraphrasing Dryden's translation of Virgil[53] and thereby ironically contrasting the " arts " of the two civilizations, fancies the Duke of Bedford being rewarded for his gaming at the coffee house precisely as the ancients were rewarded for their poetry:

> His Grace will game: to White's a Bull be led,
> With spurning heels and with a butting head.
> (55–56)

Since nobles now gamble by entering their horses instead of riding, as the ancient heroes did, in the chariot races, he imagines the uxorious Lord Bristol, to his domestic discomfort, winning whores in the sweepstakes, just as the ancient heroes were rewarded with female captives for their prowess in the heroic games. And Bristol's perfumed, effeminate son, Lord Hervey, similarly wins a herd of swine, instead of the usual horses or oxen, to take to St. James's, where, as Vice-Chamberlain, he supervises the niceties of the King's chambers.[54] But the most these Hogarthian cartoons can accomplish as satire is to point to the wide cultural gulf between the heroic games and modern gaming, and show how ridiculous a figure the pretty modern gentleman would cut if he were to revert to a Homeric civilization and its barter economy.

However, the inclusive moral preface to this

[51] Corresponding to Pope's doctrine in the *Essay on Man* that the passions, themselves morally indifferent, may produce vice or, if properly directed, the corresponding virtue. Augustine, *Enarrationes in Psalmos* (*P. L.*, XXXVI. 610): "Divitiae non iniquae, sed iniquis."

[52] *Contra Symmachum* (Loeb Classics, II. 27 ff.). In the seventeenth-century dispute over the theme of decay Prudentius' lines were translated by George Hakewill in support of his thesis that there is no " universall and perpetuall decay in the manners of men as is pretended " (*An Apologie or Declaration* [Oxford, 1630], pp. 292–93).

[53] *Eclogue*, III. 135–36:

My Pollio writes himself: a bull be bred,
With spurning heels, and with a butting head.

[54] Cp. the heroic games in *Iliad* XXIII.

strictly topical satire, together with the echo of Prudentius, suggests a purpose more serious than merely to scoff at the thought of banishing specie in order to prevent the immoral use of riches. If a barter economy, says the speaker, would be attended by indecorums that offset the virtue of making bribery more inconvenient and indelicate, a moneyed economy can be equally embarrassing to bribery, as the betraying jingle of Cato's guineas illustrates. Yet even this indelicacy has been removed by the invention of paper credit, wealth in its nearly pure and abstract form, which the speaker now apostrophizes: " Blest paper-credit! last and best supply! " (69). Value has at last been abstracted from things of value, including specie, and made available as an independent commodity having reference to nothing outside itself. Credit, as one early economist put it, had been raised " to a *Par* with Money " [55] and is the absolute refinement of wealth, being capable, unlike Cato's guineas, of permitting bribery without detection by sight or sound. It is the essence free of accidents: dishonesty can be genteel.

With this apostrophe the speaker's voice, without losing its satiric edge, takes on a renewed solemnity as he now catalogues the national enormities that mere paper credit has accomplished without the barbarities and indecorums of either barter or specie. Satirically, he sees the witty similarity between the supernaturally powerful sheets of paper money and the leaves of the Cumean Sibyl. Alluding to Virgil's lines on the Sibyl,[56] who was begged not to record her prophecies on the leaves lest the wind blow them away and disarrange the future, he recognizes that man has similarly made his economic fate subject to every wind of chance by recording his " fortune " on leaves of paper currency. But the power of the metaphor does not rest merely on the witty surface analogy. The surviving *Oracula Sibyllina* had been accepted by the Church Fathers and many of their successors as consonant with Christian prophecy, and the Sibyls were generally listed among God's prophets among the gentiles; moreover, in the preface to his *Messiah* Pope had taken the orthodox position of reading the Sibylline books as equivalent to the Old Testament in foretelling the coming of Christ.[57] The metaphor, then, runs on both sides of the road, pagan and Christian, satiric and religious. Not only is it a witty conjunction, but it also implies the blasphemy in man's using paper credit as a Christian would the *Oracula Sibyllina*; and Pope makes his language serve double duty to point to the disparity between the true faith and the false religion of money. Instead of the *Libri fatales*, which prophesied the coming of Christ and the spiritual salvation of man, one now rests his future salvation in those other Sibylline leaves, paper credit, which is " Pregnant with thousands " (of pounds —and therefore, to capitalistic society, of human destinies).[58] Paper money is his religious book of prophecy; it prophesies his salvation in the eventual Coming, not of Christ, but of " thousands "; and in this moneyed language " fates and fortunes " (76) are not tautological terms, since one's fate is decided by his " fortune."

Now that the particularized and immediate satire—on the prevalent bribery, on the aristocrats whose fragile dignity depends upon money, on the many kings who recently have been enthroned and dethroned by wealth—now that this satire has been assimilated into a religious context, the speaker assumes almost completely his preceptive voice to bring this movement to its rhetorical climax. Summarizing the ethico-financial picture he has drawn, he turns to Bathurst for evaluation of it: " Since then, my Lord, on

[55] *Remarks upon the Bank of England* (second ed., 1706), p. 13. The use of paper currency was comparatively new in England (see [Henry Pollexfen], *A Discourse of Trade, Coyn, and Paper Credit* [1697], p. 64) and, in theory, was thought to double the nation's resources, since both the specie and the paper notes representing it could circulate commercially and " do service " (*ibid.*, p. 69).

[56] Dryden's translation, *Aeneid*, VI. 116–19:

> But, oh! commit not thy prophetic mind
> To flitting leaves, the sport of ev'ry wind,
> Lest they disperse in air our empty fate;
> Write not, but, what the pow'rs ordain, relate.

See also *ibid.*, III. 448 ff.

[57] For the attitude of the Fathers toward the Sibylline oracles, see Hastings, *Encyclopaedia of Religion and Ethics*, and Mariana Monteiro, " *As David and the Sibyls Say* " (Edinburgh, 1905). The title of this book, of course, derives from the *Dies Irae*, " Teste David cum Sibylla," which alone is sufficient testimony to the Sibyl's Christian status.

[58] Cp. p. 110, line 67a: " pregnant with our fates."

such a World we fall, / What say you?" (79–80). The manifest sense is that we happen to live in such a world as I have drawn for you. And in agreeing to accept such a world (" Why take it, Gold and all"), Bathurst has at least been shaken out of his original satiric aloofness. Countering Bathurst's opinion that the game of gold is a vast jest of the gods, the speaker has translated the question from one of man's stupidity into one of ethics (it is the use to which money is put that is either good or bad) and has convincingly shown that money is now an inherent part of the culture. By being led to assent, Bathurst has been won away from his rejection of man and has consented to face seriously the question of what worthy ends riches may be made to serve.

But the recurrent religious tone of the poem compels an additional reading of "on such a World we fall." As the speaker had implied in his own account of the origin of misers and spendthrifts, this is the postlapsarian world, and ever since Adam, man has been in a state of sin. Consequently, Bathurst's assent also is an agreement to submit to our fallen state and make the best of it. The world will not be cured by tinkering with the economic machine; any economic system requires moral guidance, and the present one requires it sorely. Therefore the Prudentian satire against primitivism, which was the second phase of the movement we are tracing, is double-edged, like most of Pope's satire. In the *Rape of the Lock*, for example, he both satirized society by displaying it in incongruous quasi-heroic roles, and yet countered the satire by having Clarissa, Sarpedon-like, urge man to resign himself to his society and its culture, slight and shriveled though they are, and use them as a purposeful way of life. Correspondingly, here he has satirized the effeteness of the contemporary Herveys by fancying them in a heroic age and in a barter economy, but not in order to advocate reversion to earlier standards. The heroes are gone forever from the land, and our lesser race must both chasten its pride by recognition of its diminished state and discover the ethics appropriate to that state, just as the Christian must recognize that Eden is no more and must pursue the virtue required of a world on which we "fall."

The rhetorical curve we have been tracing is the basic pattern of the poem and constitutes the art whereby the reader becomes personally trapped in the satire. Beginning with its starkly homiletic preface, the unit has progressed gradually from gentle ridicule of particular economic foibles to increasingly more indignant and strident satire on financial corruptions; and at last it reverts to the religious theme to remind us that it is the theologian who has been speaking all the while. The reader, rising with the satire to indignation at the crimes of others, suddenly discovers, with the reappearance of the theologian's voice, that his indignation has been roused against a human condition to which he too is a party and in which he has an inescapable moral obligation. *De te fabula narratur.*

The logical argument of the next movement of the "sermon" rides forward on a similar rhetorical wave. Now that Bathurst has been led to resign himself to the fallen—that is, capitalistic—state of the world, the speaker retains for the moment his solemn and strictly analytic air. Since it is agreed that we must live in a moneyed society, what can riches provide? "Meat, Cloaths, and Fire," answers the theologian, echoing scriptural passages that were a constant reference in the sermon literature on riches. And to Bathurst's apparently hedonistic dissatisfaction with this answer he replies, "Is this too little? would you more than live?" But at this point he quickly moves into biting and narrowly personal satire: all their money could not cure the ills of Hopkins, Chartres, Crook, Cadogan, or Montagu. All this is free of religious overtones and seems merely the personal satirist's confirmation of the theologian's point that man's material needs are few.

However, Christian doctrine provides for two uses of wealth. Material goods supply the basic creature needs, but the charitable distribution of all wealth in excess of that needed to maintain one's status in life is a religious obligation. The speaker will now instruct his companion in these charitable duties; and consequently, as he passes from the first subject to the second, he correspondingly passes from mere personal satire to personal satire in a religious context. The transitional figure of Harpax, therefore, introduces the religious reference that will then dominate the rest of the satire. Since one of the rewards that Christianity promises the benefactor for his charity is the prayers and blessings of the recipients, riches " might (were Harpax not too wise to spend) / Give Harpax self the blessing of a Friend " (93–94).

Not the power of riches to supply creature needs, but their power to fulfill the Christian requirement of charity—to friends, institutions, children, and the poor—has now become the satiric theme, although the speaker continues to direct the satire against specific individuals. To ask, then, whether " the Poor might have their part " (101) of the world's goods can be only bitterly satiric, for the whole body of Christian literature holds the rich man responsible as the divinely appointed steward for the poor, as the speaker will later insist: " Who sees pale Mammon pine amidst his store, / Sees but a backward steward for the Poor " (173–74). Since the persons to be satirized in this context are arranged in terms of their various irreligious rejections of the rich man's stewardship, it is with a wonderful sense of irony that Pope chose two of them, Bond and Sutton, from the directors of the Charitable Corporation for the Relief of the Industrious Poor. Organized to provide easy loans to the poor, the corporation had actually been used by the directors and their assistants to perpetrate a notorious swindle for their private gains; and its corrupt affairs had been occupying much of the attention of Parliament. In the hands of the capitalists Christian charity had been perverted into big business, and stewardship into private profit.

Since the satirist has entered upon the strictly religious use of riches, each of the four figures satirized is assigned a different degree of irreligion in his rejection of his charitable obligations. Blatantly anti-Christian Bond " damns the Poor," whom Christ called " blessed " and the inheritors of the Kingdom of God (Luke 6: 20), and with whom Christ had identified himself (2 Corinthians 8: 9); and, inverting the scriptural injunction to " love . . . *with* all thy heart," Bond " hates them *from* his heart " (102). Atheistic Heathcote, disregarding religion entirely, in effect denies that riches are distributed by Providence, for he holds that " every man in want is knave or fool " (104). The phrases, as Pope's note points out and as the contemporary journals confirm,[59] were actually used by the scoundrels being satirized, and Pope's artistic strategy lies in organizing the specific worldly events so as to reveal their large religious implications. The Dissenter Blunt takes the Calvinist view that wealth is a sign of election, and therefore it is, in his lights, " pious " to deny those whom God starves (106). Only Sutton, the " good Bishop," knows the Christian truth that riches are no token of the elect and that the poor are entitled to their part from the stewards of riches; but instead of aiding or emulating Providence by works, he exercises only faith and " leaves them, Providence's care " (108).

Since the twofold purpose of riches has allowed the religiously oriented satirist to succeed the strictly personal satirist, the preacher's voice can now assume command and rise to serious religious indignation. Although he remains satiric, his frame of reference is now wholly religious, and although he directs himself against the whole category of uncharitable men, his generality retains the pointedness of the personal satire that immediately preceded. With irony he allows his Christian " charity " to assume that such uncharitable men as the directors of the " Charitable " Corporation must be more religious than most, not less, and must be acting on some supernatural " Revelation " hid from others (116). Not their lack of religion, but their being favored by God with prophetic vision must be responsible for their seeming avarice. And the speaker ironically seeks to be just to such misers by admitting that they adhere at least to the logic, if not to the letter and spirit, of the Commandments. For if the second greatest of the Commandments is that we should love our neighbors as ourselves (Matthew 22: 39), each of these " does but hate his Neighbour as

[59] *Fog's Journal*, 27 May 1732; *Historical Register*, 17 (1732), 268.

himself" (110) and thereby not only fails as steward of the poor but also neglects that Charity on which all the theological virtues rest. A whole texture of satiric and religious values, therefore, is interwoven by the speaker's calling such "men of pelf" "poor." In worldly terms, of course, they are rich, not poor; yet, since they are misers—that is, refuse to use their wealth and remain in "want"—they alone are truly the poor. On the other hand, since their riches are stolen ("pelf") and since they do not have Charity, the preacher can call them spiritually poor, despite their worldly wealth. And finally the speaker is both satiric and Christian in directing his own Charity toward such men: he can call them "poor" because their sins call up his pity.

But the couplet that completes this rhetorical curve is entirely free of irony or personal satire:

> Damn'd to the Mines, an equal fate betides
> The Slave that digs it, and the Slave that hides. (111–12)

As Joseph Warton pointed out long ago, a similar metaphor appears in Cowley and in Richard Allestree, but he was not necessarily right in considering the latter Pope's source. The phrase *damnare in metalla* derives ultimately from the Justinian legal code, where it designated the most severe noncapital punishment. St. Chrysostom probably was the first to adopt it as a metaphor for the condition of the covetous man and very elaborately extended the comparison to show that at every point, no matter how painful the state of the prisoner in the mines, that of the avaricious man, who has voluntarily damned himself to the mines of riches, is far worse.[60] From this common fountain, doubtless, subsequent moral and religious writers drew the metaphor. An excerpt from Chrysostom's homily appears in Joseph Lang's widely popular encyclopaedia of moral *sententiae* under the heading "Avaritia." [61] In one of his "characters" Samuel Butler defined the miser as "a Slave condemned to the Mines." [62] Cowley calls the covetous man "*ad Metalla damnatus,* a man condemned to work in Mines, which is the lowest and hardest condition of servitude; and to encrease his Misery, a worker there for he knows not whom: He heapeth up Riches and knows not who shall enjoy them; 'Tis onely sure that he himself neither shall nor can injoy them." [63] And Allestree goes beyond Chrysostom and makes identical in all details the fate of the slave damned to the mines and "the covetous mans lot." [64] Consequently, in identifying the miser, "the Slave that hides," with the slave "Damn'd to the Mines," Pope's speaker is employing a commonplace that is richly connotative of the Christian literary tradition and that redirects his satire to its homiletic ends.

Having assented, as a Christian must, to the preacher's pious exordium on the limited material use of riches, and having been engaged in its relevance to the human situation by the banter against men like Hopkins, Chartres, Crook, and Cadogan, the reader has then been roused to satiric indignation against public enemies like Bond and Sutton and against their peculations—only to be reminded at the height of his inflammation that he himself has been addressed by the homilist all the while and that he has been trapped into a personal commitment on a moral matter to which he also is a party and in which he has an inescapable religious duty. The particular corruptions of Whig economics can be hit only by direct, particularized satire, not by pious words; but to explode the corruptions, the satiric charge must be cased in the absolute ethics of Christianity.

[60] Homily 23 on 1 Corinthians (*P. G.*, LXI. 195 ff.). In his *Sermo de symbolo* (*P. L.*, XL, col. 1200) Augustine compared the luxurious dreams of those "in metallis condemnati" to the earthly life of the rich man: after his death nothing remains but penance for the past and the pains of the present.

[61] *Polyanthea nova* (Frankfurt, 1607). Jean Richard paraphrased the entire metaphor in his sermon on avarice, in *Universalis concionandi scientia* (Venice, 1747; first ed., 1700-1709).

[62] *Characters,* ed. A. R. Waller (Cambridge, 1908), p. 146. See also p. 472.

[63] "Of Liberty."

[64] [Richard Allestree], *The Causes of the Decay of Christian Piety* (1704; first ed., 1667), p. 89. The phrase "damned to the mines," applied to the miser, also appears in Charles Herle, *Worldly Policy and Moral Prudence* (1655), p. 117, and in Thomas Pierce, *The Sinner Impleaded in his own Court* (third ed., 1670), p. 30.

5

These dramatic interplays of the satiric and the theological voices have also endowed the language with rich ironic possibilities. Most obviously, the pervasive religious and moral strain can react upon any economic terminology so as to absorb it ironically into a moral sense: paper credit, for example, "*lends* Corruption lighter wings to fly!" (70). The effect of the pun is to identify the language of finance with evil and to suggest the vast discrepancy between economic values and moral ones. Concluding his scathing interpretation of the memorial statue of the miser Hopkins, the speaker exclaims:

> Behold what blessings Wealth to life can *lend*!
> And see, what comfort it *affords* our end.
> (297–98)

The clash between the financial and the religious terms reveals that, in the irreligion of the miser Hopkins, material things take the place of spiritual blessings and comfort; and inversely it implies that such economic terms can have true value only when they are metaphoric of things spiritual, just as the Christian must forego the riches of Mammon for the true riches of Heaven. Similarly, since the two voices of the speaker evoke such metaphoric possibilities, the equivocality of such a word as "fortune" can provide a significant meeting point for the economic and religious themes and establish their proper relations. Whenever virtuous men like Bathurst and Oxford shine, "oh Fortune," the poet begs, "gild the scene" (245). Pope has not eschewed worldly goods. His theme is the *proper* use of riches, not the virtues of poverty; and therefore, when such human excellence appears, it should be blessed both by Providence ("Fortune") and by the worldly fortune that Providence distributes, for such men will convert worldly gold into glittering virtue. Joining magnificence with economy, and splendor with charity, a Bathurst gains true moral wealth with his gold; and hence in equivocal senses he "shines" like the golden sun and "Fortune" gilds his scene (245). Correspondingly, the speaker begs divine aid to preserve such virtue: "And Angels guard him in the golden Mean!" (246). But since this is a virtue dependent upon the use of riches, the guardian "Angels" petitioned are also the gold coins, or angels, that were held to have the remarkable sovereign power of curing the "King's evil" and that are the instruments for liberality, the "golden Mean." [65]

The very copresence in this language of both the financial and moral senses allows the speaker immediately thereafter to turn the language of commerce satirically against itself to imply that its only valuable meaning is its moral sense: "But all our praises why should Lords *engross*?" (249). "Worth" is another such convenient economic-moral term, and Pope elsewhere complained that in these days "A Man of wealth is dubb'd a Man of Worth" (*Imitations of Horace*, Epistle I. vi. 81). Here he makes his play upon the word, not, as in his use of "Fortune," to identify the spiritual with the proper use of riches, but to divulge the current Calvinistic confusion of worldly goods with the Good:

> "Virtue! and Wealth! what are ye but a name!"
> Say, for such *worth* are other worlds prepar'd? (334–35)

By so collapsing both virtue and wealth into the one term "worth," the speaker has set the scene for the terrible disparity between riches and virtue that he will unfold when, a few lines later, he will say of Sir Balaam, "His word would pass for more than he was worth" (344). In the moral domain public reputation ("word") should be directly proportional to private virtue ("worth"), and therefore Balaam is an evil but successful hypocrite; but in the commercial world the degree to which one's credit ("word") exceeds his assets ("worth") is the established measure of success. The truth that the economic code precisely inverts the moral is contained in

[65] Cp. *Imitations of Horace*, Epistle II. ii. 218–19: "When golden Angels cease to cure the Evil, / You give all royal Witchcraft to the Devil."

The economic sense was, of course, the original Horatian meaning of the Golden Mean (*Odes*, II. x. 5).

the power of the same words to carry the two antithetical senses.

Most frequently, however, the copresence of satire and theology permits a satire in the form of inverted Christianity. As satirist-theologian, the speaker can either misapply a scriptural passage or transmogrify it so as to make it accord with contemporary corruptions. The resulting satire, because of the established double tone, becomes not blasphemy but an index both to the distance between economic and revealed ethics, and to the religious hypocrisy or false devotions of the offenders. Capitalistic Mammon-worship, like the black mass, draws its sanctions from an inverted or burlesqued Scripture, as, for example, in Pope's admitting with pseudopiety that each man of pelf "does but hate his Neighbour as himself." Or it appeals to false gods: because the younger Cotta squandered his estate in devotion to the Whiggish House of Hanover,

> 'Tis GEORGE and LIBERTY that crowns the cup,
> And Zeal for that great House which eats him up. (207–208)[66]

This technique of allowing the worshipper of wealth to indict his own sinfulness by enacting a sacrilegious parody of the worship of God also governs the portrait of the elder Cotta.[67] But since the portrait is drawn for the immediate benefit of Bathurst, the speaker also educes consent on his companion's own terms by pointedly echoing, in the description of Cotta, Virgil's "dapibus mensas onerabat inemptis": "With soups unbought and sallads blest his board" (184). By calling attention to his source in a footnote, Pope has conjured up for Bathurst-like readers the original context of the line in Virgil's fourth Georgic, where it is part of the description of an admirable old man who, owning only a few, nearly barren acres, found true happiness in the little that his labors afforded him. His content equalled the wealth of kings.[68] In the speaker's ironic application of Virgil's line, Bathurst—classicist, satirist, and philosopher—should be able to recognize that Cotta's niggardliness is a hypocritical travesty on the virtuous simple life that is taught by unaided reason.

But just as moral philosophy is subsumed under Christian ethics, so the speaker has gained Bathurst's philosophic assent in order to induce him to repudiate Cotta's avarice also on the theological grounds that Bathurst has been resisting. Although the similarity of Cotta's mean hall to "some lone Chartreux" (189) is made explicit only in a passing metaphor, actually the entire description derives from the austere rules of the Carthusians, who called themselves "Christ's poor men." According to the standard and frequently quoted description by Peter the Venerable, the Carthusians severely isolated themselves from the world and even from each other, led a remarkably ascetic life, generally maintained silence for meditation, and, like Cotta, who forgot "the use of barb'rous spits" and kept a cold kitchen (181), avoided meat entirely.[69] Like Cotta, too, they submitted to continual fasts and otherwise fed on pulse (*legumen*) and other vegetables which, like Cotta's "soups unbought and sallads," grew on their own grounds. But all this the monks did, reported Peter, for the greater glory of God and "as a check against cupidity, which is called the root of all evils, and against avarice, which is called idolatry."[70] Cotta, then, lives the stark Carthusian life in order to nurture the very avarice the monks were mortifying by that manner of life.

The monastic rules, moreover, were instituted

[66] Cp. Psalms 69: 9 and John 2: 17, where "zeal of thine house" was usually interpreted by the commentators as "dedication to the true religion."

[67] Pope's lines, "Old Cotta sham'd his fortune and his birth, / Yet was not Cotta void of wit or worth" (179–80), echo Tacitus' description of Cotta Messalinus: ". . . nobilis quidem, sed egens ob luxum, per flagitia infamis" (*Annales*, VI. vii). Tacitus also tells of the many good services Cotta had rendered Caesar (VI. v). In his edition of Juvenal and Persius ([Paris, 1658], p. 427) de Marolles glossed Persius' reference to Cotta: ". . . qui avoit fort dégeneré de la vertu et de la reputation de ses Ancestres." Aside from this one detail, however, I know of no special relevance in the name "Cotta."

[68] "Regum aequabat opes animis" (*Georgics*, IV. 132). "Few Passages in all the Writings of Antiquity," said Joseph Trapp, "delight me more, than This lovely Description of *Poverty* and *Industry*. . . . Who, that reads This, *despises* not the *Wealth*, and *pities* not the *Persons*, of all the *great ones* upon Earth?" (*Works of Virgil*, trans. Joseph Trapp [second ed., 1735], I. 214 n).

[69] *De miraculis*, II. xxviii (*P.L.*, CLXXXIX. 943–45).

[70] "Cupiditatem insuper quae radix malorum omnium dicitur, vel avaritiam quae idolorum servitus vocatur. . . ."

as a means of observing Christ's severe counsels of perfection (Matthew 19: 16 ff.) above and beyond the natural virtues and the precepts of the Gospels, which are binding on all men. Confident of philosophic Bathurst's rational agreement, the speaker has formulated the miser's portrait so as to induce Bathurst to recognize not merely that Cotta's travesty on the contented simple life is morally stupid but also, and more crucially, that in aping the perfect Christian means to eternal life for precisely the contrary ends, Cotta is sinful and his life a sacrilege. If Bathurst can read the portrait aright, he will know not merely that the perversion of the good is bad, but that the corruption of the perfect Christian way of life is the worst.

One of the more extended uses of scriptural parody to bring vice into ironic focus with a perversion of revealed religion is the sketch of Sir John Blunt. Why, it is asked, does Blunt, who cheated the public as a director of the South Sea Company, bear Britain's hate? The preacher, sustaining his "charity" and assuming a mock-sympathy, pretends that Blunt must have had some "Revelation hid from you and me." Blunt, who, according to Pope's footnote, "was a Dissenter of most religious deportment, and profess'd to be a great believer," had intended (the ironist continues) only universal good, for a "wizard" had prophesied to him that "Corruption, like a gen'ral flood, / . . . Shall deluge all" (137–39). In his canting hypocrisy Blunt, it would seem, fancied himself a latter-day Noah divinely elected to be saved and to save living things from a universal ("gen'ral") Deluge brought down by the sinfulness of the new moneyed society—in which, in fact, he was one of the most notorious offenders. It is the money-hungry Calvinist who believes he is Noah, the only man who was "perfect in his generation and . . . walked with God" (Genesis 6: 9). The metaphor of a drowning Flood of corruption, avarice, and money flows through the sketch. Since the avaricious capitalistic parvenus are "low-born," their avarice will "Spread like a low-born mist, and blot the Sun" (140); and, in another equivoque, all of Britain will ultimately be "sunk in lucre's sordid charms" (145).

However, man's "fate" has not been revealed to canting Blunt by Noah's God, but by a "wizard," one of those Old Testament figures associated with idolatry and familiar spirits. These wizards were the gentile necromancers, the "abominations" of the nations, against whom God warned the Jews, for He alone is God: "Regard not them that have familiar spirits, neither seek after wizards, to be defiled by them: I am the Lord your God" (Leviticus 19: 31).[71] Despite his seemingly religious deportment, then, Blunt is a gentile (since he is a Dissenter), his wizard is the anti-God, and his vision is a false, demonic one, derived from a false religion and hypocritical religiosity.

Consequently Pope's satire can cut in both directions. The wizard's picture of corruption is valid, and Pope can use the vision to lash at the current vices of riches. But the corrupt Blunt, the false Noah, is not the man to inveigh against them; a swindling Dissenter, he represents corruption crying out against corruption with false piety and false benevolence. In the logic of the poem, the sketch of Blunt illustrates one of the motives of avarice. Fear (117–24) and ambition (125–34) have already been examined, and unmotivated avarice will shortly be described (155–60); in this hierarchy of causes Blunt represents the avarice feigned to be necessary to survive the corruptions springing from avarice itself. Hence the propriety of casting Calvinist Blunt in the role of the false Noah, the only "good" man in a wicked world who is divinely elected to rescue mankind.

Moreover, as Pope's note points out, the prophetic words of the wizard reflect the "very style" of Blunt himself as he "declaimed against the corruption and luxury of the age." The wizard's prophecy is therefore in effect Blunt's recurrent sermon. Here, as elsewhere in the sketch, Pope is drawing both from Scripture and from the exegetical traditions. Not in Genesis, but in the words of Peter, Noah was a "preacher of righteousness" (1 Peter 3: 18–20, 2 Peter

[71] Also Leviticus 20: 6, 27; Deuteronomy 18: 9–11; 1 Samuel 28: 3; 2 Kings 21: 6, 23: 24; Isaiah 8: 19, 19: 3.

2: 5). Josephus wrote that Noah had urged his fellow men to improve their ways; two of Noah's "sermons" against the horrible sins of man appear in the *Oracula Sibyllina*; and thence there evolved a long tradition of Noah's preachings and prophecies.[72] "If "ye at last repent," Drayton has "terror-preaching" Noah say, God "will lay by his wrathfull punishment":

> Oh cry for mercy, leave your wicked wayes,
> And God from time shall separate those dayes
> Of vengeance comming, and he shall disperse
> These Clouds now threatning the whole universe,
> And save the world, which else he will destroy.[73]

Blunt's Dissenting cant against public sin, then, further qualifies him for the role of the false Noah, the unrighteous man publicly declaiming against sin and prophesying calamity. Finally, Blunt also performs the false Noah's work by bribing both political parties, for by this dishonest means he sought the "righteous end" of halting "Party-rage" and giving his country "peace." The dove and its olive branch were both symbols of the new peace; [74] the rainbow God set in the sky was a token of God's covenant of peace with man; and, according to an interpretation emphasized ever since the Midrash, Noah's very name means *quies, consolatio, pax*.[75]

But although the portrait of Blunt is the speaker's devastating attack on the religious hypocrisy at the bottom of Calvinist economics, which pretends that private lust for wealth is the divinely assigned instrument for preserving the elect from the calamities in store for the avaricious public, nevertheless Pope does not deny Blunt's lament that the public worships Mammon. The prophecy of Blunt's wizard reads as a direct assault on the widespread cupidity of the day. In Genesis the sinful generation which was "corrupt before God" and filled the earth with violence before the Flood was the product of the union of the "sons of God" and the "daughters of men." This was the generation that caused God to bring "a flood of waters upon the earth to destroy all flesh" except Noah and his family. But precisely what was meant by "the sons of God" and "the daughters of men" occasioned considerable dispute among the scriptural commentators. Matthew Poole, summarizing centuries of earlier exegesis, catalogued the four main interpretations of *filii Dei*: (1) angels or demons—an interpretation almost universally rejected in the Renaissance; (2) giants; (3) sons of judges or princes; (4) sons of the pious, or the professors of the true religion. He then explained that since such phrases as *filii hominum* really mean *homines*, (3) and (4)—which are the interpretations relevant to our purposes—are to be understood as the judges, princes, and priests who had become degenerate.[76] As Pope satirically translates these traditions into the specific corruptions rampant in eighteenth-century Mammon worship, the prediluvian class of rulers whose sins brought on the Flood become "Statesman and Patriot" (141)—that is, Whigs and Tories—who "ply alike the stocks" and the "mighty Dukes" (144) who "pack cards for half a crown." Now the "Judges job" (143). And the degenerate men of religion become the Bishops who "bite the town" (143). In his satiric construct Pope's religiously oriented speaker, through Blunt's wizard, recognizes the age before the Flood as a type of the present, and the sinful past repeats itself with notable parallelism in the current sins of capitalistic avarice. Playing the stock market, jobbing stocks, bilking the town, and cheating at cards are the "violence" that now fills the earth.

[72] Versions of Noah's sermons may be found in Athanasius Kircher's *Arca Noe* (1675); in Hieremiah Drexelius, *Noe architectus* (Antwerp, 1644), chap. VI; and in J. A. Fabricius, *Codex pseudoepigraphus Veteris Testamenti* (Hamburg, 1722), I. 229–39. For Kircher's account, see D. C. Allen, *The Legend of Noah* (Urbana, Ill., 1949), p. 184.

Cp. Pope to Lord Peterborough, August 1732 (Sherburn, II. 189): ". . . you have dwelt among us here but like a sort of Noah, preaching Sense & Honour many years, to a Generation who are doomd to be swallowd up & drownd in their own Dulness & Dirtiness."

[73] *Noahs Floud*, 221–25.

[74] See Cornelius a Lapide, *op. cit.*

[75] See Benedictus Pererius, *Commentarium et disputatio in Genesin* (Venice, 1607), II. 30–31; a Lapide, *op. cit.*, I. 104; and Matthew Poole, *Synopsis criticorum* (1669), I. 70–71.

[76] *Synopsis* (1669), I. 78. See also Pererius, *op. cit.*, II. 5. The exegetes summarized by Poole and by John Pearson (*Critici sacri* [Frankfurt, 1696]) variously define "princes" as *principii, magnati, nobilii, procures, magistrati, potentes*, and *gubernatores*.

Yet another scriptural tradition explained that the sinfulness before the Flood arose from the prohibited union of the descendants of Seth (the sons of God) and the descendants of Cain (the daughters of men). Whereas the former were of the tribe of rulers, judges, and priests, the latter were of the lower orders, the rabble (*plebiae*, according to a Lapide; *subditii*, according to de Lyra). These God had forbidden to unite; [77] but they lusted after each other and violated God's mandate—some exegetes like de Lyra calling this an unlawful coupling and some like Drusius even considering it rape.[78] In Pope's version of this libidinous social miscegenation the sexes are interchanged: "Peeress and Butler share alike the Box" (142). In the total context the main allusion is to the dice box, since all the surrounding references are to other forms of gaming and swindling; [79] and it is this common lust after money that now unnaturally unites royalty and mob. But the reference is also to the theater box, where the leveling process of capitalism is obliterating the traditional sharp distinctions among the social ranks. And finally there is a nuance of the popular sexual pun on "box" [80]—shortly to be reinforced by the picture of "Britain sunk in lucre's sordid charms"—that echoes the lust of the sons of God for the daughters of men and that was given special social point for the eighteenth century by the recurrent tales of noble ladies who found illicit pleasures with their footmen and butlers. The corruption that the capitalistic culture has brought about not only has degraded the leaders of state, court, and church, but also has broken the hierarchy, which, to the Tory mind, is essential to a sound social structure. As in the days of the antediluvian giants, God might justifiably see again that "the wickedness of man was great in the earth, and that every imagination of the thoughts of his heart was only evil continually."

[77] See, e.g., *Critici sacri*, I. 138.

[78] Quoted in *Critici sacri*.

[79] Cp. Dryden, "Third Satire of Persius," 95–96: "And watch the box, for fear they should convey / False bones. . . ."

[80] Cp. [James Bramston], *The Man of Taste, Occasion'd by an Essay of Mr. Pope's on that Subject* (1733), pp. 3–4:

> My Father was a play'r in Drury-lane,
> Pears and Pistachio-nuts my Mother sold,
> He a Dramatick-poet, She a Scold,
> His tragic muse could Countesses affright,
> Her wit in boxes was my Lord's delight.

The poem was occasioned by Pope's epistles to Bathurst and Burlington.

6

To this point we have been examining the satiric rhetoric of the epistle, rather than its ethical content as oration or sermon. What is the ethical frame on which Pope is weaving his satire and from which the satire gains its meaningful design, rather than merely its persuasive force? Unsatisfactory answers to this question have long been a barrier to an appreciation of the poem, largely, I believe, because the efforts to read it with too simple and naïve a set of premises or within strictly Mandevillian terms cannot fail to make it an incoherent statement. Courthope's almost perverse misreading has been the prototype of the argument for thematic inconsistency:

> The philosophical defects of this Essay are obvious. Pope's reasoning is self-contradictory. He starts with what is in effect an attack upon luxury and civilisation (for no refined community can dispense with the use of a currency, which Pope regards solely as an instrument of corruption); yet he afterwards asserts that the constitution of society, which he has thus condemned, is ordained and promoted by Heaven itself. . . . His doctrine about the operation of extremes is not supported by facts. Misers do not always have prodigal sons, and, even if they had, it would be very unjust to make Providence responsible for the blundering scheme of distributing wealth which Pope imagines to proceed from the relationship. He wishes us to believe that the miser, under divine direction, hoards up his money only for his heir to dissipate it so lavishly that "men and dogs may drink him till they burst!" Such "extremes" would scarcely seem to "concur to general use."

Putting aside Courthope's almost willful errors (for example, Pope obviously does *not* regard currency "solely as an instrument of corruption "), nevertheless does not Pope's doctrine that God created misers and spendthrifts for the same reason that he "bids the Ocean ebb and flow" relieve man of all moral responsibility and make divinely necessary the very corruptions Pope is attacking? Why satirize miserly Cotta and his prodigal son if collectively they are carrying out God's scheme of reconciling extremes? Since, Courthope believed, Pope accepted Mandeville's paradox, "private vices, public benefits," he failed to see that "to impute this supposed social law to the wisdom of the Creator . . . would be in effect to deny the moral nature of God." The inconsistency Courthope and succeeding critics have thought to find in the epistle is identical in kind with the supposed philosophic inconsistency of the *Essay on Man*: if a Borgia and a Catiline are necessary to God's scheme because "partial Evil" is "universal Good," man can have no moral responsibility for his actions. Then why enjoin him to virtue by the exercise of his conscience if "whatever is, is right"?

Put in this way, the problem is a false one. To avoid Courthope's initial blunder, it would be well to recognize first that the opening eighty lines of the *Epistle to Bathurst* constitute a prologue—or rather, the *exordium* and *narratio*—and not a part of the main argument. The purpose of this preparatory section is to determine the grounds and premises for the central problem, the proper *use* to which riches should be put. In addition to generating the satiric rhetoric of the poem, the prologue advances two points, each punctuated by explicit agreement between Bathurst and Pope. First, mere possession of wealth is unrelated to private virtue or spiritual worth, riches being distributed by some providential plan ("We find our tenets just the same at last"). Therefore riches, like the passions, are the morally indifferent means of a moral act. Second, in ascertaining his moral norms man must do so within the limitations of a postlapsarian world, the boundless opportunity for dishonesty released by paper credit being the economic expression of that fallen state. Pope, then, is not condemning the mere existence of a moneyed culture any more than he could condemn his contemporaries for original sin. "Better for Us," he wrote in the *Essay on Man*, "Were there all harmony, all virtue here"; but he is sane enough—and religious enough—to know that Adam lost Eden for us and that sin is, and must be, loose in the world. Correspondingly, he can think wistfully upon precapitalistic days, but he knows it would be as ridiculous for Worldly to cry coals from street to street as for a farmer to expect the eternal spring of the Garden of Eden. It is within the confines of these realistic—and Christian—admissions that Pope will seek the morality and theology of riches: What is the supreme ethics of wealth possible in a fallen world?

Nevertheless, the dilemma of determinism and moral freedom seems to remain, for if God's management of the fallen world consists of reconciling misers and spendthrifts, just as he reconciles seedtime and harvest, together with all other contraries in nature (161–70), must not all men belong necessarily to one category or the other by divine decree? This problem, however, can arise only if one—heretically—assumes that God's perfection can in any way be affected by man's conduct and that God's mode of sustaining His fallen creation implies the obligation that human conduct conform to that mode. From the fact that God, in His perfection, harmoniously reconciles extremes it does not follow that His perfection is contingent upon man's pursuing the extremes; for this would imply that perfection depends upon evil. Indeed, Pope has been careful to explain that God's purposes are a mystery, not to be questioned or sought by man, whose duty is merely to accept them as perfect. One manuscript version records that God's reconciliation of the extremes in man serves "some *mysterious* use." [81] And even in the published version he answers with a tautology the question, "what makes one keep, and one bestow?": "That Pow'R who bids the Ocean ebb and flow" (166). He who makes and reconciles extremes is He who makes and reconciles extremes; for it is sufficient that God know His purpose in permitting the poten-

[81] That is, the same line that appears in *Essay on Man*, II. 206. See below, p. 86.

tiality of sin and, in His foreknowledge, the fulfillment of the potentiality. But the impossibility of man's fathoming God's mysterious but necessarily perfect purpose does not free individual man from the responsibility to know and strive to fulfill that degree of perfection remaining to his fallen nature. Briefly, the essential Christian dilemma that Pope is facing consists of acknowledging on the one hand that, despite man's fall, God, and therefore His total creation, must be perfect ("All partial evil, universal good"); and that, on the other hand, the moral duty of the individual man is to strive to fulfill the final end for which he was created, regardless of God's economy of the whole.

Perhaps the least difficult way of gaining access to Pope's solution of this dilemma is to examine a memorandum Spence recorded of Pope's conversation on this very epistle:

> We s^{d} not speak agst one large Vice, without speaking agst its contrary.—As to ye General Design of Providence ye two Extremes of a Vice, serve like two opposite biasses to keep up ye Ballance of things. Avarice, lays up (w^{t} w^{d} be hurtful;) Prodigality, scatters abroad (w^{t} may be useful in other hands:) The middle ye point for Virtue.[82]

The sentences are sadly jumbled, but the language is precise enough to allow us to reorganize them. The first and last sentences speak of the means of defining virtue and therefore are concerned with private morality; but the central two sentences describe the way in which Providence operates to the good of the whole. It is fundamental to all of Pope's ethical works that these two perspectives—God's and the individual man's—be discriminated.

God's general Providence works with the "two Extremes of a Vice," such as prodigality and avarice, reconciling them to sustain the "Ballance of things." This is the postlapsarian system of harmony that Providence employs, now that there can no longer be "all harmony, all virtue here"; for it is inconceivable to Pope that man's vices can disturb the perfect wisdom and goodness of God, whose "great view is One, and that the Whole" (*Essay on Man*, II. 238). In the *Epistle to Bathurst* this "truth" is announced in this way:

> 'Tis Heav'n each Passion sends,
> And diff'rent men directs to diff'rent ends.
> Extremes in Nature equal good produce,
> Extremes in Man concur to gen'ral use.
> (161–64)

Consequently in His economy God employs misers and spendthrifts in the same way that He

> bids the Ocean ebb and flow,
> Bids seed-time, harvest, equal course maintain,
> Thro' reconcil'd extremes of drought and rain,
> Builds Life on Death, on Change Duration founds,
> And gives th'eternal wheels to know their rounds. (166–70)

However, it must be noticed that in thus accounting "for moral as for natural things" Pope has reference only to the moral condition of mankind as a whole, not to the morality requisite for individual man. Moreover, this reconciliation of extremes is a supernatural act, and to propose that the individual attempt it could be only blasphemy. In Spence's memorandum, therefore, the statement that "Avarice, lays up (w^{t} w^{d} be hurtful;) Prodigality, scatters abroad (w^{t} may be useful in other hands:)" pertains not to private morality, but only to God's total economy in the management of fallen mankind. Nor, it should be obvious by now, is it a Mandevillian expression of the public value of private vices. Mandeville was a political economist; Pope, a Christian moralist. As economic theorist, Mandeville was concerned with the thesis that what Christianity calls a private vice works to the *material* good of society, and his end is homocentric. Pope, on the other hand, is dealing in these last sentences with the sum total of mankind *sub specie aeternitatis,* as the object of God's concern and management: that which is truly Christian vice is disposed by God into a total good in terms of God's mysterious purpose.

Behind this definition of God's providential plan lies the traditional belief that the universe

[82] Quoted in Bateson, p. xxii.

is a *concordia discors,* a doctrine that helped shape Pope's customary cosmology and metaphysics.[83] In the writings of the Pythagoreans, of Heraclitus, Plato, Cicero, Plutarch, Ovid, Plotinus, and many others, the theory was developed that the harmony of the universe is the product of the clash of contraries. As Pope expressed it in *Windsor Forest,* the world is " harmoniously confus'd," and in it, " tho' all things differ, all agree." The doctrine appears in the writings of many of the Fathers and spread widely in the Renaissance to account not only for the form and operation of the material universe but also for politics, commerce, ethics, and art. Yet the general assumption remained that this is God's art, not man's. William Ayloffe, for example, drew the analogy between the fact that " The whole Universe subsisteth but by the contrariety of the Elements " and the fact that man is both beast and angel, adding that the wisdom and power of God are manifest in His " union of these two Parts so highly disagreeing in themselves." [84] And Sir Francis Fane, commending Charles II, God's vicegerent, for harmonizing the oppositions in his state, spoke of it as " the praeternatural art of uniting Contraries." [85] This is God's " Eternal Art " of " educing good from ill " in a world of sin. Behind Pope's explanation of the divine and cosmic role of misers and prodigals, considered *en masse,* lies the authority of a long ideological tradition that had already been adopted by Christianity; and this interpretation of God's Providence Pope uses as the insulating frame within which to consider, not the role of Providence, but the private morality of riches.[86]

Private morality, on the other hand, is provided for by the other standard in Spence's memorandum: " The middle ye point for Virtue." Whereas God's harmony of corporate fallen mankind results from *concordia discors*—the supernatural reconciliation of extremes—private virtue rests in striving for the mid-point between extremes; and therefore " We s^{d} not speak agst one large Vice, without speaking agst its contrary," since virtue lies between the opposite extremes. Consequently Pope sharply draws the distinction between God's production of total harmony through " reconcil'd extremes " (168) and the fact that Bathurst, as the individual moral norm, knows " That secret rare, *between* th'extremes to move " (227).

If, indeed, we needed aid in uncovering the basic ethical system governing the poem, an entry in the manuscript of the *Essay on Man* should remove all doubt: " Arist. l. 7 reduces all ye Passions under Pleasure and Pain as their universal Principles. The mean between opposite Passions makes Virtue, ye Extremes Vice." [87] With wonderful ingenuity and, so far as I know, with great originality, Pope has brought together two loosely related ideas deeply rooted in Western thought: *concordia discors,* or the supernatural harmony of the contradictory extremes of this world; and the Aristotelian ethical tradition of *mediocritas,* or the definition of virtue as the mean between opposing vices. The two traditions share a kind of geometric metaphor, and yet, by approaching the same metaphor from contrary directions, they make possible Pope's absolute differentiation of God's perspective from that of individual man.[88]

[83] See my chapters on Denham and Pope in *The Subtler Language* (Baltimore, 1959).

[84] *The Government of the Passions* (1700), pp. 22, 73.

[85] *A Panegyrick to the Kings most excellent Majesty* (1662). Francis Osborn, *Advice to a Son,* in *Works* (1704), p. 174: ". . . wise Providence hath matched every thing's strength, in their respective Gradations, with such proportionable Antagonists, that they are all contained within the compass of a just proportion." Cp. Pope, *Essay on Man,* III. 293–95: " 'Till jarring int'rests, of themselves create / Th'according music of a well-mixd State. / Such is the World's great harmony. . . ."

[86] Nor was Pope by any means the first to apply the doctrine of *concordia discors* to God's reconciliation of vices. In his very popular handbook of religion, Daniel Dyke had claimed that God " can make sin, contrary to his own nature, to work to our good, driving out one poyson with another " (*Mystery of Selfe-Deceiving* [1642]; quoted by Bernard Kay in his ed. of Mandeville's *Fable of the Bees,* I. 107 n., where he uses it to illustrate a similar passage in Mandeville).

In a sense, Pope has transformed the very common doctrine that God has distributed riches unequally but has harmonized rich and poor into a *concordia discors.* For these economic terms Pope has substituted the moral ones, prodigality and avarice. See Henry Peacham, *The Worth of a Penny* (1677), p. 8; Thomas Clutterbuck, *Spittle-Sermon* (1687), pp. 18 ff.; Robert Moss, *The Providential Division of Men into Rich and Poor* (1708), reprinted in *Twenty-Five Sermons* (1729).

[87] See the Twickenham edition of the *Essay on Man,* ed. Maynard Mack, p. 69 n.

[88] It should now be possible to understand why Pope's thesis has been confused with Mandeville's and also to recog-

With the Renaissance the *Nicomachean Ethics* of Aristotle was revived and became the basic ethical textbook. It was endlessly paraphrased, interpreted, expanded, transformed into ethical catechisms, and, upon the authority of Aquinas' adaptation, was reinforced with scriptural and patristic parallels, and assimilated into treatises on Christian ethics. Now, just as for Pope, who would speak not only against a vice but also against its contrary, so for Aristotle virtue is the mean between two contrary vices, one of excess and the other of defect. And, like Pope, Aristotle devoted considerable attention to the vices and virtues relating to riches, insisting, as Pope does in his prologue, that only the use of riches, not the mere possession of them, is an ethical problem: "wealth is not the Good we are in search of, for it is only good as being useful" (I. v. 8; see also IV. i. 6).[89]

But Aristotle distinguished between two virtues in the use of riches: liberality, which is the mean between prodigality and niggardliness; and magnificence, which is called into play when large sums are involved and which lies between vulgar display and shabbiness (II. vii. 4–6). Hence Pope has supplied us with two epistles on the "Use of Riches," one to Bathurst on liberality, and another to Burlington on magnificence. Even the summaries later added to the poems testify to their relation to each other and to Aristotle's *Ethics*. The summary of the first states that "The true Use of Riches is known to few, most falling into one of the extremes, Avarice or Profusion"; that of the second notes that "The Extremes of Avarice and Profusion being treated of in the foregoing Epistle, this takes up one particular Branch of the latter; the Vanity," and it then identifies this vanity with "the false Taste of Magnificence." The two poems, taken together, constitute Pope's satiric adaptation of Aristotle's analysis of the ethics of wealth. But since Aristotelian liberality had long been integrated with Christian charity, Pope appears in the epistle to Bathurst as a lay theologian, and the whole bias is Christian. Magnificence necessarily remained a purely worldly virtue that could not be assimilated into a theological virtue, and the speaker in the poem to Burlington is the tasteful and polished aristocrat.

To determine the extent to which the Aristotelian ethics is the ideological framework of the two poems, it would be helpful to linger for a moment over the *Epistle to Burlington*. Of the two extremes of magnificence—shabbiness, or deficiency of expenditure, and vulgarity, or tasteless extravagance—Pope's poem concerns itself with the latter. Since magnificence has its proper decorum which requires that the donor be an "artist" in taste, vulgarity consists, says Aristotle, not in "spending too great an amount on proper objects, but [in] making a great display on the wrong occasions and in the wrong way" (IV. ii. 4). Both public dinners and wedding banquets are proper objects of magnificence, but vulgarity of taste appears when one confuses the two and gives a dinner at his club on the scale of a wedding banquet, or when one supplies a comic chorus with the trappings appropriate to tragedy. For, Aristotle adds, "the same gifts are not suitable for the gods and for men, and the same expenditure is not appropriate to a sacrifice and a funeral" (IV. ii. 17). Magnificence becomes vulgar display when things truly great in themselves are assigned to equally great objects to which, however, they are inappropriate; or, as Pope puts it, when one loads "some vain Church with old Theatric state" (*Epistle to Burlington*, 29).

This Aristotelian definition of vulgarity underlies much of the satiric artistry in Pope's

nize how unlike the two actually are. For Mandeville also uses the Aristotelian mean and the doctrine of *concordia discors* as counters in his argument. But whereas Pope distinguishes them as the human norm and the divine economy, Mandeville draws from the Aristotelian doctrine of the mean merely the terminological distinction between vice and virtue, and considers *concordia discors*, not as the work of Providence, but as an excellent economic program for society to pursue. That is, he accepts the term "virtue" for the Aristotelian mean, which he calls "frugality," but he rejects this "virtue" as economically unsound. On the other hand, he accepts the term "vice" for the Aristotelian extremes, avarice and prodigality; but he claims that the harmonious clash of these "vices" is man's device, not God's, for creating an economically prosperous society: ". . . I look upon Avarice and Prodigality in the Society as I do upon two contrary Poisons in Physick, of which it is certain that the noxious Qualities assist each other, and often make a good Medicine between them" (I. 106; see also I. 104).

[89] All quotations of Aristotle are taken from the Loeb translation.

description of Timon's estate, but it is so adapted that bad taste becomes identified with sacrilege. Echoing Aristotle's statement that what is suitable for the gods is not suitable for men, Pope outfits Timon's chapel with all the luxuries of a great hall. The frivolous, abruptly shifting music has the sprightliness of a jig, instead of the solemnity of spiritual meditation, and the chapel becomes a ballroom. The ceilings are richly painted with scenes suggesting luxurious bodily rest, and the cushions invite, not to kneeling prayer, but to repose.

Conversely, the dining hall has the attributes of a church, and the meal is conducted in the manner of a Roman sacrifice, but with notable overtones of the Christian Mass. Since both religious sacrifices and public banquets are, according to Aristotle, proper objects of great expenditure, Pope is illustrating Timon's vulgar confusion of the two. The "chiming Clocks" that call to dinner (151) are only disguises for the chapel bell calling the hundred faithful to prayer in the marble hall of God's dining room. Here, in this "Temple" (156), the lavish dinner is truly a Roman "Hecatomb," or, like the Mass, a "solemn Sacrifice" (156–57), the *sacrificium sollemne corporis et sanguinis Christi sub speciebus panis et vini.* Timon's meal therefore becomes the Host, distributed to those at his Communion Table with all the ceremonial punctuality of the Communion: "You drink by measure, and to minutes eat" (158). Even the servants, as attendant ministers, are properly moved by the presence of the Godhead so that their salvers ring with their fervent "trembling." At length this ritualistic dinner, like the Communion, comes to an end with the drinking of sweet wine and "God bless the King": *Deo gratias.*

The Aristotelian ethics is also the ground for Pope's preferring the vulgarity of misapplied riches to niggardliness:

> Yet hence the Poor are cloath'd, the Hungry fed;
> Health to himself, and to his Infants bread
> The Lab'rer bears: What his hard Heart denies,
> His charitable Vanity supplies. (169–72)

For the spendthrift "benefits many people," but the niggard "benefits nobody, not even himself," according to Aristotle (IV. i. 32).[90] Aristotle also had emphasized that in the building of great houses the magnificent man will prefer to spend on "permanent objects" (IV. ii. 16), and Pope underscores the fragile transitoriness of Timon's estate, soon to be erased by the living power of Nature: "Deep Harvests bury all his pride has plann'd" (175). Finally, the poet looks forward to a return of the Golden Age, when England will have kings who will lead their nobles to the greatest public benefactions of magnificence. Aristotle had established three categories of magnificence, religious, public, and private; and as examples of public works he had listed only the equipping of a chorus, the fitting out of warships, and the offering of public banquets. To this list the successive commentators on the *Ethics* added greatly, and the public works that Pope would have a Burlington perform in a better age derive from these accumulated extensions: theaters, aqueducts, paved roads, bridges, temples, and moles ("moles in mare iactae").[91]

> Bid Harbors open, public Ways extend,
> Bid Temples, worthier of the God, ascend;
> Bid the broad Arch the dang'rous Flood contain,
> The Mole projected break the roaring Main;
> Back to his bounds their subject Sea command,
> And roll obedient Rivers thro' the Land.
> (197–202)

By means of these derivative themes the *Epistle to Burlington* affiliates with the Aristotelian ethical system, and, since magnificence is a special mode of liberality, it is an appendage to the *Epistle to Bathurst.* In this sense, the former poem is at least incipient in the latter, for the Man of Ross, in his liberality, also per-

[90] Hence, too, Pope's original intention in the *Epistle to Bathurst* to identify his speaker and Bathurst as "strict Follow'rs of the former Sect" (i.e., prodigals), or as "somewhat leaning to ye former Sect." See below, pp. 74, 104, 106.

[91] See Giovanni Pontano, *Opera* (Basileae, 1538), I. 240–54; and Agostino da Sessa, *Ragionamenti* (Parma, 1562). See also Pope's mock catalogue of the works of magnificence in his letter to Bathurst, 11 September 1730 (Sherburn, III. 130).

forms many of the tasks of magnificence, and Bathurst himself joins "with Œconomy, Magnificence." It is because Pope's ethical conception derives from Aristotle that he seeks to identify liberality as the mean by speaking not only against "one large Vice" but also against "its contrary"; and the ethical principle of the mean between vicious extremes determines also his system of portraiture. Buckingham the wastrel is set off against miserly Cutler; Balaam the miser, against Sir Balaam the spendthrift. For we can know the middle course by steering away equally from the two opposing excesses. Hence the double thematic function of the two Cottas. In the divine scheme the Cottas, taken together, give evidence that Providence uses "y[e] two Extremes of a Vice" to "serve like two opposing biasses to keep up y[e] Ballance of things"; and therefore Providence needs a prodigal Cotta to balance a miserly Cotta in order to shape the total *concordia discors* of a fallen world. But in the system of human morality the Cottas are merely the treacherous opposing shores that give the moral navigator bearings for a safe channel, "y[e] point for Virtue." However, Aristotle added, since vice is multiform, and good is a single mid-point, it is "easy to miss the target and difficult to hit it"; "it is hard to be good, for it is hard to find the middle point in anything" (II. vi. 14; ix. 2). Correspondingly, although young Cotta recognized the error of his father's avarice and revolted against it, he sinned by mistaking "reverse of wrong for right" (200), instead of seeking the mean between excesses:

> For what to shun will no great knowledge need,
> But what to follow, is a task indeed.
> (201–202)[92]

There is, then, no thematic inconsistency in the poem. In explaining God's reconciliation of extremes, Pope is stepping outside the bounds of his immediate moral theme momentarily to locate securely his human bearings and to assure himself and the reader that morality is to be ascertained within the assumption of a "careful," not an indifferent, Heaven and within an organization that, in its totality, is perfect.[93] The world is in God's hands, which can, preternaturally, reconcile vicious extremes. But morality is an affair of the private individual, and it is his duty to "ease" the care of Heaven by reducing the need for *concordia discors*: for if man were to follow the mean between extremes, there would be no need for Heaven to balance and harmonize vices. So long as men are in a state of sin, Heaven will maintain a total perfection through "reconcil'd extremes"; and yet man is not thereby relieved of his necessity to be a Bathurst, who knows to "speak against" opposite vices by negating them—wealth is "*Not* meanly, *nor* ambitiously pursu'd"; he is "*Not* sunk by sloth, *nor* rais'd by servitude" (221–22)—and who knows, not to reconcile extremes, but "between th'extremes to move."

With this essential distinction between God's economy and man's morality we can see more readily the subtle and intricately overlapping organization of Pope's total argument. The *exordium*, we have already observed, results in agreement that possession of wealth is no sign

[92] Cp. Pope's expansion of Horace's "Sordidus a tenui victu distabit, Ofello / judice: nam frustra vitiam vitaveris istud, / si te alio pravum detorseris":

> 'Tis yet in vain, I own, to keep a pother
> About one Vice, and fall into the other:
> Between Excess and Famine lies a mean,
> Plain, but not sordid, tho' not splendid, clean.
> (*Imitations of Horace*, Satire II. ii. 45–48)

See also Virgilio Malvezzi, *Discourses upon Cornelius Tacitus*, trans. Sir Richard Baker (1642). Discourse 42 is entitled, "That it is easier to passe from one extreame to another, then from an extreame to the middle"; and Averroes is quoted: "Facilius est a superabundantia ad defectum venire; & ab hoc ad illam, quam ad medium." Horace's *Satires*, I. i and I. ii are also relevant here.

After the couplet quoted, Warburton added the following from Pope's manuscript (see below, pp. 88, 118):

> Yet sure, of qualities deserving praise,
> More go to ruin Fortune, than to raise.

Bateson is certainly right in rejecting this as lacking Pope's authority, but he has no ground for considering it an "alternative" reading for 201–202. The manuscript gives no evidence that it was to be a substitute for 201–202; and it does not, as Bateson claims, merely repeat the sense of the couplet, but supplements it. Moreover, it, too, stems directly from Aristotle: the spendthrift "benefits many people," but the miser "benefits nobody, not even himself" (IV. i. 32). See footnote 90 above.

[93] Cp. *Rape of the Lock*, III. 21–24, where Pope glances out at the surrounding world in which "Wretches hang that Jury-men may Dine" in order to locate the secure fashion able world of Belinda and her friends.

of grace (Pope's theology is one of faith and works, not faith alone), that riches are morally indifferent (virtue is a moral act), and, most important, that man must accept his fallen state and pursue the highest ethics possible in it. With this much granted, Pope's speaker develops a series of satiric attacks around the two uses of riches: they can supply the basic requirements of life (81–100); and the excess beyond what is needed to maintain one's status in life should be distributed as charity (101–12). Since the second of these uses of riches is elaborated by way of satire against the avariciously uncharitable, the speaker now examines the psychology of the various whimsical motives of avarice—fear, ambition, hypocritical pretense to public good—ending with the worst, avarice for its own sake (113–60). At this stage of his argument, the speaker, continuing to observe the neatly organized structure characteristic of the sermon, is required to recognize that since he has been examining human causation it would be appropriate to take note also of the final cause; and at this point, therefore, he explains that God reconciles the extremes of vices.

Moreover, the lines on the divine reconciliation of vices not only are the high point of the argument and its theological drift but are also appropriately climactic in the rhetorical suasion of Bathurst. After the opening epitrope which skillfully granted "that which hurteth him to whom it is graunted," the speaker and Bathurst found their ground of agreement in rejecting Calvinism, and Bathurst was then persuaded to concern himself with the fallen state of man, from which he had held himself satirically aloof, in order to seek out the worthy purposes of riches. With this concession Bathurst learned, apparently to his surprise, that the essential private uses of riches are few ("would you more than live?" [83]), and thereby he made himself available to instruction in the theology of almsgiving ("Perhaps you think the Poor might have their part?" [101]).[94] It is after this instruction, conveyed by satire of irreligious men of avarice, that the speaker turns to Bathurst to declare unequivocally:

> Hear then the truth: . . . .
> Ask we what makes one keep, and one bestow?
> That POW'R who bids the Ocean ebb and flow.

But this is the very doctrine that he had agreed not to press at the beginning of the poem and had pretended to pass off lightly as a disagreement of the Doctors, a matter of hair-splitting. For the sake of an area of mutual agreement, Bathurst had seemed to be allowed his belief that for their own sport the gods created men miserly and prodigal fools. But the Christian doctrines ironically concealed in that concession have progressively been rising to the surface, and Bathurst has been so swayed toward Christian principles and toward charity to man that the rhetorically convincing theologian at last dares repudiate bluntly his original concession: misers and spendthrifts were created by a "careful Heav'n" to effect a harmony in the postlapsarian moneyed world. And Bathurst now does not protest.

7

It is noticeable that after this thematically climactic passage the remainder of the poem—slightly more than half its length—consists almost entirely of a series of portraits. In terms of the satire, they are Theophrastian "characters"; in terms of the sermon, they are *exempla,* applied instances of the lay apostle's argument that contribute to rhetorical effectiveness, or, as Pope described them, "living examples, which enforce best."[95] The *exemplum* had always played a large part in homiletic literature, usually to supplement and reinforce moral and religious generalizations. For example, in the many works that elaborated on the *Nicomachean Ethics* it was customary to add a series of such portraits to each of Aristotle's general topics; and Pope was following a recognized rhetorical pattern in

[94] *Erotesis,* or rhetorical interrogation, wrote John Ward, serves "to press and bear down an adversary. . . . Such a way of pushing an antagonist shews the speaker has great confidence in his cause; otherwise he would never lay himself so open, if he was not assured the other party had nothing to reply" (*System of Oratory* [1759], II. 97–98).

[95] Pope to Caryll, 27 September 1732 (Sherburn, III. 316).

thus ending his sermon.[96] Moreover, Pope organized these "characters" into a dialectic that continues his analysis of the theme of riches and brings it to its final satiric fulfillment.

However, we must suspend, for a moment, further pursuit of the dialectic of the "characters" to determine the relation of the praise of Bathurst to the portrait of the Man of Ross. For is there not an artistic and rhetorical lapse in Pope's turning away from Bathurst and the nobility to find his exemplary figure in this humble and most exceptional country squire? This simple benefactor may serve to shame the negligent Bathursts; but the rarity of such a figure seems to reduce greatly his rhetorical effectiveness as a rebuke, and, if we take the poem as a social commentary, it is anticlimactic to find public salvation in the lesser squirearchy after having sought it in the nobility.

Everything in the poem, however, has indicated its primary concern with personal, not societal, ethics; and to that end the portrait of the Man of Ross is essential. The praise of Bathurst as the virtuous man (219–48) has powerful effect in the speaker's rhetorical course, for it serves to dispose sweepingly of almost all previous differences between Bathurst's philosophy and the speaker's Christian theology. Bathurst has been successfully moved to the position where it is profitable for the speaker to remind him that his practice belies his beliefs. The nobleman who has claimed to be a cynical misanthrope has been charitable in fact and has exercised the virtue of liberality, moving between the extremes "Of mad Good-nature, and of mean Self-love." The beliefs that Bathurst has professed to entertain must collapse now under the proved insincerity. And the theologian can draw Bathurst even closer to himself by adding that such acts are religious, for they ease or emulate "the care of Heav'n," which Bathurst, like Momus, had called careless.

Here we might expect the speaker to rest, since the two men now seem to be in nearly total accord on the speaker's own ethical terms. But clearly his premises everywhere have been Christian, and as yet he has merely brought Bathurst around to full agreement on the virtue of liberality, the golden mean required of all moral men and evident to the rational mind. And this is still far short of the theologian's goal, as the undercutting of his praise shows. There is an ominous threat in his tempering his acclamation of Bathurst's liberality with the qualification that he is "*yet* unspoil'd by wealth!" (226); and if Bathurst's and Oxford's charity to the oppressed and despairing is their "better part" (243), the speaker is warning against a deficiency as much as he is praising a virtue. For the moral virtues have no safeguard in themselves and, laudable though they are, are far short of the theological virtues. To be won over wholly to the speaker's Christian views, which have been evident from the beginning, Bathurst must be won to the Christian life. It is to this end that he is confronted with the extraordinary Man of Ross.

The striking and unusual modulation of that portrait is carefully calculated to provide us with its proper significance. For example, the Man of Ross did not merely plant a grove of elms; he "hung with woods yon mountain's sultry brow" (253), not because the poet here needs a theatrical effect, but because the heroic language supplies the necessary evaluation of the act. The seemingly hyperbolic, quasi-pastoral language asserts a superhuman status and power: Kyrle sympathized with the sweltering mountain as one sympathizes with a weak creature, and he had the godlike strength to shade the personified mountain. Whatever it is he represents, he stands at the opposite extreme from the misers and spendthrifts whose vices grotesquely debased human nature to the status of landscape features; his virtuous perfection raises inanimate nature to the level of his own abun-

[96] Fénelon in his discussion of pulpit oratory had urged the use of such portraits to make real and experiencable to the auditor's imagination the moral and religious truths (*Dialogues on Eloquence*, trans. W. S. Howell [Princeton, 1951], pp. 92–93). For such portraits, Boileau had praised the sermons of Bourdalou (*Satire*, X. 345–49). And one of the appealing features of William Law's *Serious Call* was its abundant use of character sketches to supplement each of its religious principles.

But almost any typical handbook of ethics—Vincent of Beauvais' *Speculum morale*, or Peter de la Primaudaye's *The French Academy* (1614), for example—will illustrate the standard practice of appending biographies and characters to each unit of moral doctrine.

dant humanity. He did not merely contribute funds for a taller church; he "taught that heav'n-directed spire to rise" (261). For, saint-like in his religious virtues, he could instruct the symbol of man's aspiration to God to ascend even higher toward the spirit's goal.

Nor did he merely erect a local waterworks: "From the dry rock" he "bade the waters flow" (254). This, of course, repeats the miracle of Moses, type of the Redeemer;[97] and the essence of the wifeless, childless Man of Ross's portrait is that beneath the surface language is a current of references to Christ's life and miracles. When Christ drove the money-changers from the temple, the children greeted the deed by exclaiming, "Hosanna to the son of David"; and Christ commented, "Out of the mouth of babes and sucklings thou hast perfected praise" (Matthew 21: 1–16). The analogous accomplishment of the Man of Ross was to drive out the quacks and "vile attornies"; and, when asked who had accomplished all the charitable marvels, "The MAN of ROSS, each lisping babe replies" (262), thereby not only revealing how widely his charities were known and felt, but also perfecting the praise of his Christ-like character. Like Christ, he brought peace and, without other human aid, effected cures, he himself relieving, prescribing, attending, and making and administering the medicine (269–70). And just as Christ miraculously multiplied the five loaves by breaking them to feed thousands, so, to feed the entire almshouse, "The MAN of ROSS divides the weekly bread" (264).

To the extent of human limitations, the scriptural echoes reveal, the life of the Man of Ross has been an *imitatio Christi,* and Bathurst's liberality is to this man's self-denying charity as the Commandments are to the Counsels of Perfection. Perhaps one of the most helpful explanations of the relation of the Man of Ross to Bathurst, now the laudable symbol of *mediocritas,* is to be found in the gloss to the emblem of Spenser's July eclogue, which reads, "*In medio virtus; in summo felicitas*": ". . . according to the saying of olde Philosophers . . . vertue dwelleth in the middest, being enuironed with two contrary vices: . . . albeit all bountye dwelleth in mediocritie, yet perfect felicitye dwelleth in supremacie. For they say, and most true it is, that happinesse is placed in the highest degree. . . ." It is not the function of the speaker's sermon to carry the conversion this far, but to make available to Bathurst the revelation that beyond mediocrity is supremacy, a Christ-like state of being which is beyond the danger of being spoiled by wealth. Only in the knowledge of Christ and in the aspiration to imitate the perfection of His life can one be truly guarded in the golden mean between vicious extremes. The speaker has here reached outside the limits of rhetorical persuasion and has displayed the Man of Ross to Bathurst in order to draw the curtains for him upon the supernatural sanctions that give human virtues their total meaning in the framework of ultimate truth and eternal life. Through a Miltonic echo the preacher invites Bathurst, whose firmament has been the "little Stars" (282) that decorate the nobility, to gaze on the perfect Man of Ross, that sun "with surpassing Glory crown'd" (*Paradise Lost,* IV. 32). And Bathurst responds with the light-blinded awe of a man who has observed a supernal glory, first assuming that only great wealth could perform "that boundless charity" (278) and then bewildered by the intimation of a value beyond earthly fame that can motivate and justify such abundant self-denial (283–84).

In the dialectical arrangement of the "characters," then, the Man of Ross is both climactic and transitional. The pageant had begun with the Cottas, who are transitional between the two halves of the poem. Taken together, they give flesh to the preceding thesis that Providence reconciles extremes, avarice and prodigality. But individually they dramatize the two extremes of private vice and consequently prepare for the praise of Bathurst, who, moving midway between their extremes, fulfills the normal requirements of natural ethics in this postlapsarian world. The succeeding portrait of the Man of

[97] Richard Kidder's gloss on Moses' striking the rock (Exodus 17: 6) represents the customary interpretation: "This speaks the Power of God, and does also represent *Christ,* and the Benefits which we receive by him" (*Commentary on the Five Books of Moses* [1694], I. 354).

Ross then reaches out beyond human life, to the area of eternal life and the spiritual perfection it demands and justifies, in order to supply the final sanctions for moral conduct. But the successive portraits also move forward and overlap to form an argument; and, like almost all these portraits, the climactic one of the Man of Ross faces in two directions. Exemplifying the human life in imitation of Christ, he conjoins both human existence and the eternal life promised after death, man's immediate end and his final end. And therefore it is appropriate that the theologian conclude his epistle by evaluating the next series of men—Hopkins, Buckingham, and Cutler—in the perspective of their deaths, the moment when the moral worth of a man's deeds can be tallied as he is about to stand before his ultimate Judge.[98] We have seen in the poem up to this point " what blessings Wealth to life can lend "; now we must find " what comfort it affords our end " (297–98). Consequently the word " end " runs like a theme through the last section (290, 292, 298, 314, 329), bringing to a full stop the portraits of the Man of Ross, Hopkins, and Buckingham.

Thus, while the life of the Man of Ross is the climax of one unit of portraits, his " end " introduces the next; and the Man of Ross and Hopkins are companion pieces drawn after their deaths to contrast the conceptions of fame entertained by the follower of Christ and by the follower of Mammon. Next, Buckingham and Cutler, symmetrically balancing the two Cottas, enact the miserable ends of prodigality and miserliness, just as the Cottas had enacted the wretched lives they afford. Finally, all the satiric venom of the poem will be drained into the ultimate object of the satire, Sir Balaam. The first four portraits—the Cottas, Bathurst, and the Man of Ross—have moved forward to propose a code and a sanction for virtuous conduct; and were the poem merely preceptive it might profitably have ended here. But its goal is corrective satire, and the portraits of Bathurst and the Man of Ross are not an end, but a means to that end. Consequently at this point the speaker has reversed the direction of his pageant to drive toward the satiric version of his ethical goal. Beginning again with Buckingham and Cutler, a pair of extremes like the Cottas, he now, instead of finding the mean between their excesses, collects their two vices in Sir Balaam, the cumulative climax of his religiously motivated satiric wrath. For Sir Balaam stands in vivid contrast to the virtuous Bathurst and the saintly Man of Ross, who culminated the first movement of the portraits. He combines in his early and later careers both the avarice of the elder Cotta and Cutler, and the prodigality of the younger Cotta and Buckingham; and he illustrates both the wretched existence (the Cottas) and the wretched death (Buckingham and Cutler) that the vicious extremes of liberality purchase.

To establish the full ironic sense that " end " is to carry, the portrait of the Man of Ross concludes with a highly moving play on the word. The only record left of him is to be found in the register in the parish church; there the distinctions between rich and poor are leveled, since it records only the dates of birth and death, regardless of earthly status: " to be born and die, / Of rich and poor makes all the history " (287–88). The house of religion, concerned only with the soul, disregards the things of the world:

> Enough, that Virtue fill'd the space between;
> Prov'd, by the ends of being, to have been.
> (289–90)

In the parish register, only these two terminal dates prove that one has been. But if, like the Man of Ross, one has filled the space between these two ends with virtue, he has fulfilled the " ends " of man's earthly existence. The record of birth and death alone, which proves that one has been, is the church's testimony to the irrelevance of wealth and earthly fame. For it is the space between these " ends " that permits one to fulfill his true " ends." One's unrecorded virtuous acts are his true fame and the ultimate testimony to his having been.

The ensuing portrait of Hopkins inverts that of the Man of Ross to display the vicious opposite of his virtues; and the transition to the

[98] Ecclesiasticus 11: 28: " Call no man happy before his death, for by his end shall a man be known."

following unit of portraits is provided by the attitudes of the two men toward church and fame—or, more inclusively, toward the relation of the earthly to the spiritual world. Being complete in his charity, the Man of Ross eschewed not only avarice for wealth but also that other form of avarice, desire for earthly fame; and therefore he has left no monument to himself. " His race, his form, his name " are " almost unknown " (284) —and the poet has been careful to call him only " the Man of Ross." For this life is only a preparation for the next, and all its vanities must at last be thrown aside. Therefore, one who despises earthly fame will, in his devotion, build a church to God but " Will never mark the marble with his Name " (286) .[99] Although the surface of the line merely states he has not caused his name to be cut into the marble to record his gift, the word " mark " carries strongly unpleasant overtones and suggests the notorious practice of scribbling on the walls of London houses.[100] The implication is that if to scribble one's name on buildings is defacement, to mark one's name on a church is desecration; and therefore to memorialize one's gift to a church is a wall-scribbling sacrilege that quite belies the presumed religious charity.

By contrast, whereas the saintly Man of Ross gave everything in life to remain anonymous after death, Hopkins was a miser in life who left his fortune to be squandered on his funeral and his statue. The Man of Ross built a church unmarred by his name, but Hopkins has had his statue intruded into the church, " Should'ring God's altar " (293), as though intending the idol of himself to be worshipped instead of God. And whereas he was uncharitable in life, his false image in the church, striking the customary statuary pose, " extends his hands " (294), intimating the charity he had never performed. Inverting the career of the Man of Ross, Hopkins has fulfilled none of his spiritual duties and yet has assumed that the final good is to purchase worldly memorials which will " spiritualize " him in the sense of materializing him for enduring earthly fame. The miser had preserved a " live-long wig " (295), and now that he has been reproduced in marble (the marble that the Man of Ross would not mar even with his name), the frizzles have become " Eternal " curls in the Parian stone (296). Moreover, like the serpent-haired head of the Gorgon, which transformed all who gazed on it into stone, Hopkins' stringy wig, " which Gorgon's self might own," has metamorphosed itself and its owner into unfeeling marble. The object of Hopkins' contemplation had been himself, and his Gorgon self has lapidified " live-long " into " Eternal "—a span of life into an enduring earthly existence —so as to perpetuate material things, instead of translating mortal life into the only true eternity, the immortal spirit. Instead of recognizing that eternity is spiritual, the miser can conceive of it only as the postmortal perpetuity of the material things he had avariciously preserved throughout life, including his physical self; and, knowing that the church houses the eternal, he expects to endure forever by placing there his own marble image. Eternizing himself in stone, he persists and now possesses his wig forever. It is only fitting that Pope's preacher ridicule Hopkins' expectation that wealth will *lend* blessings to life and *afford* comfort to our end, since Hopkins has gained blessings and comfort in neither their material sense nor, what he confuses with the material, their spiritual sense.

8

By his skillful reversal in the drama of character presentations, the poet can now draw his Whig capitalist in full-length portrait. In Sir Balaam the poet will hang in effigy the arch-representative of the corrupting power of capitalistic theology and ethics. It is for this dramatic

[99] Matthew 6: 1, 2: " Take heed that ye do not your alms before men, to be seen of them: otherwise ye have no reward of your Father which is in heaven. Therefore when thou doest thine alms, do not sound a trumpet before thee, as the hypocrites do in the synagogues and in the streets, that they may have glory of men."

[100] Cp. *Imitations of Horace*, Satire II. i. 98: " Or whiten'd wall provokes the skew'r to write "; *Epistle to Arbuthnot*, 215: " What tho' my name stood rubric on the walls "; *ibid.*, 19–20: ". . . scrawls / With desp'rate charcoal round his darken'd walls." See Dekker's *Gull's Hornbook*, chap. 4, where Dekker urges the gull to become fashionable by cutting his name inside St. Paul's steeple—" indeed the top of Paul's contains more names than Stow's Chronicle."

purpose that the speaker, having reached with seeming solemnity a "knotty point," abruptly cuts off the serious theological drift of his argument and agrees to lighten his subject with a "tale," which, the less homiletic the speaker's tone makes it appear, the more it is a bitterly satiric parable. Since his final mode is satire, the speaker will never answer his question: for virtue and wealth "are other worlds prepar'd? / Or are they both, in this their own reward?" (335–36). But through Sir Balaam we will know that such "worth" as his purchases only unhappiness here and the custody of Satan hereafter; the preceptive implication is obvious.[101]

Pope's Balaam is identified in large part by his scene. The Monument, near which he lives, is at the heart of London's commercial district, and, as Pope's note pointedly tells us, was "built in memory of the fire of London, with an inscription, importing that city to have been burnt by the Papists." At the time of the Titus Oates affair the inscription was added to this second tallest and most conspicuous structure in the City, accusing "the Popish faction" of having set fire to London in a plan to destroy "the Protestant religion and old English liberty." [102] Subsequently sentiment over the inscription ran high. It was erased in the reign of Catholic James II and restored in that of vigorously Protestant William. Thomas Ward divulged how painful "this damn'd lie" was to Catholic sensibilities.[103] And Defoe reported there once had been a foolish rumor that Papist Frenchmen had tried to steal away the Fire Monument; the moral, he added, is plain: how easily "may the common People in England be imposed upon in the abstruse Points of High-Flying and Low-Flying, Toleration, Moderation, Persecution, and zealous Adhering." [104] The Monument, therefore, was an acknowledged symbolic focus not only of Protestant-Catholic antagonism, but also of the clash between High Church and Low, Anglicanism and city Dissent. Both its location and the inscription it bore made it a monument to Nonconformity. It often was alluded to in the annual September sermons commemorative of the Fire, but seldom was it as inflammatory as it was for such as Matthew Henry when he preached on that occasion at his nearby meeting-house. To him it is the token that the Dissenter is the true Protestant and the sure protection against the Romish idolators.[105] It was, then, no idle fancy that led Addison's visiting country Tory, as he looked down from the top of the Monument upon the surrounding warehouses, to confess "His heart misgave him that these were so many meeting-houses." [106] For the Monument symbolically places a particular economic code in a particular sectarian context. Balaam's residence near "London's column," which, "pointing to the skies / Like a tall bully, lifts the head, and lyes," locates him at the heart of the Whiggish merchant Dissenters, whose Calvinistic doctrine of election justified their capitalistic morality and set them off from the landed Anglo-Catholics on whom Pope pinned his faith for the preservation of Christian culture and ethics. And by seeming like one falsely swearing to heaven, the Monument symbolizes the religious hypocrisy Pope means to fasten on these capitalistic Dissenters.

The basis for Pope's choice of Balaam as the typically corrupt Puritan merchant is not only the Book of Numbers, in which the rewards offered Balaam to curse the Israelites are not the essence of the events, but especially references in the New Testament, where he is castigated because he "loved the wages of unrighte-

[101] Pope to Bethel, 17 June 1728 (Sherburn, II. 501): "It is by Belief and firm Hope, that men are made happy in this life, as well as in the other." Pope to Caryll, 1 January 1733/4 (Sherburn, III. 400): "To the best of my judgment the author [of the *Essay on Man*] shews himself a Christian at last in the assertion, that all *Earthy Happiness* as well as *Future Felicity* depends upon the doctrine of the gospel, love of God and man, and that the whole aim of our being is to attain happiness here, and hereafter by the practice of universal charity to man, and entire resignation to God."

[102] John Entick, *A New and Accurate History and Survey* (1766), II. 272.

[103] *England's Reformation* (Hamburg, 1710).

[104] *The Review*, IV, no. 133 (1707).

[105] "A Memorial of the Fire of the Lord: a Sermon, Preached September 2nd, 1713, being the day of the commemoration of the burning of London," in *Complete Works* (Edinburgh, London, and Dublin, 1853), II. 427 ff.

[106] *Freeholder*, no. 47 (1 June 1716). Upon reading the inscription on the Monument, this Tory and obviously High-Church gentleman was startled by the accusation against the Catholics, since he had often heard "it was the Presbyterians who burned down the city."

ousness" (2 Peter 2: 15) and where "the error of Balaam for reward" is condemned (Jude 11). Philo also laid Balaam's eagerness to curse the Jews to greed for Balak's gifts; [107] many Churchmen held that his sin was simony; [108] and on the basis of such interpretations subsequent commentators defined Balaam as a type of the avaricious man who employs dishonest means—none of the exegetes ever failing to make the point. Pope therefore was following a clear tradition in selecting Balaam as the representative of the corrupt Puritan money-culture; indeed, to the scripture-minded speaker of the poem no other figure could have appeared more appropriate.

For the character of Balaam as it was shaped by the Biblical commentators was a complex of related roles, almost all of which are pertinent to the archetypal contemporary whom Pope was seeking to draw. Most notably, the scriptural Balaam was a gentile, an enemy of the Israelites, and in the religious milieu of the poem the gentile is the Calvinist outsider from whom Pope is sharply distinguishing himself and his audience. He is the Dissenting London merchant caught up in a false religion of capitalism and its fiscal ethics, unlike God's chosen, the Tory nobility and landed gentry who observe (or who, above all others, have the revelation to observe) the orthodox Christian interpretation of riches and charity. That Pope has chosen a gentile as his paradigm of the corrupting power of modern money-grubbing is of considerable consequence, for, together with the Monument, it identifies the Calvinist frame in which the portrait of Sir Balaam is to be read.

Yet this is to state much too simply the relation of the gentile Balaam to the London merchant. For although a gentile, the scriptural Balaam had been used by God to utter a true prophecy, and consequently there had been considerable debate over his religious status. One traditional interpretation held that, although a gentile, he had worshipped the true God and therefore had been granted the true power of prophecy; only on succumbing to avarice did he fall from grace. St. Jerome, the major proponent of this interpretation, described him as "primum vir sanctus, et prophetes Dei, postea per inobedientiam et desiderium munerum, dum Israel maledicere cupit, divini vocabulo nuncupatur." [109] This is essentially the tradition Pope is following in his account of Balaam's final abandonment of the last traces of his thin Christianity. Completely corrupted by Satan, Balaam

> Ascribes his gettings to his parts and merit,
> What late he call'd a Blessing, now was Wit,
> And God's good Providence, a lucky Hit.
> (376–79)

The good gentile of the Book of Numbers had also known the true God; but at last, persisting in his attempt to curse the Jews despite God's prohibition, he must have assumed that the power lay in his own will. In Symon Patrick's expansion of Jerome's interpretation one can recognize the exegetical background of Pope's lines: Balaam

> had been formerly a good Man, and a true Prophet, till loving the *Wages of Unrighteousness,* he apostatized from God, and became a . . . *Diviner*: That is, . . . an Astrologer; who, observing when Men were under a bad Aspect of the Stars, pronounced a Curse upon them; which sometimes coming to pass, gained him a great Reputation. . . . And it is likely, while *Balaam* . . . continued a good Man, he blessed and cursed no other Way, but by Prayer to God, and by Imprecations in his Name. . . . But when *Balaam* degenerated into a false Prophet, and became a Diviner, then he used Spells and Inchantments . . . and such Rites and Ceremonies as were the Invention of wicked Spirits.[110]

However, although many, especially writers on pagan theology such as Eugubius and Collius, continued to list Balaam as one of the true prophets among the pagans, Jerome usually was quoted by the exegetes only to be refuted: Balaam was from the beginning a false prophet,

[107] *Life of Moses* (Loeb Classics), I. 48 ff.
[108] E. g., Suarez, *Opera omnia* (Paris, 1859), XIII. 645.
[109] *P. L.*, XXIII. 972.
[110] *A Commentary upon the Fourth Book of Moses* (1699).

wizard, and soothsayer (*hariolus*).[111] These contradictory traditions left Balaam in a highly ambiguous position, so that it could be said neither that he was wholly divided from God nor that he was truly a man of God. This is the ambiguity reflected in Pope's description of his " plain good man " as " Religious, punctual, frugal, and so forth " (343). Religion is worth only as much as any one of the commercial virtues justified and exalted by Calvinism; and the shrug with which the line ends makes Balaam's virtues rest so indifferently upon him that they are nearly unseated. For since he is a Dissenter, he outwardly professes Christianity and yet is not truly Christian, just as Balaam knew and was used by the true God and yet was a gentile and wizard. Henry Ainsworth's representative summation will do to suggest the excellent grounds for labeling the Dissenter a Balaam: ". . . it appeareth, that Balaam the Syrian (and so the people to whom he was a Prophet) did know and worship the true God, though corruptly, and it may be other gods also with him." [112] Briefly, the Calvinistic piety of the London merchant that is the source of his capitalistic ethics is only a thin façade of Christianity and therefore justifies the ambiguity of Pope's portrait. His Balaam has not yet wholly turned from God, but being equally " Constant at Church, and Change " (347), holds the un-Christian position that he can serve both God and Mammon. He is not totally lacking in charity, but his givings are " rare, save farthings to the poor " (348), since he observes the outward form of almsgiving, not its spiritual intent; and he " solemnizes " the Lord's day with an extra pudding (346). The capitalistic, worldly basis of Calvinism is so little Christian that, like the Balaam of the exegetical tradition, he totters on the brink of diabolism.

But Pope's London merchant can be defined even more precisely and damningly. Because of the ambiguous relation of the scriptural Balaam to God, it was possible to deny that he was religious in any way and to dispose of his calling upon God for aid as mere religious hypocrisy. Augustine had laid the ground for Pope's use of the scriptural Balaam as a schismatic who, like the Puritans, separated from orthodoxy in order to use religion as a mere pretext for material gains: " He is an Heretike that for temporal commodities sake either coineth or followeth new opinions." [113] Balaam is, declared Henry Ainsworth, " a picture of covetous hypocrites, which pretend they would not doe against the Word of God, for an house full of Gold, when they will doe it for a handfull: as this Prophet laboured with all his might to doe the thing which God had forbidden him." [114] Balaam, wrote John Diodati, had some knowledge of the true God and did sometimes receive prophetic revelations from Him; but, " being a wicked man, he mixed Pagan superstitions and diabolicall witchcraft therewith, which he covered all with the cloak and colour of divine revelations." [115] And Pelargus, like Pope, used the avaricious Balaam to lash out at the avaricious religious hypocrites of his own day.[116] In this setting the religiosity of Pope's Calvinistic Balaam is a sham that he employs to cloak his covetous labors in his counting house. The Puritan doctrine of election is but a religious pretense that makes publicly respectable his worldly interests, just as the scriptural Balaam pretended to be God's prophet to gain Balak's rewards.[117] It is especially this tradition of the

[111] " Verum dico, Balaam fuisse prophetam non Dei, sed diaboli " (Cornelius a Lapide, *Commentaria* [1700], I. 677).

[112] *Annotations upon the Five Books of Moses* (1639), on Numbers 22: 18. Approximately the same words appear in Arthur Jackson's *A Help for the Understanding of the Holy Scripture* (Cambridge, 1643), p. 404.

[113] I quote the passage from the Reims translation of the New Testament (1582), where it appears as a gloss on Jude 11.

[114] *Op. cit.*, on Numbers 22: 18. See also Johannus Piscatorius, *Commentarii in omnes libros Veteris Testamenti* (Herbonae, 1646), I. 360.

[115] *Pious and Learned Annotations upon the Holy Bible* (second ed., 1648), p. 102.

[116] Christophorus Pelargus, *In Numeros Sacros quartum librum Mosaicum* (Lipsiae, 1606), p. 252. Of Balaam's hypocrisy in calling on God when his heart was on the wealth of the world, Matthew Henry wrote: " It is an easy thing for bad men to speak very good words, and to make a shew of piety, from the teeth outward. There is no judging of men by their words, God knows the heart " (*An Exposition of the Old and New Testament* [fifth ed., 1761], on Numbers 20).

[117] This interpretation of the Nonconformist's Christianity as merely a disguise for his ungodly pursuits receives excellent support from the manuscript of the poem (p. 128). In describing the Fire Monument, Pope at one stage contem-

religious hypocrisy of Balaam, now become the representative Puritan, that explains the sneer in the word " saintship " when the Devil, observing the few virtues of Pope's Balaam, " was piqu'd such saintship to behold " (349). The word directly identifies Balaam with the Puritans, who, because of their doctrine of election, persisted in calling themselves " the Saints," to the amusement and annoyance of the Anglicans; and since Balaam's small and merely utilitarian virtues by no means entitle him to the honor, the irony unfolds the false appearance of religion assumed by Balaam and the Puritan merchants to gain their material ends.

In the light of this definition of Balaam we can also better grasp the full significance of the fact that his " word would pass for more than he was worth " (344). We have already observed that the line brilliantly indicts capitalistic standards as the inverse of the true ethical code. Applied to the world of finance, the words constitute the highest praise, since if Balaam's credit

plated adding: " Edwyn reard ye Monumt so high." There is no evidence that Sir Humphrey Edwyn (see *DNB*) had any part in constructing the Fire Monument, although the notorious inscription accusing the Catholics may have been restored while he was alderman for the ward of Cheap. Yet, Edwyn was especially relevant to the symbolic significance Pope intended to attach to the Monument and to Balaam. Almost immediately upon being elected Lord Mayor of London (1697), this vigorous Dissenter gave great scandal by first attending church, as his office legally required, and then worshiping at a Nonconformist meetinghouse, wearing his civic robe and preceded by his official sword-bearer. This notorious act of religious hypocrisy stirred up heated debate and played a large part in the subsequent controversy over occasional conformity that came to a head in the Parliament of 1703. Thereby Edwyn became a symbol of hypocritical Dissent.

We can best understand Pope's intent in identifying Sir Humphrey with Balaam's Monument when we recall that Swift repeated the story of Sir Humphrey's " Insolence " in going " in his Formalities to a Conventicle, with the Ensigns of his Office," and, associating the event with the Geneva Bible and the inner light, ascribed the deed to Jack, Swift's image of the mad Dissenter (*Tale of a Tub*, ed. Guthkelch-Smith, pp. 204, 279). Defoe also, among many others, attacked Edwyn for his hypocrisy in his city office: ". . . to make the matter a Game, to dodge Religion, and go in the Morning to Church, and in the Afternoon to the Meeting; to Communicate in private with the Church of England, to save a Penalty, and then go back to the Dissenters and Communicate again there: This is . . . a Retrograde Devotion" (*An Enquiry into the Occasional Conformity of Dissenters* [1697], p. 152).

But although Edwyn's occasional conformity is wonderfully apposite to the hypocrisy of the Calvinist, " gentile " Balaam, it is unnecessary to Pope's portrait, which otherwise sufficiently establishes the religio-economic ambience intended.

(" word ") is even greater than his assets (" worth ") he has achieved success as it is understood in the commercial world; applied to ethics, they damn Balaam as notably less virtuous (" worth ") than his false words would make him out to be. The ironic relation of the two readings asserts that man cannot serve both God and Mammon, since to love the one is to hate the other. But the line also faithfully describes the scriptural Balaam whose malediction (" word ") falsely passed among the heathen Moabites as all-powerful, since, not following the true God, they could not know that the power to curse and bless was God's, not Balaam's. The entire capitalistic society therefore is identified with the gentile Moabites, the enemies of God's chosen people; and the worship of the immoral power of commercial success is made one with the faith of the idolatrous gentiles in the power of the false prophet's malediction. To this must also be added the Calvinistic hypocrisy of Balaam's religion, for his claim to religion, his occasional alms, and the attendance at church are but professions that passed for a religion he did not have.

However, it is obvious that only a small part of the London merchant's character is drawn from that of the scriptural Balaam; and on the surface it would appear that the scriptural Balaam is only a slight pretext for a wholly original creation. Or so it might appear if it were not evident that the theologian's voice is heard everywhere in the poem and that the poem is repeatedly informed by scriptural and homiletic allusions. Much of the satire of the poem, we have already seen, springs from the appositeness of contemporary corruptions to an inverted Scripture; and the scriptural inversion providing most of the substance of Sir Balaam's career is explicitly motivated. Because the mercantile Dissenter had at least a trace of virtue,

> The Dev'l was piqu'd such saintship to behold,
> And long'd to tempt him like good Job of old:
> But Satan now is wiser than of yore,
> And tempts by making rich, not making poor.
> (349–52)

When we add to this that in the end "sad Sir Balaam curses God and dies" (402) and recognize that thereby Sir Balaam, contrary to Job, has followed the advice of Job's wife, the method of portraiture is evident. If the Devil has turned upside down his methods of temptation in order to provide for the change from an agrarian society, which could withstand the pains of poverty, to a moneyed society, which cannot resist the seductions of riches, then his successful strategy for corrupting the Balaam of capitalism must reverse his unsuccessful attempt against Job. And therefore the poet can build his story of Sir Balaam's ruin-through-riches by inverting at every relevant point Job's resistance to temptation-through-poverty. By portraying Sir Balaam as the capitalistic anti-Job the speaker has provided a measure not only of Sir Balaam's ungodliness but also of the inclination toward sin in a society founded on the ethics and theology of money, as opposed to the lesser temptations in a precapitalistic culture. As one exegete had written in a commentary on Job's loss of his wealth: "Olim enim divitiae fere in pecoribus et armentis erant. Et ibi avaritia minus locum habebat, quam hodie, ubi auri argentique acerui, insatiabili et insana cupiditate colliguntur." [118]

This method of satiric portraiture by inversion had been formulated by Pope from the beginning and undoubtedly was the original germ of the poem. In early 1730, apparently before the *Epistle to Bathurst* had separated itself from the inclusive plan for a great moral poem to which the *Essay on Man* was to be an introduction, Spence recorded that "Mr. Pope is now employd in a large design for a Moral Poem: there will be several Behaviors flung into Fables: one in particular on the Misery of Affluence (pland just like y[t] of Job only wth y[e] Contrary point in view), w[ch] Mr. Pope says he foresees already will take up at least a thousand verses." [119]

There are many reasons why Job and Balaam would have been thought of as related figures. The most obvious is that Balaam, who "loved the wages of unrighteousness," is the direct antithesis of Job, who was remarkable for his charities and singularly unaffected by the loss of his wealth. Francis Quarles, for example, singling this out as one of Job's most notable virtues, devoted his poetic commentary on the first chapter of the Book of Job to a meditation on avarice and contempt for riches,[120] just as others treated Balaam as the typical worshipper of Mammon. In addition, Jerome, following a rabbinical tradition handed down from the Jerusalem Sota, identified Balaam with Elihu, one of Job's friends; [121] and although later commentators tended to deny the identification, they at least repeatedly called attention to Jerome's words.[122] But even more important than this recurrent conjunction of Job and Balaam, another rabbinical tradition preserved by Baba Bathra declared that God raised up seven prophets among the heathen nations: Balaam and his father, and Job and his four friends.[123] This tradition persisted, and writers on the pagans, such as Franciscus Collius, consistently assumed that Job and

[118] Lucas Osiander, *Esdras, Nehemias, Esther, Job* (Tubingae, 1578), p. 184.

[119] This information came to Spence from Robert Hay-Drummond, nephew of the Earl of Oxford. I am indebted to Aubrey Williams for calling the entry to my attention, and to James M. Osborn both for his kindness in transcribing the passage for me from the Spence notebooks in his possession and for granting me permission to quote it. The entry will appear as No. 293 in Osborn's forthcoming edition of the Spence manuscripts.

Since early 1730 Pope had earnestly busied himself with the task of encouraging subscriptions for Samuel Wesley's *Dissertationes in librum Jobi*, which was finally published in 1736 (see Pope to Swift, 14 April 1730 [Sherburn, III. 95] and subsequent similar letters). Undoubtedly Pope knew the contents of this learned work, which examines almost all the exegetical traditions concerning Job and which also contains a chapter on Balaam as a prophet of God. It may well be that his acquaintance with the treatise led him to conceive of a satirical portrait of an anti-Job.

[120] *Job Militant.*

[121] K. Kohler, "The Testament of Job," in *Semitic Studies in Memory of Rev. Dr. Alexander Kohut*, ed. G. A. Kohut (Berlin, 1897), p. 285. Jerome wrote that Balaam "in libro Job dicitur Eliu" (*P.L.*, XXIII. 1021).

[122] For a summary of the arguments, see Franciscus Collius, *De animabus paganorum* (Mediolandi, 1622), III. xi. According to J. A. Fabricius (*Codex pseudoepigraphus Veteris Testamenti* [second ed.; Hamburg, 1741], III. 104), Thomas Hyde, in his *Itinera mundi Abrahami*, p. 73, claimed that although the Septuagint version of the Book of Job states that Job succeeded Balak as king of Edom, "*Bileam*" (Balaam) should be read there instead of "*Balac*." Balaam and Job, therefore, were at different times occupants of the same throne.

[123] Kohler, *op. cit.*, p. 269. The passage from Baba Bathra is translated in *The Babylonian Talmud*, ed. Rabbi Dr. I. Epstein (1935), pt. IV, vol. III, p. 74. Also J. A. Fabricius, *Codex*, II. 812.

Balaam were among the most important of God's prophets among the gentiles.

Since Job and Balaam, although both gentile prophets, were of opposite moral characters, the close exegetical bonds between them allow Pope to flesh out his account of Sir Balaam with an anti-Job. For if Satan has reversed his strategy of seduction, Pope's effigy of the merchant class is simultaneously the evil Balaam of a money culture and the opposite of the good Job of an agrarian culture. The opening evaluation of Pope's Balaam, for example, accords superficially with Jerome's description, " primum vir sanctus, et prophetes Dei ":

> A plain good man, and Balaam was his name;
> Religious, punctual, frugal, and so forth.[124]

We have already seen that the praise is severely undercut by the succeeding lines on the moral worthlessness of Balaam's " word," as it is by the shrug with which the lines end, so that these virtues are reduced to mere outward display. However, the biting irony of the evaluation arises mainly from the fact that the lines are not drawn from any scriptural account of Balaam, but from the opening verse of the divine book of his antitype: " There was a man in the land of Uz, whose name was Job; and that man was perfect and upright, and one that feared God, and eschewed evil." [125]

More precisely, Pope is echoing the Vulgate, which, for the " perfect " of the Authorized Version, here reads " simplex " (rendered in the Douay as " simple "). And thereby he has concentrated in his corresponding phrase, " plain good man," the overlapping ironies of the entire portrait. In the moral and religious traditions the *simplicitas* attributed to Job was understood as the virtue of artless innocence, the instinctive goodness of the prelapsarian Adam; and Pope's formulation, " plain good man," is calculated to render this idea exactly.[126] But obviously neither the prudentially punctual and frugal Balaam of the poem nor the wily Balaam of scripture is " simplex " in this sense; and " plain good man " can be only ironic. Indeed, the irony points tacitly, but directly, to the true character of Balaam, for it was a commonplace of moral theology that human virtue rests in the conjunction of *simplicitas* and its contrary, *prudentia*; and Gregory's gloss on " simplex " in Job 1: 1 makes this very point: " Necesse est ut simplicitatem columbae astutia serpentis instruat, et astutiam simplicitas temperet." [127] Because of the ironic inappropriateness of applying Job's *simplicitas* to Pope's commercial Balaam, the term directs attention to Balaam's true characteristic, the complementary contrary of *prudentia*—but prudence in its completely worldly sense as businesslike wiliness, craft, and cunning (*prudentia carnis*). Only in the forms of his low-church religion is Puritan Balaam simple, or " plain "; and therefore he serves to satirize his Christian sect both for its pretense to *simplicitas* and for the actual worldly prudence of its commercial ethics.

In his first effort to reduce Job through poverty, Satan destroyed his property by slaughter, lightning, and theft, and his children by means of " a great wind from the wilderness " (Job 1: 19). The context makes it evident that the

[124] Cp. Symon Patrick, *op. cit.*: " [He] had been formerly a good Man, and a true Prophet."

[125] Assuming an ideal contemporary audience, Pope's words must have been felt as more than a mere verbal echo, for the scriptural commentators never wearied of analysing Job 1: 1 as though it were a pattern for describing a man. The following from the *Annotations upon all the Books of the Old and New Testaments Authorized by the Westminster Assembly* (1651) is typical: " In this first verse, the principle object of the ensuing History, is set forth by his nature and sex, *A Man.* By his habitation, *In the land of Uz.* By his name, *Job.* By his virtues and good qualities, *perfection, uprightness, fear of God,* and *care to avoid evil.*" In Johannes Cocceius, *Commentarium in librum Jobi* (1701), the verse is analyzed at great length under the heads, *subjectum, patria, nomen, mores.*

Pope, therefore, was not merely imitating the passage in Job but was also fulfilling a formula for identification directly associated with the opening of the Book of Job: (1) " a Citizen "; (2) " Where London's column . . . lifts the head, and lyes "; (3) " Balaam was his name "; (4) " sober," " plain good," " Religious, punctual, frugal, and so forth."

[126] The " vir simplex " of Genesis 25: 27 is translated as " a plain man " in both the Douay and the Authorized Version.

[127] Gregory's comment was incorporated in the *Glossa ordinaria* (*P.L.*, CXIII. 751). Cp. Jerome on Hosea 7: 11: " Praecepit Dominus in Evangelio ut simus simplices quasi columbae, et astuti quasi serpentes, ut imitantes simplicitatem columbarum, et serpentis astutiam, nec aliis nocere possimus, nec ab aliis patiamur insidias, sed simplicitate et prudentia exhibeamus hominem temperatum; quia prudentia absque bonitate, malitia est: et simplicitas absque ratione, stultitia nominatur " (*P.L.*, XXV. 878).

destructive wind is wielded by Satan, but the Biblical commentators wished to determine more specifically how and why the devil could control the winds for evil. The answer lay in Ephesians 2: 2, where he is called " the prince of the power of air, the spirit that now worketh in the children of disobedience." Here, in the region of air, the explanations ran, the devil and his fellow demons were placed, ready at hand to tempt mankind and do mischief through storms, whirlwinds, and other meteorological disorders. Consequently, among the Biblical exegetes and demonologists the passage in Ephesians was regularly linked with the whirlwind that destroyed Job's children. Matthew Poole is typical in explaining the passage in Ephesians as alluding to the prince of the demons " that work so many effects in the air, raise storms and tempests, etc. as in the case of Job and his children." [128] Conversely, George Hutcheson glossed the passage in the Book of Job: Satan's " power to vex [virtuous men] if not hindered by God, appears in the command he hath in the Air, Eph. 2. 2 to raise Tempests, Whirlwinds and Lightnings." [129] Because of this customary cross reference, Pope's identification of Satan as " the Prince of Air " (353) who brought " whirlwinds " evokes not merely the term from the Pauline Epistle but more especially the tragedy of Job and transfers it to Sir Balaam.

But whereas the devil had used the whirlwind to make Job poor by destroying his children, the Prince of Air now, in accordance with the complete reversal of his evil stratagem to take advantage of the corruption potential in a money economy, uses the whirlwinds to destroy Balaam's father, instead of his children; and the successful consequence is that through inheritance Balaam has made his first step toward riches, instead of poverty. Correspondingly, just as Satan's lightning had consumed Job's sheep, the Prince of Air employs the same whirlwind not only to destroy Balaam's father but also to wreck two ships on the Cornish coast; but it is an ironic commentary on the topsy-turvey character of a capitalistic morality that the wreckage of one man's property can be the occasion of another's wealth. Not God, as we would expect, but the Devil's wreckage of property " blesses " [130] with wealth by providing opportunity for plunder. In his ascent to riches Balaam is climbing a ladder of sinfulness. For his father's death, which supplied him with an inheritance, he is not responsible, and yet it has been brought about by the Devil as a powerful temptation to sin. But of the sinfulness of claiming shipwrecked property, no matter what the laws, the casuists left no doubt. The whole history of the subject is summed up by Bishop Hall in a passage which also echoes Pope's ironic use of " bless ":

> . . . no words can express the horrible cruelty and injustice, that is wont to be done in this kind, not only on our shores, but in other nations also, upon the shipwrecked goods, both of strangers and our own compatriots; while, instead of compassioning and relieving the loss and miseries of our distressed brethern, every man is ready to run upon the spoil; and, as if it were from some plundered enemy, is eagerly busy in carrying away what riches soever come to hand; which they falsely and injuriously term " God's grace," when as indeed it is no other than the Devil's booty. This practice can pass for no other than a mere robbery. . . .[131]

Balaam has sinned by a form of theft, and yet the wrecking of the ships was not his work. He has sinned, but only in claiming property that

[128] *Annotations upon the Holy Bible* (1688).

[129] *An Exposition of the Book of Job* (1669), p. 13. See also Johannes Piscatorius, *Commentarii in omnes libros Veteris Testamenti* (Herbonae, 1646); Westminster Assembly, *Annotations upon all the Books of the Old and New Testaments* (1651), on Ephesians 2: 2; Matthew Henry, *An Exposition of the Old and New Testament* (fifth ed., 1761), on Job 1; Joseph Caryl, *An Exposition . . . upon . . . the Book of Job* (1669), pp. 162, 171, 175–76.

[130] Cp. Proverbs 10: 22: " The blessing of the Lord, it maketh rich. . . ."

[131] Joseph Hall, *Cases of Conscience*, in *Works* (1837), VII. 392. See also Johannes Caramuel, *Theologia intentionalis* (Lugduni, 1664), III. 88; Gulielmus Herincx, *Summa theologica* (Antwerp, second ed., 1680), III. 304; Bartholomaeus Mastrius, *Theologia moralis* (Venice, fourth ed., 1700), p. 75; Paul Laymann, *Theologia moralis* (Patavii, 1733), I. 244; and Jean Pontas, *Dictionarium casum conscientiae* (Venice, 1757), II. 616. All of these also list the major casuists on the subject.

came to him, as the Christian moralists classified it, *inventione*. Now, however, he both accepts a stolen gem and, exercising bad faith, refuses to allow the pledged diamond to be redeemed; and the moralists allowed only one answer to the question, "Whether I may lawfully buy those goods, which I shall strongly suspect or know to be stolen or plundered." [132] The hierarchy corresponds to that concerning the status of goods elaborated by the casuists in their discussions of *dominium*: inheritance, possession of goods of uncertain status, acceptance of stolen property, and violation of contract. At last, by this gradual progress through indirect theft, corresponding to Job's increasing poverty, Balaam has been prepared for open and willful theft: he deals in stocks and serves as director of the new corporations.

Balaam further inverts Job's history, for whereas Job had to resist his wife's evil advice to sink under his misfortunes—"curse God, and die"—Sir Balaam yields to his wife's contrary advice—"Live like yourself" (359)—and thereby gives himself wholly to things of the world. Moreover, one aspect of Job's perfection that especially struck the commentators was his extreme solicitude for his children, for we are told that when they feasted, "Job sent and sanctified them . . . and offered burnt offerings . . . : for Job said, It may be that my sons have sinned, and cursed God in their hearts" (Job 1: 5). Such scrupulous, supererogatory care for his family convinced the commentators of Job's saintliness, since, although he "knew no particular sin" in his children, he feared even the danger of their "secret sins." [133] On the contrary, instead of exercising such "great care . . . to keep his children in the favour of God," [134] Sir Balaam was far too busy in his counting house on Sunday and "sent his family and wife" to church (382) to save their own souls as best they could without his assistance.

However, Balaam will not be completely Satan's until, through worldly success and love of riches, he has been swallowed up in the machinery of capitalism. To that end Satan devotes himself by pouring "Stocks and Subscriptions" around him; and having created these temptations,

> all the Dæmon makes his full descent,
> In one abundant show'r of Cent. per Cent.,
> Sinks deep within him, and possesses whole,
> Then dubs Director, and secures his soul.
> (371–74)

Professor Maynard Mack quite properly has made us aware of the presence of the Danaë legend in these lines. Satan is playing Jove to Sir Balaam's Danaë, impregnating him with the golden shower of rich investments. To this it must be added that the myth had long had approximately the allegorical value that Pope is here assigning it. Horace, for example, had used the story of Jove and Danaë to illustrate the power of bribery to penetrate all barriers and corrupt every virtue.[135] The allegory was adopted among the Church Fathers, was constantly repeated in subsequent Christian writings, and persisted as the primary meaning of the myth.[136] Pagan in origin and substance and yet absorbed into the Christian treatment of riches, the myth readily lent itself to Pope's humanistic-Christian poem on avarice; and Pope's artistry of poetic assimilation lies in his telling the story in the terms, not of the myth, but of the allegorical meanings which the original myth concealed, yet without losing allusive contact with the myth.

However, there is also a larger artistry here that aligns the classical myth with the entire religious context of the account of Balaam and anti-Job in which it appears. Since the tradition of angelology held that the pagan gods were various forms assumed by the Devil,[137] Pope is

[132] Joseph Hall, *op. cit.*, X. 393.

[133] James Durham, *Exposition on the whole Book of Job* (Glasgow, 1759), pp. 3–4; also, e.g., George Abbot, *Whole Book of Job Paraphrased* (1640).

[134] Westminster Assembly, *Annotations* (1651).

[135] *Odes*, III. 16.

[136] Evidence is so widespread that it is almost pointless to document it, but the following list will indicate the range: Lactantius, *Divine Institutes*, I. chap. xi; Augustine, *City of God*, XVIII. 13; Richard Cobet, *Times Whistle* (EETS, XLVIII. 42); Joshua Poole, *English Parnassus* (1677), s.v. "Gold"; Sir George Mackenzie, *The Moral History of Frugality* (1691), p. 30; and Swift, "Critical Essay upon the Faculties of the Mind."

[137] Emil Schneweis, *Angels and Demons According to Lactantius* (Washington, D.C., 1944), pp. 143–53. See also

merely stripping away the Jupiter-disguise of the classical myth to reveal the true identity of the malefactor as " the Dæmon." He is not coyly concealing the presence of the Danaë-Jupiter myth, but is restoring the myth to its true Christian character by assigning it to Satan. The wealthy purchaser of Danaë's chastity therefore is identical in the Christian tradition with the false gods invoked by the wizard Balaam and with the Satan who sought to tempt Job. Moreover, the Devil who has set out to gain Sir Balaam by inverting his unsuccessful devices against Job has already appeared in his role of " Prince of Air " and has effected his evil work by his control over the storms. Consequently, the meteorological Jupiter-Demon who came to Danaë as a rain of gold and to Sir Balaam as a " show'r of Cent. per Cent." is the same meteorological Satan who destroyed Job's children and Sir Balaam's father in a whirlwind.

If now we recognize Pope's thorough absorption of the Danaë myth and its moral allegory into Christian demonology, we are led to read his Jupiter-Demon as also the Devil in the form of the incubus following the fixed steps in his routine of capturing a human soul. The " Tempter " first besieges, or " obsesses," his victim by the usual method of surrounding him: " Stocks and Subscriptions pour on ev'ry side " (370).[138] Obsession was understood to be the limit of Satan's power over the virtuous, but Sir Balaam is an easy and willing victim; and Satan proceeds to inhabit, or " possess ": as the Jupiter-incubus, he " Sinks deep within him, and possesses whole " (373). But the essence of witchcraft is the *pactum cum daemonibus*, the agreement to renounce God and to serve the Devil in order to gain his aid in this world at the expense of the next.[139] Consequently, Satan finally " secures " Balaam's soul when he " dubs " him director of a corporation, for the necessary implication is that *Sir* Balaam has sworn fealty and homage to the Devil and is now his vassal. In accord with the general maneuvering of the poem, the classical myth of Danaë has been restored to its inherent Christian terms and assimilated to the ritual of witchcraft so as to draw Bathurst's classical prejudices into the speaker's Christian assumptions.

Like the scriptural Balaam, who sought to curse the Israelites for Balak's rewards, Sir Balaam now " takes a bribe from France " (396). He has been both the miser and the prodigal and has enacted the fact that both of these extremes of liberality are sins. Finally, condemned for the sins that his decline into riches has driven him to, Sir Balaam falls to his lowest satanic depths by adopting the evil advice of Job's wife to " curse God and die." The Devil has succeeded so well with his new capitalistic stratagem that Sir Balaam not only accedes to the diabolical advice his antitype had rejected, but in this act, with terrible irony, also persists in his own wicked wizardry; for the Balaam whose efforts to curse the Israelites were transformed by God into blessings has attempted, at his end, to turn his malediction against God Himself. Nay, more; for Pope has wrung from his final line every possible horror. In cursing God, Balaam has given testimony that Satan has succeeded with him precisely as he had failed with Job. Given an anti-Job, a hypocritical, Calvinistic capitalist with only the ethics of Cheapside, instead of a true worshipper, Satan has proved the validity of his devilishly Hobbesian philosophy that had failed against Job. " Doth Job fear God for nought? " Satan had asked God. " Hast not thou made an hedge about him, and about his house, and about all that he hath on every side? thou hast blessed

Burton, *Anatomy of Melancholy,* I. ii. 1. 2: until Christ's Coming, the " Devils of the Air " domineered as the " gods of the pagans." The same idea is used by Milton (*P. L.*, I. 364 ff.) and appears regularly in the glosses on 1 Chronicles 16: 26 and Psalms 96: 5: " For all the gods of the nations are idols." E. g., Guillielmius Estius, *Annotationes* (Moguntiae, 1667), p. 426.

[138] Dr. Johnson defined *obsession* as " The first attack of Satan, antecedent to possession." See also Rossell Hope Robbins, *Encyclopedia of Witchcraft and Demonology* (New York, 1959), s. v. " Possession "; and *OED*, s. v. " obsess " and " obsession."

[139] Sir Robert Filmer, *An Advertisement to the Jurymen of England touching Witches* (1652), p. 9: ". . . the witch as a slave binds herself by vow to believe in the Devil, and to give him either body or soul, or both [so as to gain the Devil's promise] to be ready at his vassal's command . . . to consult and to aid him, for the procuring of pleasure, honor, wealth, or preferment. . . ."

the work of his hands, and his substance is increased in the land." Man fears God only that, selfishly, he might prosper in the world. "But put forth thine hand now, and touch all that he hath, and he will curse thee to thy face" (Job 1: 9–11).

These interplays of Scripture and the machinations of finance, together with its social and political frippery, not only shape and then hang the typical Dissenting Whig merchant who combines in his life the sins both of avarice and prodigality; they also form a texture for a disconnected assortment of further threads of irony, such as the threefold pun whereby the speaker describes as "now a man of spirit" (375) the spirited parvenu who, by his pact with the Devil, has lost his immortal spirit and is possessed by demonic spirits. With similar irony, when Satan the incubus possesses Sir Balaam he "Then dubs Director, and secures his soul" (374). By raising Sir Balaam to this honor and thereby gaining his fealty, Satan not only "secures" (gains possession of) Balaam's soul but also makes it secure in a thoroughly devilish sense, for Balaam's soul is not "secure" but lost. Against the grain of these religious meanings of the line runs its economic sense, the theme of the poem having consistently been that the two are intimately related: the title of "Director" of a corporation is the sound security, or bond, guaranteeing that the Devil will ultimately have the soul.

But the sharpest thrust is made by the couplet on Sir Balaam's election to Parliament—

> In Britain's Senate he a seat obtains,
> And one more Pensioner St. Stephen gains.
> (393-94)

For it directs the satire toward Sir Robert Walpole, whose shadowy figure has hovered in the background of the entire poem, just as it hovered over the politico-economic morality of the age. Indeed, it may be said that by indirection the entire poem is really an attack on Walpole, leader of the Whigs, friend of Chartres and other villains in the poem, patron of Phryne, screener of the directors of the South Sea Company, proponent of the Excise Bill. When Sir Balaam becomes a Member of Parliament, "one more Pensioner St. Stephen gains" because Walpole, who, as Lord Treasurer, completely dominated the government, used to a notorious degree his access to the nation's funds to make hirelings (or "pensioners") of the House of Commons, whose meeting place was St. Stephen's Chapel in Westminster. It was at this very moment that the word "pension" was gaining its Johnsonian definition as "pay given to a state hireling for treason to his country"; for Parliament had recently been debating the Pension Bill, designed to prevent its members from holding government grants, which, said the *Craftsman*, are intended not to reward a man for "his Service, but to corrupt his Conduct." [140] To be of the group meeting in the chapel once dedicated to St. Stephen is, therefore, to be a hireling of that other patron saint to whom the House of Commons is now dedicated and who is its presiding spirit, the Lord Treasurer.

We have repeatedly seen that much of the art of the poem lies in energetic interplays among vast, complex areas of allusion evoked with gentlemanly ease and the greatest verbal economy. The areas most frequently evoked are classical and Christian, so that the first may congenially draw assent from the classicist Bathurst and that the second may transform his assent into a similar commitment on Christian grounds. The speaker, therefore, has here cast his language into a particularly significant form, and in a footnote Pope was careful to let us know that "And one more Pensioner St. Stephen gains" echoes Juvenal's "atque unum civem donare Sibyllae": and one more citizen the Sibyl gains. Thereby he delicately tips the mirror of the line to reflect the entire context of Juvenal's third satire, together with the strong bitterness usually associated with the Juvenalian manner. Just as Sir Balaam has made his progress from the City to St. James and thence to St. Stephen's Chapel in Westminster, where Walpole performs his mysteries, so Juvenal's friend, Umbritius, is escaping Rome to live in Cumae, where the Sibyl has her shrine and prophesies

[140] No. 203, 23 May 1730.

men's futures. Juvenal's satire is leveled mainly against the avarice then governing Rome, where the power of money was corrupting the old culture and where those "gentiles," the immigrant Greeks, like the Calvinists, were gaining control of wealth by hypocritically cloaking their vices under pretenses to the Stoic philosophy. Juvenal's decaying Rome, the speaker is saying to Bathurst—who would by nature be sympathetic to the classical allusion—was the type of modern London; but the irony, of course, lies in the fact that whereas Umbritius was escaping to the simple, agrarian culture of Cumae, Sir Balaam has fled from sordid London to the very source of its corruption.

Rome, however, is merely the secular analogue of modern London and comments only on moral virtues. The same line of verse also points to a scriptural analogue, and St. Stephen is not only a ridiculous substitute for that prophetic Sibyl, Sir Robert Walpole, but is also, in a bitterly ironic way, his scriptural type. Modern London is not only the classicist's second-century Rome but also the Christian's first-century Jerusalem. When, according to Acts 6, the populace—especially the Greek converts—began to murmur over their poverty, the Apostles decided to confine themselves to their spiritual task and not to "serve tables." Therefore, just as the king's chief minister, the Lord Treasurer, is chosen as leader by his party but is appointed to his official post by the king, so the Apostles ordered the multitude: "look ye out among you seven men of honest report, full of the Holy Ghost and wisdom, whom we may appoint over this business [of distributing alms]" (Acts 6: 3). These seven the commentators took as the first deacons of the church, the secular stewards whose duty was to parcel out the church's temporalities to the "pensioners" (i. e., the dependants on charity). And of these deacons the most important was Stephen, a man "full of faith and power" who "did great wonders and miracles among the disciples." [141]

Here is Pope's satiric technique of montage in its most telling and triumphant form, as the overlay of the scriptural St. Stephen upon his modern counterpart, the corrupt Lord Treasurer, divulges the painful distance between Christian alms and the spoils system of capitalistic government. As the play on "pensioner" asserts, the recipient of alms has become the political hireling, and political bribery is the only acknowledged form of "Christian" charity in a capitalistic government. Behind the veil of the words, the First Lord of the Treasury, Deacon Walpole—that man of honest report and full of the Holy Ghost—distributes to the muttering politicians the largess of the state as patronage, bribery, propaganda, and espionage, and thereby produces great wonders and miracles among his disciples. Although only a ghostly presence, as he is throughout the poem, and although shaped only by the most delicate, indirect intimations, this latter-day St. Stephen whose spirit pervades the chapel of his prototype is one of Pope's greatest satiric portraits. The power to create him by implication only and with a mere half-dozen words is the touchstone of the success of the poem's complex "voice," blended by the opening interplay between the follower of Momus and the theologically well-informed, religiously committed speaker.

[141] In view of the recurrently implied identification in the poem of the Israelites with the Tory Anglicans and the gentiles with the Whig Dissenters, it probably is significant that the deacons were appointed because of the "murmuring of the Grecians [i. e., the Hellenic converts] against the Hebrews, because their widows were neglected in the daily ministration" (Acts 6: 1).

In the first edition of 1732 the personal names in the poem appeared in such elliptical forms as "W–rd," "W–t–rs," and "Ch–rs" (20). These were undoubtedly recognizable to Pope's London contemporaries after a little speculation, and in subsequent editions the names were mercifully printed in full as "Ward," "Waters," and "Chartres." But even if we were to misunderstand the nature of Pope's rhetorical art, the manuscripts make it plain that the poem does not exist to satirize these public characters. Pope's culture had provided him with a reservoir of *exempla* that he drew on for the figures that would best illustrate his moral themes. "I shall make living examples, which enforce best," he wrote Caryll.[142] The manuscripts show, for example, that instead of Ward, Waters, and Chartres, he might have included Bladen, Jansen, Knight, Blunt, Bond, and the mysterious "M–n & D–y." In a similar way, we see the poet turning over tempting possibilities—Cutler, Demar, Selkirk, Heathcote, and Coleby—before he decided that "Plum" Turner was the man for his line: "Alas! 'tis more than Turner finds they give" (84). Undoubtedly Pope properly described the roles of these names when he wrote of his "Moral Book," ". . . many exemplary Facts & Characters fall into it daily." [143] The life about him was persistently supplying the exemplary confirmation of the moral doctrines which are the purpose of the poem.

Some of the names, however, are those of types—Harpax, Uxorio, Phryne, Sir Morgan, Adonis—and consequently are more ambiguous. "Narses" (91), for example, was Justinian's general, but the manuscript reading, "C x x n," shows that Pope originally had Farl Cadogan in mind; and the descriptive details in the published version no doubt were sufficient for Pope's better-informed readers to name the man. Similarly, the knowing could probably find Walpole's mistress, Molly Skerrett, in "Phryne" (121), Sir Christopher Musgrave in "Old Cato" (68), and Lord Hervey in "Adonis" (61). Certainly the poet's introduction of many explicit proper names encourages the search for the identity of all the characters; and even Swift wished the names were spelled out in full because of his "ignorance in facts and persons, which make us lose abundance of the Satyr." [144] But who shall we say is such a figure as "S–l–k" (117)? The manuscript (p. 114) suggests that Pope first had the Duke of Marlborough in mind as his *exemplum*—a fact that has no bearing on the final poem, however interesting to the biographer. Pope's contemporaries would have recognized "S–l–k" as the Earl of Selkirk, whose avarice was notorious, and undoubtedly the reader was being asked to make this identification. On the other hand, the reader was also being intentionally befuddled, for thirty lines earlier in the published version there appeared another miser, "wretched Shylock" (96), and after the first edition "S–l–k" of line 117 was filled out to "Shylock," whom Pope in his edition of Shakespeare had listed, not surprisingly, as the type of the avaricious man.[145] Are both Shylocks now to be read as Selkirk, or is neither? If we should assume that all the names are removable masks foı real individuals and that the critic's task is to search out the thinly veiled victims, the problem is further complicated by the fact that in the manuscript (p. 78) Pope first assigned line 96—"Of wretched Shylock, spite of Shylock's Wife"—to one "Gu–" and then to "W–y," which in the later manuscript (pp. 76, 110) becomes "Worldly." This is the same Worldly who cries "coals from street to street" in line 50 and whom the circumstances identify as Edward Wortley Montagu, husband of Lady Mary and the devoted owner of rich coal mines. But certainly, then, the Twickenham editor cannot be right in making Shylock at one point Wortley and at another

[142] 27 September 1732 (Sherburn, III. 316).
[143] Pope to Bethel, 8 September 1731 (Sherburn, III. 227).
[144] Sherburn, III. 343.
[145] See his letter to Tonson (Sherburn, II. 214).

Selkirk; and, no matter what individuals may have run through Pope's mind in the various stages of composition, the editor must be wrong in identifying " wretched Shylock " (96) so precisely as Wortley Montagu, since he could equally well be " Gu—" or Selkirk—and is indeed, in the printed text, only Shylock.

Such an identification with particular persons confuses rhetoric with biography and history—and the facts of art with the facts of life. For just as the specifically named individuals are moral *exempla,* not the subjects of the satire, so all the names are pawns in a brave rhetorical gambit. The problem Pope was solving was how to make his satire both general and particular: how to attack generally and yet not lose contact with the recognizable data of contemporary life, and how to be specific without producing exclusively personal satire. The presence of such clearly identifiable names as " Sir G—t," " Bl—t," or " Bond " encourages a sense that particular individuals are to be the consistent butts of the poem. But Shylock may and may not be Selkirk or Wortley Montagu, and the reader is to be tantalized into seeking the precise person, even though Shylock resists final identification and remains a type. In each of these inexact names the poem offers only a category, but the artistry effectively drives the reader to the effort to translate it into a specific person. When Pope's enemies insisted that Timon was meant for the Duke of Chandos, Pope protested against " so great a stupidity in the point of comprehending a poet's manner (being the ignorance of the very principle of that sort of writing) ." [146]

In his rhetorical intent Pope succeeded admirably, and his contemporaries strained to find the persons supposedly aimed at in the larger portraits of Cotta and Sir Balaam.[147] A detail seemed to label the elder Cotta as Sir John Cutler—or perhaps the Duke of Newcastle—and really neither will do. Sir Balaam is Thomas Pitt—although not exactly. Bateson therefore, like Pope's contemporaries, has proved an excellently responsive audience and an admirable victim of Pope's rhetoric. To say, as Bateson does, that Sir Balaam is " a generalized portrait " and yet " a good case has been made " for identifying him as Thomas Pitt, is to fulfill the orator's intent that his audience experience the character simultaneously as a type and yet as flesh and blood. This is to respond as Lady Anne Irwin did when the poem first appeared. After identifying the characters, she added, " The last character does not hit in every particular, but I think where 'tis disguised 'tis with a design it mayn't be fixed." [148] But this is not to perform the duties of the critic, who is required to stand apart from orator and audience, and to recognize the rhetorical procedures whereby the suasion of the audience is effected.[149] When Spence asked whether the two Cottas were the Duke of Newcastle and his heir, Thomas Pelham-Holles, " Mr. Pope did not confirm it outright, . . . but spoke of their characters in a manner that seemed not at all to disown it." [150] Any other answer would have distorted the poetic truth. For the poem completes its own inner rhetorical and poetic requirements and is self-sufficient, so that, like the names it employs, it both grew out of a moment in time and yet is available and pertinent to man at any time.

[146] Pope to Caryll, 29 March 1732 (Sherburn, III. 279) .

[147] See Bateson, pp. 105 n., 118 n.

[148] Bateson, p. 118 n.

[149] In an intricate, yet indecisive effort, Bateson tries to identify the Cottas on the basis of a very literal reading of the manuscript lines (p. 90) :

> How Providence once more shall shift the Scene?
> And, showing Harley, show the Golden Mean! . . .
> Where one lean Herring furnish'd Cotta's Board, . . .
> There gracious Oxford, acting God's own part,
> Relieves th' oppress, and glads the Orphan's heart.

Bateson takes this to mean that Oxford now owns Cotta's country seat and by this means tries to identify Cotta. But " Providence once more shall shift the Scene " prevents such a reading, and the stage metaphor clearly means that with Oxford the curtains are raised on a wholly different scene. The allusion is not to a place, but a moral condition; and it is the very nature of Providence, or Fortune, to change conditions. Compare Lord Lansdowne's epigram on Walpole: " Good unexpected, evil unforeseen, / Appear by turns, as Fortune shifts the scene."

Moreover, Bateson's proposal collapses in the face of the supplementary manuscript revision which would have the Cottas succeeded by both Oxford and Chandos, who could not both have gained Cotta's country seats; and that " Scene " refers not to an estate, but to the moral " scene " each Cotta symbolizes, is made clear by the revision, " Who next appear, & gladden either Scene? "—i. e., the miserly " scene " of the elder Cotta and the prodigal one of the younger.

[150] Spence, *Anecdotes*, ed. S. W. Singer (1820) , p. 300.

The Manuscripts

Although any assignment of dates to the three Huntington manuscripts here reproduced must be largely conjectural, there is sufficient circumstantial evidence to establish the outer limits of each of them. The first is obviously a supplementary revision of an unknown earlier version. Since this pair of leaves corresponds roughly to lines 237–388 of the first edition of 1732 and begins with a revision of page 5 of the earlier manuscript, the unknown version probably was between one-half and three-quarters of the length of the poem as it was first published.

The earliest references to the contents of the poem appear in Spence's memorandum of early 1730 on a poem on Job (see above, p. 49) and the following entry in Spence's papers:

> . . . Sr Balaam: The man of Ross: The Standing jest of Heaven. And sure ye Gods & We are of a mind. The Man posses^d of Debts & Taxes clear, Children & Wife—Five hundred pound a year (Publ: Buildings Alms Houses, Walks, Road;) The man of Ross divides ye weekly bread: Public Table twice a week for Strangers &c.—Will give w^t we desire; Fire, Meat, & Drink—What more? Meat, Drink, & fire.[1]

These portions of the poem, therefore, were in existence before the date of the Spence entry, 1–7 May 1730, and probably were the germs of the poem, although the full entry suggests they had not yet been separated in Pope's mind from the inclusive philosophic poem he intended to write. The first of the Huntington manuscripts undoubtedly was written after this date. Its terminal date is supplied by line 50, " W^ch Villers lost, & W— cannot find," for the Duke of Wharton was to die on the Continent on 30 May 1731, and Pope must have learned of it shortly thereafter.

Since the second manuscript contains a similar line, " Which Villers mist and Wxx ner shall find " (279), it also was composed before this date, no doubt as a clean copy from the unknown manuscript of which the first Huntington draft is a revision. Page 346* (p. 80), however, is a supplementary revision of page 346^v and was written between 30 May 1731, when Wharton died (line 109 reads, " Which Wh—n mist ") and 24 August 1731, when the Marquis of Blandford died (the same line reads, " and B—d ner shall find ").[2] But line 117 (" Japhet Ears & Nose ") fixes even narrower limits, since it was on 10 June 1731 that Japhet Crook suffered the loss of these features on the pillory.[3] If on this page the revision, " not Vultur Breath " (116a), means that John (" Vulture ") Hopkins is dead,

[1] Quoted in Bateson, pp. xxii–xxiii.

[2] Courthope's proposal (III. 148 n.) that the reference is to the Duke of Bedford seems most unlikely. The marginal additions on page 348^v, " What losing, saving, B—d ner c^d hit " and " Which Wh— lost, and B— ner could find," are obviously rewritings of line 109 and mean that " B—d " is now dead. But since the entire marginal passage undoubtedly predates 22 January 1731/2 (see p. 60), it cannot refer to Bedford, who died in Spain on 23 October 1732.

On the other hand, Blandford, the grandson of the Duke of Marlborough, had been on Pope's mind. On 8 September 1731 (Sherburn, III. 227) he wrote to Bethel: " I have been busy in the Moral Book I told you of: many exemplary Facts & Characters fall into it daily, but which render it less fit for the Present Age. The Fate of the Marlborough family is a Great one, which the death of the Marquess of Blandford has renewd my Reflections on. *Solus sapiens dives* is very true." The paragraph then goes on to discuss the Man of Ross.

Blandford, who had a large fortune in his own right, was a notorious drunkard and died as a result of a drinking bout at his Oxford club (A. L. Rowse, *The Early Churchills* [1956], pp. 406–407). Pope's reference to him seems part of a continued campaign—in his manuscripts—to attack the Marlborough family. For suppressed and discarded attacks, see Courthope, frontispiece of vol. III, and III. 527–28; and in the following manuscripts, pp. 84, 114. For a further discussion of Pope's satire of Marlborough, see Bateson, pp. xii–xiv, 162.

[3] *Gentleman's Magazine*, 1 (1731), 218, 263–64.

it was added after 25 April 1732. But it may allude only to some difficulty Hopkins had in breathing or speaking, which seems to be the sense of Gay's line of 1721: "Let Vulture *H—ns* stretch his rusty Throat." [4] The marginal additions on page 348v of this manuscript would seem to predate 22 January 1731/2, when Pope wrote Oxford that he had included a celebration of both Oxford and Chandos, and they probably were added shortly after the first public identification of Chandos as the Timon of the *Epistle to Burlington* (published 13 December 1731). Since Pope wrote Tonson on 7 June 1732 that he would put "into a note, perhaps into the body of the poem itself" the fact that the Man of Ross had no monument, it seems reasonable to believe that the addition to that effect in the note on page 349 was added at about that date.[5]

The third draft, originally a clean copy of the second, was perhaps written at about this last date, but there appears to be nothing in its contents to date it more precisely. There must have been at least one subsequent working manuscript in which Pope brought the poem to its final published form.

Although the *Epistle to Bathurst*, dated 1732, was not published until 15 January 1732/3, on 2 November 1732 Pope expected it to appear "next week" (letter to Jonathan Richardson). The poem, said Pope, was "the work of two years by intervals," and "I never took more care in my life of any [other] poem." [6]

The Huntington Library manuscripts (HM 6007 and 6008) were available to Jonathan Richardson, Jr., who transcribed readings from them to a copy of the 1735 edition of Pope's *Works* (also in the Huntington Library collection). Later they were used by Warburton for his 1751 edition of Pope's *Works* and by Elwin, since Courthope acknowledged use of his transcriptions of the "Chauncy MS." (*Works of Alexander Pope* [1881] III, x). The Pope manuscripts in the possession of Dr. Charles Chauncy were finally dispersed on 30 July 1889 at the Nassau Lees sale. There appears to be no reference thereafter to the manuscripts of the *Epistle to Bathurst*, and the Huntington Library has no record of their acquisition.

[4] "A Panegyrical Epistle to Mr. Thomas Snow," line 30.

[5] In the third manuscript he added marginally (p. 124) the passage that fulfills his promise to incorporate the information in the body of the poem.

[6] Pope to Caryll, 8 March 1732/3 (Sherburn, III. 353); to Swift, 16 February 1732/3 (Sherburn, III. 348).

I am indebted to Mr. H. C. Schulz, Curator of Manuscripts of the Henry E. Huntington Library, for the following bibliographical information. What is here recorded as the first version is portion of HM 6008:

"Page 5" (pp. 64, 66)
$12\frac{1}{2}$ x $7\frac{7}{8}$, fol.
Wmk. Pro Patria, Heawood 3690–3718, without initials, faces left

"Page 7.8.5 *" (pp. 68, 70)
$11\frac{1}{2}$ x $7\frac{7}{8}$, fol.
Countermark, similar to Heawood 3702

The second version is HM 6007:

Leaves "345"–"350" (pp. 72–78, 84–98)
$9\frac{3}{8}$ x $7\frac{3}{8}$ 4to.
Wmk. similar to Heawood 1743, countermark "IV"

Leaf "351" (pp. 100, 102)
9 x $7\frac{1}{4}$, 4to.
Countermark only, "IV"

Leaf "346*" (p. 80)
$8\frac{3}{4}$ x $7\frac{3}{8}$, chain lines are vertical
Countermark only, "LV"

The third version is also part of HM 6008:

Leaves "1"–"5" (pp. 104-130)
$12\frac{1}{2}$ x $7\frac{7}{8}$, fol.
Wmk. lion similar to Heawood 1348, countermark "LVG"

Page 132 is the conjugate of leaf "1"

Information readily available in Bateson has not been repeated in the notes to the manuscripts.

The letter *a* following a line number indicates

a revision above the line; the letter *b*, a revision beneath it.

⟨ ⟩ encloses illegible passages and especially dubious readings.

Following is a list which correlates as closely as possible the line numbers of the several manuscripts with the line numbers of the 1732 edition of the poem.

Manuscript I	*1732*
1–2	237–238
3–6	241–244
7–8	——
9–14	247–252
15	254
16	253
17–38	255–276
39	226
40	225
41–42	227–228
43–44	213–214
45–49	217–221
50	——
51	293, 328
52–55	329–332
56–59	329–332
60–91	335–366
92–111	369–388

Manuscript II	*1732*
1–4	1–4
5–6	——
7–8	5–6
9–10	——
11–18	7–14
19–43	17–41
44	——
45–53	42–50
54–71	53–70
72–73	——
74–79	77–83
80–89	85–96
90–91	——
92–93	107–108
94–97	111–114
98–99	121–122
100–101	77–78
102	213
103	——
Manuscript II (cont.)	*1732*
104a–108	216–221
109	——
110–127	79–96
128–129	——
130–131	107–108
132–135	111–114
136–137	121–122
138	——
139	116
140–145	——
146–147	127–128
148–152	133–137
153–155	141–142
156–171	145–160
172–177	163–168
178–191	171–184
192–193	101–102
194–199	185–190
200–201	195–196
202–203	193–194
204–205	191–192
206–209	197–200
210	——
211	201
212–219	203–210
220–223	——
224–225	239–240
226–227	——
228	222
229	——
230–231	237–238
232–267	241–276
268	226
269	225
270–271	227–228
272–273	——
274–278	217–221
279	——
280–295	293–308
296–297	315–316
298–303	309–314
304–307	317–320
308–317	323–332
318–349	335–366
350–374	369–393
375–376	——
377	394

Manuscript III	*1732*
1–14	1–14
15	——

Manuscript III (cont.)	*1732*
16–48	18–50
49–66	53–70
67–88	77–98
89–90	——
91–92	107–108
93–98	111–116
99–100	121–122
101	——
102	116
103–104	121–122
105	——
106	116
107–111	133–137
112–114	141–142
115–138	145–168
139–144	171–176
145–146	169–170
147–148	177–178
149–150	101–102
151–162	179–190
163–164	195–196

Manuscript III (cont.)	*1732*
165–166	193–194
167–168	191–192
169–172	197–200
173–175	——
176	201
177–178	203–204
179–193	207–221
194–196	——
197–200	221–224
201–202	237–238
203–238	241–276
239	226
240	225
241–244	227–230
245–262	291–308
263–264	315–316
265–270	309–314
271–286	317–332
287–318	335–366
319–344	369–394

The Manuscripts

Page 4.5.

There gracious × × acting Gods own part,
Relieves th' Opprest & glads the Widows heart;
There English Bounty yet a while shall stand,
And Honour lingers, ere ~~she~~ it leaves the land.
[Yet all our Incense why should Lords engross?
Rise, honest Muse! and sing the Man of Ross;
The Man of Ross! ~~his is~~ ~~[illegible]~~ ~~[illegible]~~ unknown. / The Man from Vaga to Sabrina known
~~Trace humble Worth beyond Sabrina's Shore~~:
whose joy was Good, his ~~[illegible]~~, and Virtues all his own.
× ~~Who sings not him, Oh may he sing no more!~~
Round the white ~~Town~~ Church on yonder ~~Sunny~~ airy brow,
Who ~~hung~~ spread the Woods, and bad the waters flow?
Not to the Skies in useless columns tost,
Or in vast proud Sheets Falls magnificently lost,
But clear and artless, pouring thro' the Plain
Health to the Sick, and Solace to the Swain?
2 Whose Seats the weary Wanderer repose?
1. Whose ~~Trees divide the~~ Causeways ~~[illegible]~~ yon Vale in ~~equal~~ with shady rows?
Who ~~rais'd~~ feeds that Almshouse, neat, but void of State,
Where Age & Want sit smiling at the Gate?
Who taught yon' Heav'n-directed Spire to rise?
The Man of Ross, each lisping child replies.
Behold the Market-place with Poor o'erspread!
The Man of Ross divides the weekly Bread.
Him portion'd maids, apprentic'd Orphans, blest,
The Young who labour, & the Old who rest.
Is any Sick? the Man of Ross relieves,
Prescribes, attends; the med'cine makes, and gives:
Is there a Variance? enter but his door,
The Courts are baffled, and the Contest o'er:
Despairing Quacks with Curses left the place,
And vile Attorneys fled, an useless Race.

Twelve for Children

Thrice

Page ~~6~~. 5.

There gracious xx acting Gods own part,
Relieves th'Opprest & glads the Widows heart;
There English Bounty yet a while shall stand,

it
And Honour lingers, e're ~~she~~ leaves the land.
5 [Yet all our Incense why should Lords engross?
Rise, honest Muse! and sing the Man of Ross;

His
he Man of Ross? ~~*And*~~ *is* ~~*that*~~ *name*
~~*real*~~*unknown / The Man from Vaga to Sabrina known*
~~Trace humble worth beyond Sabrina's shore~~:

sole joy,
Whose joy was Good his ~~Delight~~, *and Virtue all his own.*
X ~~Who sings not him, oh may he sing no more!~~

Church *airy*
Round the white ~~Town~~ on yonder Sunny brow,

~~*spread*~~
10 Who hung the Woods, and bad the Waters flow?
Not to the Skies in useless columns tost,

proud Falls
Or in vast Sheets magnificently lost,
But clear and artless, pouring thro' the Plain
Health to the Sick, and Solace to the Swain?
15 2 Whose Seats the weary Wanderer repose?

Causeways parts ~~—~~ */⟷/yon* ~~*with*~~ *shady*
1.Whose ~~Trees divide the~~ ^Vale in ~~equal~~ ^rows?

feeds
Who^ ~~rais'd~~ that Almshouse, neat, but void of State,
Where Age & Want sit smiling at the Gate?
Who taught yon' Heav'n-directed Spire to rise?
20 The Man of Ross, each lisping child replies.
Behold the market-place with Poor oe'rspread!
The Man of Ross divides the weekly Bread.
Him portion'd Maids, apprentic'd Orphans, blest,
The young who labour, & the old who rest.
25 Is any Sick? the Man of Ross relieves,
Prescribes, attends; the med'cine makes, and gives:
Is there a Variance? enter but his door,
The Courts are baffled, and the Contest o'er:
Despairing Quacks with Curses left the place,
30 And vile Attorneys fled, an useless Race.

Trustee for Children

Thrice

16a: Causeways] originally *Causeway*.
The deleted word may be *raise*.

7

* Thrice happy Man! enabled to pursue
What all so wish, but want the Powr to do.
O say what Sums thy genrous hand supply?
What Mines, to swell thy boundless Charity?
Of Debts and Taxes, Wife & Children clear, [interlined above: Taxes, Debts, and]
This man possest — five hundred pound a year.
Blush Greatness, blush! false Pride ~~withdraw~~ [interlined: contract] thy blaze!
Ye Little Stars! hide your diminishd Rays. +

\+ The Man of Ross was a name given by way of Eminence
to a private Country Gentleman of that Place, who ~~but have~~ did all
~~name was~~ the good works abovementiond: His true name was,
Cairls. he lived to ye age of yrs. and dyed 172

Those, Bathurst! these alone, give Riches Grace
Whose measure falls oertlast on human race,
Force them to virtue; temperd & diffusd;
As Poisons heal, in ~~just~~ due proportion usd.
What & how great, the Virtue & ye Art,
To bear our Fortunes in our head, not heart,
Large Wealth to sanctify with just Expence
Join with Oeconomy Magnificence
yet keep our Fame our Reason & our Health
Oh teach us, Bathurst! yet unspoild by wealth.
That secret, rarely with Good fortune joind,
with Villers lost, & to — cannot [interlined: never shall] find.
Pag 6. In ye worst Innes worst room &c. To Virtue & Wealth! wt are ye but a Name?
[Say, for such Worth are other worlds prepard?
Or are they both, in this, their own reward?
A knotty Point! on wch we now proceed —
But you are tird. Ill tell a Tale. — agreed. 7. A plain good Citizen

7

✳ Thrice happy Man! enabled to pursue
What all so wish, but want the Pow'r to do.
O say what Sums thy gen'rous hand supply?
What Mines to swell thy boundless Charity?

Taxes, Debts, and
35 Of Debts and Taxes, Wife & Children clear,
This man possest -- five hundred pound a year.

contract
Blush Greatness, blush! false Pride withdraw thy blaze!
Ye Little Stars! hide your diminish'd Rays. +

\+ The Man of Ross was a name given by way of Eminence
who did all
to a private Country Gentleman of that Place, ~~his true~~ ^
the good
~~name was~~ works abovementiond: His true name was
Cairls, he lived to y^e age of y^{rs} and dyed 172

Those, Bathurst! those alone, give Riches Grace
40 Whose measure full oerflows on human race,
Force them to virtue, temperd & diffusd;
As Poisons heal, in ~~just~~ due proportion usd.
What & how great, the Virtue & ye Art,
To bear our Fortunes in our head, not heart,
45 Large Wealth to sanctify with just Expence
Join with Oeconomy Magnificence
Yet keep our Fame our Reason & our Health
Oh teach us, Bathurst! yet unspoild by Wealth.
That Secret, rarely with good fortune joind,

ner shall
50 W^{ch} Villers lost, & W-- cannot find.
Pag 6. In ye worst Innes worst room &c. to -- Virtue & Wealth! w^t are ye but a Name?
[Say, for such Worth are other Worlds prepard?
Or are they both, in this, their own reward?
A knotty Point! on wch we now proceed--
55 But you are tird. Ill tell a Tale--agreed. 7. A plain good Citizen

Footnote: to a private] Instead of *private*, Pope first wrote *G*, probably intending *Gentleman*.

43: This line, repeated throughout these manuscripts, is a translation of the opening line of Horace's *Satires*, II. ii. It does not appear in the published version of the *Epistle to Bathurst*, but was to serve as the first line of Pope's 1734 imitation of Horace's poem.

44: Swift to Bolingbroke and Pope, 5 April 1729 (Sherburn, III. 28): ". . . I have made a maxim, that should be writ in letters of diamonds, That a wise man ought to have Mony in his head, but not in his heart."

45: This line, repeated throughout these manuscripts, became the basis of line 179 of the *Epistle to Burlington:* "In you, my *Lord*, Taste sanctifies Expence" (later, "'Tis Use alone that . . . .").

50: W--] Philip, Duke of Wharton.

— But a name. [Say, for such worth are Other worlds prepar'd?
Or are they both, in this, their own reward?

A knotty Point! on wch we now proceed— | wch shall I now discuss
But you are tir'd— I'll tell a Tale— Agreed. | or tell a Tale?— A Tale.— it follows thus.

A plain good Citizen, of Sober fame,
In Cheapside dwelt, and Balaam was his name.
Religious, punctual, frugal, and so forth:
His Word would pass for more than he was worth.
One solid Dish his each day Meal affords,
An added Pudding solemniz'd the Lord's.
Constant at Church and Change: His Gains were sure,
His Givings rare, save farthings to the Poor.

The Devil was piqu'd, his Saintship to behold,
And long'd to tempt him, like good Job of old;
But knew (for now the Devil was grown a Witch)
The way was not, to make him Poor, but Rich.

Rowz'd by the Prince of Air, the Tempests sweep
The Surge, and plunge his Father in the Deep:
Then, full against his Cornish Lands they roar,
And two rich Ship-wrecks bless the lucky Shore.

Sir Balaam now, he lives like other folks;
He takes his chirping Pint, he cracks his Jokes:
Live like yourself, was now my Lady's word;
And lo! two Puddings smoak'd upon the Board.

Asleep, and naked, as an Indian lay,
An honest Factor stole a Gem away;
He pledg'd it to the Knight; the Knight had Wit,
So robb'd the Robber, and was rich as[x] —— P—t
Some Scruples past, but thus he eas'd his thought.
"I'll now give Sixpence where I gave a Groat

~~—but a name~~
⟵⟶ [Say, for such Worth are Other Worlds prepard?
—But a name. Or are they both, in this, their own Reward?
A knotty Point! on wch we now proceed—— / wch shall I now discuss
But you are tird——Ill tell a Tale——Agreed. or tell a Tale?——A Tale.——
it follows thus.

60 A plain good Citizen, of Sober fame,
In Cheapside dwelt, and Balaam was his name.
Religious, punctual, frugal, and so forth:
His Word would pass for more than he was worth.
One solid Dish his each day meal affords,
65 An added Pudding solemniz'd the Lord's.
Constant at Church and Change: His gains were sure,
His Givings rare, save farthings to the Poor.
The Dev'l was piqu'd, his Saintship to behold,
And long'd to tempt him, like good Job of old;
70 But knew (for now the Dev'l was grown a Witch)
The way was not, to make him Poor, but Rich.
Rowz'd by the Prince of Air, the Tempests sweep
The Surge, and plunge his Father in the Deep:
Then, full against his Cornish Lands they roar,
75 And two rich Ship-wrecks bless the lucky Shore.
Sir Balaam now, he lives like other folks;
He takes his chirping Pint, he cracks his Jokes:
Live like yourself, was now my Lady's word;
And lo! two Puddings smoak'd upon the Board.
80 Asleep, and naked, as an Indian lay,
An honest Factor stole a Gem away;
He pledg'd it to the Knight; the Knight had wit,
So robbd the Robber, and was rich as x— P—t
Some Scruples past, but thus he eas'd his thought:
85 "I'll now give Sixpence where I gave a Groat

71: Poor, but Rich] originally *poor, but rich.*
Margin: under —But a name] in pencil, *What & how great*
Under this, also in pencil, *But.*

83: P—t] Thomas Pitt.

9

"Where once I went to Church, I'll now go twice;
"And am so clear too, of all other Vice." [from written above "of"]

The Tempter saw his time: the work he ply'd;
Stocks and Subscriptions pour on ev'ry side;
And all the Dæmon makes his full Descent,
In one abundant Show'r of Cent per Cent.

Behold! Sir Balaum turns a man of Spirit,
Ascribes his gettings to his Parts & Merit;
What once he call'd a Blessing, now was Wit, [late written above "once"]
And Gods good Providence a lucky Hit.
Things chang'd their names & took another turn; [a worldly written above "another"]
His Counting-house employ'd the Sunday morn;
Seldom at Church, 'twas such a busy life;
But duely sent his Family and Wife.
Till (so the Devil ordain'd) one Christmass tide,
My good old Lady there catch'd Cold, and dy'd.

A Nymph of Quality admires our Knight:
He marries, bows at Court, & grows polite
Leaves the dull Cits, and joins (to please the Fair)
~~The~~ your well-bred Cuckolds of St. James's Square:
First, for his Son, a gay Commission buys;
Who drinks, whores, fights, and in a Duel dies.
His Daughter shines a Viscount's tawdry Wife;
She bears a Coronet and Pox for life.
In Britains Senate He a Seat obtains;
And one more Pensioner St. Stephen gains.

When

"Where once I went to Church, I'll now go twice;

from
"And am so clear too, of all other Vice."
The Tempter saw his time: The work he ply'd;
Stocks and Subscriptions pour on ev'ry side;
90 And all the Dæmon makes his full Descent,
In one abundant Show'r of Cent per Cent.
Behold! Sir Balaam turns a Man of Spirit,
Ascribes his gettings to his Parts & Merit;

late
What once he calld a Blessing, now was Wit,
95 And Gods good Providence a lucky Hit.

a worldly
Things chang'd their names & took another turn;
His Counting-house employ'd the Sunday morn;
Seldom at Church, 'twas such a busy life;
But duely sent his Family and Wife.
100 Till (so the Dev'l ordain'd) one Christmass tide,
My good old Lady there catchd Cold, and dy'd.
A Nymph of Quality admires our Knight:
He marries, bows at Court, & grows polite
Leaves the dull Cits, and joins (to please the Fair)

Your
105 ~~The~~^well-bred Cuckolds of St. James's Square:
First, for his Son, a gay Commission buys;
Who drinks, whores, fights, and in a Duel dies.
His Daughter shines a Viscount's tawdry Wife;
She bears a Coronet and Pox for life.
110 In Britains Senate He a Seat obtains;
And one more Pensioner St. Stephen gains.

When

96a: worldly] originally, in error, *word*.

Of the Use of Riches.

An EPISTLE

To the Rt Honble ALLEN Lord BATHURST.

What can be judg'd, when Doctours disagree
And ye most thoughtful doubt, like You and me?
You hold the Word ~~express~~ from Jove to Momus given,
That Man was made the standing Jest of Heaven,
And this proud Creature (to define him flat)
Is not [less a] the Thing that [to] laughs but [than be] is laugh'd at.

and Gold bestow'd to keep
the Fools in play,
For half to heap, & half
to throw away.

To keep these Fools (say you) in constant play,
Jove gave them Gold, to heap, & throw away,
One half employ'd to hoard the precious Evil,
The other half to send it to the Devil.

But I, who think more highly of our Kind,
(And surely Heav'n & I are of a mind)
Opine, that Nature (as in Duty bound)
Deep hid from Man his Mischief under ground.
But when (observe) the flaming Mine [flagrant ore] begun
To give [Shine] a Rival to its Sire the Sun, Ital.
See! Providence two sorts of men ordain,
To scatter ~~one~~, & ~~one~~ to hide again.
these, & those

of the Use of Riches.

An

EPISTLE

To the Rt Honble

ALLEN Lord BATHURST.

What can be judg'd, when Doctours disagree
And ye most thoughtful doubt, like you and me?

from Jove
You hold the Word ~~express,~~ to Momus given,
That Man was made the standing Jest of Heaven,
5 And this proud Creature (to define him flat)

less a *to* *than be*
Is not the Thing that laughs but is laughd at.
To keep these Fools (say you) in constant play,
Jove gave them Gold, to heap, & throw away,
One half employ'd to hoard the precious Evil,
10 The other half to send it to the Devil.
But I, who think more highly of our Kind,
(And surely Heav'n & I are of a mind)
Opine, that Nature (as in Duty bound)
Deep hid from Man his Mischief under ground.

and Gold bestowd to keep
the fools in play,
For half to heap, & half
to throw away.

~~*flagrant Ore*~~
15 But when, (observe) the flaming Mine begun
Ital
~~*shine*~~
To give a Rival to its Sire the Sun,
See! Providence two sorts of Men ordain,
To scatter ~~one,~~ & ~~one~~ to hide again.
< > *these, & those*

1: Doctours] originally perhaps *Doctrines*.
13: in] originally perhaps *is*; Duty] originally *duty*.
15: when,(observe)] originally *when, observe!*; erasure over *observe* perhaps *my Lord*.

18: scatter] perhaps altered from *waste ye*.

Can we, brave Followers of the former sect
Think Gold (my Lord) a mark of God's Elect?
we, who see the dirty blessing light
On such as Chartres w—rs, W—rd,
see but to whom he gives ye precious evil?
To W—d, to W—rs, Ch—s, & ye Devil.

now we,
We both, strict Followers of these former Sect,
Agree, this Gold's no Mark of God's Elect
For if His Blessing, could it ever stay / light
With Ward and Chartres, or with M—n & D—y? Bl. & Kn:
[What Nature needs, they tell us, it Gold bestowd;
Thro' that, man eat the Bread he never sow'd:
But eat he, then, not more than he deserv'd?
And was it just, if he who sow'd it, starv'd?
What Nature needs, (a Phrase I much distrust)
Extends to Luxury, extends to Lust;
And if you count among the Needs of Life
Another's Toil, why not another's Wife?
But grant it useful to what Life requires,
yet baneful too, the Murderer it hires:
Trade it may help, Society extend;
But lures the Pyrate, and corrupts the Friend:
It raises Armies in a Nations aid,
But bribes a Senate, and the Land's betrayd.

Oh! that such bulky Bribes as all might see,
Still, as of old, encumberd Villany.
In vain now Heroes fight, & Patriots rave;
When secret Gold saps on from Knave to Knave.
Twoud poze a head, dear Lepidus! like thine,
Shoud once Ambassadors be payd in Wine.
What could it more, than Knights & Squires confound,
And hurl the Horse & Horseman to the ground,
Or water all the Clergy ten mile round?

Flx

may Preachers sweat,

To break a Trust, were Peter brib'd with Wine,
Peter! 'twoud pose as wise a head as thine.
What more could Wine, do more yn

Sect
Can we, brave Follow'rs of the former ^
Think Gold (my Lord) a mark of
God's Elect?

We, who behold
~~When still we see the dirty~~
blessing light

Ch–s W–rs
On such as ~~Bl–n, Ja–n, W–rd,~~
~~or K–t.~~

See *whom*
~~Mark~~ but to ~~what hands~~ he
gives ye precious evil?
To W~~x~~d, to W~~xx~~s, Ch^x–r–s, & ye Devil.

Now we
~~We both~~, strict Follow'rs of the former Sect,
Maintain *Gift*
Agree, this Gold's no Mark of God's Elect — 20
For if His Blessing, could it ever stay / *light*
On *on* *Bl. & Kn.*
With Ward and Chartres, or with M–n & D–y?

needs, they tell us, ~~*it,*~~
[What Nature<—>~~needs, we grant them~~, Gold bestow'd;
Thro' that, man eat the Bread he never sow'd:
But eat he, then, not more than he deserv'd? — 25
And was it just, if he who sowd it, starv'd?
What Nature needs, (a Phrase I much distrust)
Extends to Luxury, extends to Lust;
And if you count among the Needs of Life
Anothers Toil, why not another's Wife? — 30
But grant it useful to what Life requires;
Yet baneful too, the Murderer it hires:
Trade it may help, Society extend;
But lures the Pyrate, and corrupts the Friend:
It raises Armies in a nations aid, — 35
But bribes a Senate, and the Land's betrayd.
Oh! that such bulky Bribes as all might see,
Still, as of old, encumber'd Villany.
May Preachers sweat, ~~divines~~ — In vain now Heroes fight, & Patriots rave,
When *saps*
~~If~~ secret Gold ~~mines~~ on from Knave to Knave. — 40
Twou'd poze a head, dear Lepidus! like thine,
Shou'd once Ambassadors be payd in Wine.

To break a Trust, were Peter
brib'd with Wine,
Peter! twou'd pose as wise a head
as thine.
~~For~~ What<—>coud Wine, than *do more y^n*
more

it ~~*do*~~, ~~*but*~~ *Knights &*
What could ~~they~~ more, than ~~Country~~ Squires confound
And
~~Than~~ hurl the Horse & Horseman to the ground,
~~*And*~~
Or water all the Clergy ten mile round? — 45

Flx

23: Nature–] written over *What Nature.*

Margin: Can we] Erasure over these words is *For we.*

22: M–n & D–y] I am unable to identify these two names with complete assurance. Two very likely candidates are Robert Mann and Thomas Day, both of whom held posts in the Customs.

Robert Mann married Eleanor Guise and fathered Horace Mann, friend of Horace Walpole (*Horace Walpole's Correspondence with Sir Horace Mann,* ed. W. S. Lewis, W. H. Smith, and G. L. Lem, I. xxix). He was intimate with his distant relative, Sir Robert Walpole, who secured for him the post in the Customs, and by some device or other gained a considerable fortune. When Walpole was Secretary at War, Mann served as his major agent for two profitable foraging contracts distributed by Walpole; and he testified before Parliament to this effect when Walpole was tried for having corruptly profited in his office (*Cobbett's Parliamentary History of England* [1810], VI. 1067-75). The subject of these events of 1712 was revived in the periodicals in 1731 (*Gentleman's Magazine,* I [1731], 248).

J. H. Plumb (*Sir Robert Walpole* [1956], p. 180) writes: "There is nothing . . . to show that Walpole himself took any bribes or percentages on contracts. But . . . his wealth grew immeasurably during these years and just how this happened we do not know. Certainly 'Cousin' Mann knew, for he continued to act as Walpole's banker."

Thomas Day, father of the author of *Sandford and Merton,* was Collector Outwards for the Port of London, a lucrative office that allowed him to accumulate a more than comfortable estate.

22a: Bl. & Kn.] Sir John Blunt and Robert Knight.

41: Lepidus] Marcus Aemilius Lepidus, the Triumvir.

Margin: Ch–s . . . W–rs] Francis Chartres; Peter Walter, or Waters.

Margin: Bl–n, Ja–n, W–rd, or K–t] Martin Bladen and Sir Theodore Jansen, for whom see Elwin-Courthope; John Ward and Robert Knight.

Margin: W~~x~~d, W~~xx~~s, Ch^x–r–s] John Ward, Peter Waters, Francis Chartres.

Margin: Peter] Peter Waters.

A Statesman's ~~English~~ Visions

Fl××y's deep Quiet how this Speech w^d spoil!
"Sir, Spain has sent the thousand Jarrs of Oil:
"The English Broadcloth, Sir, blocks up the door:
"An hundred Oxen at your Levee roar.

Poor Avarice one Torment more w^d find,
Nor could Profusion squander all in Kind.
To ~~selling~~ Cheese, Sir ~~Gripus~~ might we meet,
And W×××y ~~driving~~ Coals ~~along the~~ Street.
~~Were G××e to sell his Cattle and his~~ Hogs,
~~Could G××e have sent~~ his Fortune to the Dogs?
My Lord will game: To White's a Bull be led
With spurning heels & with a butting head;
To White's be carry'd, as to ancient Games,
Fair Coursers, Vases, and alluring Dames.
& Shall then ~~Uxorio~~, if the Stakes he sweep,
Bear home six Whores, & make ~~my~~ his Lady weep?
Or ~~his soft Heir~~, so essenc'd and so fine,
Drive to St. James's a whole Herd of Swine?
Oh vile Incumbrance on industrious Skill!
To spoil the Nation's last great^est Trade, Quadrille!
Once, when the Patriot bore beneath his Cloak
The latent Bag, the dropping Guinea spoke,
And gingling down the Back-stairs, told the Crew,
"Old Cato is as great a Rogue as you."
Blest Paper-Credit! that advanc'd so high
Now lends Corruption lighter wings to fly!
Pregnant with thousands, flits the Scrap unseen
And silent, sells a King, or buys a Queen.

What Bane to all Trade, in Burroughs, & Quadrille!

[well then, since with ye world

Visions
A Statesman's ~~*Projects*~~
Flxxy's deep Quiet how this Speech w^{d} spoil!
"Sir, Spain has sent the thousand Jarrs of Oil:

Bales of
"The English Broadcloth, Sir, block~~s~~ up the door:
"An hundred Oxen at your Levee roar.
50 Poor Avarice one Torment more w^{d} find,
Nor could Profusion squander all in Kind.

Astride a / On heaps of *Morgan*~~*Humphry*~~
~~So selling~~ cheese, Sir ~~Gripus~~ might we meet,

orldl *crying* *from street to*
And Wxxy ~~driving~~ Coals ~~along the~~ Street.

Could Moore, were Mo-re to sell his Hops &
~~Were Gxe^to sell his Cattle and his~~ Hogs,

send in one year
55 ~~Could Gxe have sent^~~his Fortune to the Dogs?
My Lord will game: To White's a Bull be led
With spurning heels & with a butting head;
To White's be carry'd, as to ancient Games,
Fair Coursers, Vases, and alluring Dames.

~~*good*~~ *Bxx*
60 &Shall then Uxorio, if the Stakes he sweep,

his
Bear home six Whores, & make ~~my~~ Lady weep?

thou, sweet Vx
Or ~~his soft Heir~~, so essenc'd and so fine,
Drive to St. James's a whole Herd of Swine?

~~*What*~~ ~~*such*~~ *filthy check to all*
Oh vile Incumbrance on industrious Skill!

~~*Might*~~ *est*
65 To spoil the Nation's last great ^ Trade, Quadrille!

What ~~Bane~~ to *all* ~~Trade~~, in
Burroughs, & Quadrille!

Tis true that once
Once, when the Patriot bore beneath his Cloak
The latent Bag, the dropping Guinea spoke,
And gingling down the Back-stairs, told the crew,
"Old Cato is as great a Rogue as you."
70 Blest Paper-Credit! that advanc'd so high

Since lent
X Now lends Corruption lighter wings to fly! [Well then, since with ye world
Pregnant with thousands, flits the Scrap unseen
And silent, sells a King, or buys a Queen.

62a: thou] written over *that*.
68: Back-stairs] *Back* written over *stair*.
73: silent] altered from *secret*.

46: Flxxy's] André Hercule de Fleury. Cardinal and major political adviser to Louis XV of France.
53: Wxxy] Wortley.
54: Gxe] Joseph Gage, who made and lost a great fortune in the Mississippi Scheme (*DNB*).
54a: Moore] James Moore Smythe, who inherited his grandfather's estate in 1720 and soon squandered it.
60: Uxorio; 60a: B~~xx~~] John Hervey, Earl of Bristol.
62a: Vx] Vice; that is, Lord Hervey, Vice-Chamberlain and son of Lord Bristol.

[However, as by the World we stand or fall
Come, take it as we find it, Gold & all.
But what ye Virtue, & how great y Art,
To bear our Fortunes in our head not heart
Large Wealth to sanctify wth just expence,
Join with Oeconomy Magnificence,
And keep each Bound of Reason, Fame & Health

2 The noble Villers had to boast at last
It ne'r to man gave more than common
Not that, or to ye Miser.

Wise was the Pray'r of Profuse Heaven blend them if it can
"And of two Wretches make one happy man!
[What sh'd it give? &c.

since things so fall

But yield we to the World: our Party's small,
Come, take it as we find it, gold and all.
What Wealth can give us? let us then inquire:—
Meat, Fire, & Clothes—What more? Meat, Clothes, & Fire.
How? think we this too little? loth we grave?
'Tis more than Cutler found it gave.
[What should it give? Greek,
Ears to deaf A—y, to Rose?
Fire to pale H—r in the Gem bestrew?
In Fulvia's Buckle ease the throbs below?
or heal C×××n thy obscener ail
With all th' Embroid'ry plaister'd at thy Tail?
It might (could S—k be so mad to spend) give S—k's self the Blessing of a Friend,
It might, to W—y (spite of W—y's Wife) Give such a Doctor as w'd save his life,
But thousands dye, without or this, or that,
And leave it to a College, or a Cat.

Why then the poor and needy Rich revile?
They only claim our Pity, or our Smile:
The Man who gives not, ne'r enjoys his self,
And does but hate his Neighbor as himself.

Damn'd to the Mines an equal fate betides
The Slave that digs it & the Slave that hides.

Such Suff'rings lead Charity to doubt
They may have reasons others ne'r find out;
Some War, some Plague, some Famine may foresee,
Some Revelation hid from you and me:
Why heaps Nigrinn such a monstrous Sum?
She fears, perhaps, a . will cost a Plum.

Why

[Howere, as by the World we stand or fall,
Come, take it as we find it, Gold & all.
But what ye Virtue, & how great ye Art,
To bear our Fortunes in our head, not heart
Large Wealth to sanctify wth just Expence,
Join with Oeconomy Magnificence,
And keep each Bound of Reason, Fame, & Health,
Instruct us Bathurst yet unspoild by Wealth
That ~~this~~ secret hard with affluence rarely joind
Which Villers mist and ner shall find

2 The noble Villers had to boast at last

~~To Man~~ It ne'r ^to man gave more than comon use.
~~Know, 'twill~~ Nor that, or to ye Miser, or Profuse.
Wise was the Pray'r "Heav'n blend them if it can,
"And of two Wretches make one happy man!
[What shd it give? &c.

since things so fall
But yield we to the World: our Party's small,

Come, take *'em* it as we find *em* it, Gold and all. 75

What Wealth ^*can* give us let us then inquire:–
Meat, Fire, & Clothes–What more? Meat, Clothes, & Fire
How? think we this too little? look we grave?
What Wealth can give us, let us then inquire: Meat fire–How?–
Know this is
~~Tis more, much~~ more, than Cutler found ~~they~~ *it* gave.
1 Know this is more than all his glory past

[What ~~can they~~ *should it* give? ~~not Bu–y~~ *to P–ke* Greek, ~~God knows~~ *(suppose)* 80

Ears to deaf A–y,
~~Not Eyes to H Ears~~ to Bubo Nose?

Fire to pale H–r in the Gem bestow?
~~Can Goldn gems make Remp's hand encase~~?

In Fulvias Buckle ease what throbs below?
~~Make Dutchess his less~~ *the*

Or heal Cxxxn thy obscener Ail
~~Or wrought in Cushions ease Cxxxn's Ail~~

With all th'Embroid'ry Plaister'd at thy Tail? *his*
~~In~~ *broad*
~~Or spread in broad Embroidry o'er his tail~~? 85

our gaudy Gen'rals awkwd Ail

rpax

It might (could S–k be so mad to spend) Give S–k's self the Blessing of a Friend;
~~They might to Gu–, (were he so mad to spend)~~

ylock

It might, to W–y (spite of W–y's Wife) Give such a Doctor as wd save his life,
~~Give a safe Doctor, or a pitying Friend~~
But thousands dye, without or this, or that,

And leave ~~them~~ *it* to a College, or a Cat.
Why then the poor and needy Sick revile? 90
They only claim our Pity, or our Smile:
The man who gives not, ne'r enjoys his pelf,
And does but hate his Neighbor as himself.

Damnd to the Mines an equal fate betides
The Slave that digs it & the Slave yt hides.

^Such Suff'rings ~~make it~~ *lead my* Charity to doubt

They may have reasons ~~we can scarce~~ *others n'er* find out; 95
Some War, some Plague, some Famine may foresee,
Some Revelation hid from you and me:
Why heaps Nigrina such a monstrous Sum?
She fears, perhaps, a will cost a Plum.

Why

76: Wealth] altered from *Riches*.
80: Bu–y] originally *G*, perhaps intending *Greek*.
82: make] altered to an illegible word; *encase*] altered from *dress*.
91: They only claim] originally *He only claims*.

94a: my] originally *one's*.
95: They] originally *He*.
Margin: [Ha] rpax; [Sh] ylock. Manuscript torn.
Margin: opposite line 99] *100* in pencil.

I have been unable to identify Bu–y (80); A–y (81a) – Atterbury and Abergavenny seem unlikely; H– (81); H–r (82a) – unless this is Hanmer; Gu– (86).

79: Cutler] Sir John Cutler.
80a: P–ke] Thomas Herbert, Earl of Pembroke; satirized by Pope in the *Epistle to Burlington*, 8.

82: Remp's] If this is *Kemp*, instead of *Remp*, it may allude to the "keeper of an assembly" mentioned in Edward Young's *Love of Fame*, VI. 469-78.
84: Cxxxn's] William, Earl Cadogan.
86a: S–k] Charles Douglas, Earl of Selkirk.
87a: W–y] Edward Wortley Montagu.

346*

Howe're, as with the World we stand or fall,
Come, take it as we find it, Gold and all.
What, and how great, the Virtue and the Art,
To bear our Fortunes in the Head, not Heart;
But Wealth to sanctify by just Expence,
Join with Oeconomy Magnificence,
With Splendor Charity, with Plenty Health;
Oh teach us, Bathurst, yet un-spoil'd by wealth!
That Secret rare, with Affluence hardly join'd,
Which Bi[illegible] mist, and B[illegible] ne'r shall find.
What Riches give us, shall we first enquire?
Meat, fire, and clothes — What more? — Meat, clothes & fire.
How? think you this too little? look ye grave?
'Tis more, much more than [illegible] found they gave:
'Tis more, than all his Dream of Pleasure past
unhappy Wh[illegible] wak'd, & found at Last.
What can they give? not [illegible] Breath, God knows,
Not Ch—rs Vigor, Japhet Ears & Nose:
Could they, in Gems, bid pallid Wippia glow?
In Fulvia's Buckle ease the Throb below?
Or heal our gawdy Gen'rals aukward Ail,
With all the Embroid'ry plaister'd at his Tail?
They might (were Harpax not too wise to spend)
Give Harpax self the Blessing of a Friend:
They might, to W[illegible] (spite of W[illegible]'s Wife)
Give such a Doctor as wd save his life:
But thousands dye, dying without or this or that,
And leave them — to endow a College, or a Cat.
Why then the poor & needy Rich revile?
They claim our Pity, or at worst our Smile:
The wretch who gives not, ne'r enjoys his Pelf,
And does but hate his Neighbor as Himself.
Such Sufferings lead my Charity to doubt,
They may have Reasons none of us find out;
Some War, some Plague, or Famine they foresee,
Some Revelation hid from you or me:

Why

Bet: meanly gain'd / not greedily pursued
They ne'r [illegible] use more common / Nor that [illegible] ye Miser or Profuse.
Saved they heal
Or such a Dr as wd save thy Life [illegible] — k
Of wretched Worldly spite of Worldly wife
To some, [illegible] —
[illegible] the happier fate
To bless a Bastard or a Son they hate
T'enrich
Damnd to ye mines, an equal fate betides
The Slave that digs it, & the Slave that hides.

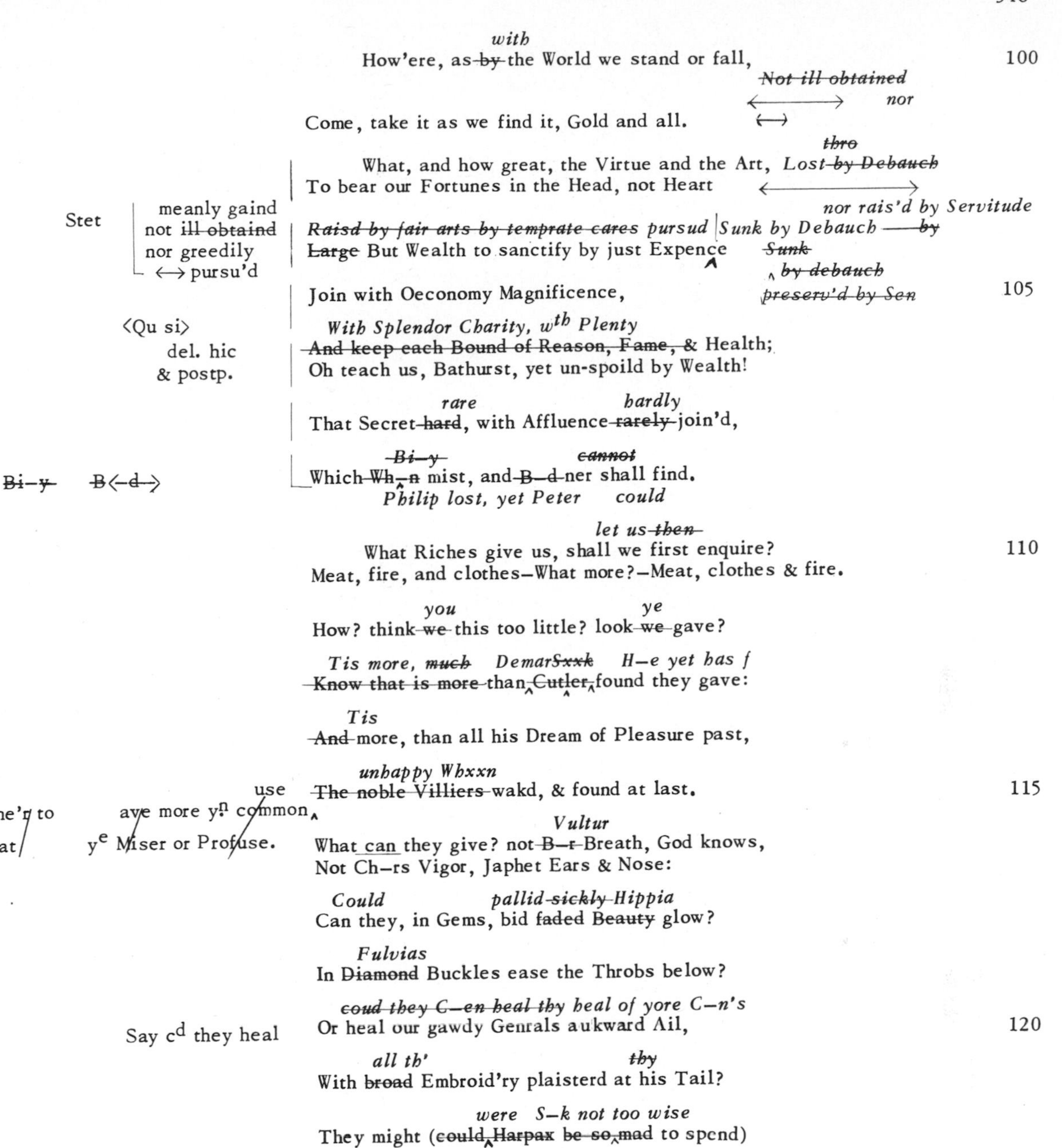

110: shall we] originally probably *let us*.
118a: Hippia] originally *W*—.
Margin: Qu si] If this is the reading, Pope is asking himself whether to delete the marked passage and add it farther on in the poem.
Margin: They ne'r . . . or Profuse.] manuscript torn.

109a: Bi—y] Robert Benson, Baron Bingley (1676-1731). See *DNB*.
109: Wh—n] Wharton
B—d] The Marquis of Blandford. See above, p. 59, note 2.
109b: Peter] Peter Waters.
113a: Demar] Joseph Damer, or Demar (1630-1720), a wealthy, miserly Irish usurer. Swift alluded to him in "Character of an Irish Squire" (Temple Scott, XI. 193) and satirized his miserliness in "An Elegy on the Much Lamented Death of Mr. Demar, the Famous Rich Man" (*Poems*, ed. Harold Williams, pp. 232-35).
Sxxk] Selkirk.
H—e] Sir Gilbert Heathcote.
116a: Vultur] John ("Vulture") Hopkins.
116: B—r] unidentified.
117: Ch—rs] Chartres; Japhet] Japhet Crook.
120a: C—en] Cadogan.

Or such a D[r] as w[d] save y[e] Life
Of wretched Worldly spite of Worldlys wife

To some, indeed Heavn grants —
or whom Heavn alas denies
~~To whom hard Heavn denies~~
⟵⟶ ~~alas denyd~~ the happier fate
To bless a Bastard or a Son they hate
T'enrich

Damnd to y[e] mines, an equal fate betides
The Slave that digs it, & the Slave that hides.

W— W—
They might, to ~~Shylock~~ (spite of ~~Shylock's~~ Wife)
Give such a Doctor as w[d] save his life: 125
dying
But thousands dye, without ~~or~~ this or that,
endow
And leave them—to a College, or a Cat.
Why then the poor & needy Rich revile?
at worst
They ~~only~~ claim our Pity, or ^ our Smile:
Wretch
The ~~Man~~ who gives not, ne'r enjoys his Pelf, 130
And does but hate his Neighbor as Himself. ^^
^Such Suffrings lead my Charity to doubt,
They may have Reasons none of us find out;
Some War, some Plague, or Famine they foresee,
Some Revelation hid from you or me: 135

Why

Margin: Worldlys] originally *W—y.*

Margin: alas denyd] altered to *alas denys.*

124a: W—] Edward Wortley Montagu.

The verso of this leaf contains only one line: How'ere as by the World we stand or fall.

Why heaps Nigrina such a monstrous Sum?
a Stallion's Price may be a Plum
The fears, perhaps, a man may cost a Plum.
Why rais'd old Helluo that prodigious store?
He heard, a Goose w.d rise to tenpence more.
You wonder much, a Gen'ral of renown
Shou'd save a Sixpence rather than a Town:
He reason'd thus. "If Crowns, w.ch long have roll'd
"From head to head, by Auction shou'd be sold—
"If frugal Didius Rome's great Lord c.d be—
but
"If my Prætorians were at true to me—
"The Polish Sceptre's sold some twice an age,
"And very near its purchace came Jo: Gage.

Why bears Sir John the Nations Curse & hate?
it
A Wizard told him in these words our Fate.
"At length Corruption, like a gen'ral flood,
"(By S××× and W×× long with-stood.) By Statesmen, Churchmen, Patriots, long withstood
deluge What shall not then
"Shall rush oer all: then all things shall be sold,
"× Bishops buy Betts
when trade in Stocks Bishops job, and Chancellors take on Gold,
"Then Dukes shall pick the pockets of y.e Town;
"And Duchesses pack Cards for half a crown."
2 not city- not lordly
Not sordid Gain, no paltry Vanity;
What [illegible]
1 ^ Push'd, the great Scrivner's thy brave genrous Views so high?
thy generous
No: 'twas his honest aim, asham'd to see
Senates so sunk, & Patriots dis-agree,
And nobly wishing Party-Rage to cease;
thy
To buy both sides, and give his ^ Country Peace.

All

Why heaps Nigrina such a monstrous Sum?

a Stallion's Price may be a Plum
She fears, perhaps, a . may cost a Plum.
man

Why raisd old Helluo that prodigious store?
He heard, a Goose w[d] rise to tenpence more.
140 You wonder much, a Gen'ral of renown
Shou'd save a Sixpence rather than a Town:
He reasond thus. "If Crowns, wch long have roll'd
"From head to head, by Auction shou'd be sold–
"If frugal Didius Rome's great Lord c[d] be–

but
145 "If my Prætorians were ~~as~~ true to me–
"The Polish Sceptre's sold some twice an age,
"And very near its purchace came Jo: Gage.
Why bears Sir John the Nations Curse & hate?

~~its~~
A Wizard told him in these words our Fate.
150 "At length Corruption, like a gen'ral flood,
"(By Sxxx and Wxx long with-stood)

By Statesmen, Churchmen, Patriots, long withstood

deluge *What shall not then*
"Shall ~~rush o'er~~ all: then all things shall be sold,

Bishops buy Bears *take*
"x ~~trade in Stocks,~~ and Chancellors ~~in~~ Gold,
When Bishops job,

"When Dukes shall pick the pockets of y[e] Town,
155 "And Duchesses pack Cards for half a crown."

2 ~~*Not*~~ *city-* *nor Lordly*
Not ~~sordid~~ Gain, ~~no~~ ~~paltry~~ Vanity;

What ~~*w[t] pushd,*~~ *thy brave*
1 ^push'd, ~~the~~ great Scriv'ner's ~~s~~ ~~gen'rous~~ Views so high?

thy genrous
No: 'twas ~~his honest~~ Aim, asham'd to see
Senates so sunk, & Patriots dis-agree,
160 And nobly wishing Party-Rage to cease;

thy
To buy both sides, and give ~~his~~ ^ Country Peace.

All

153a: Bears] originally *Bulls*.
154: When] originally *Then*.
157: push'd] originally *Push'd*.

140: a Gen'ral] the Duke of Marlborough.
147: Jo: Gage] Joseph Gage.
148: Sir John] Sir John Blunt.
151: Sxxx] Charles Spencer, Earl of Sunderland.
Wxx] Sir Robert Walpole.

"All this is madness" cries ~~some~~ sober Sage.
But who, my Friend, has Reason in his Rage?
Each ruling Passion, be it what it will,
That ruling Passion conquers Reason still:
Less mad the wildest Whimsy ~~that Man~~ we can frame,
Than ev'n that Passion, if it have no aim;
~~And if~~ 'Tis true such Motives folly you may call,
~~Tis~~ But still ~~a~~ 'tis greater to have none at all.

Hear then the truth. 'Tis Heav'n each Passion sends
And diff'rent men directs to diff'rent Ends:
Ask we, what makes one keep, & one bestow?
That Pow'r, who bids the Ocean ebb & flow;
2 Thro' reconcil'd Extremes of Drought or Rain;
1 Bids Seedtime, Harvest, still their course maintain,
Builds Life on Death; on Change Duration founds;
And gives th' Eternal Wheels to ~~run~~ know their Rounds.

Who sees pale Mammon pining on his Store,
Sees but a backward Steward for the Poor;
This year, a Reservoir to keep & spare,
The next, a Fountain spouting thro his Heir,
In lavish Streams to quench a Country's thirst,
And Men and Dogs ~~to~~ shall drink him till they burst.

Old Cotta sham'd his Fortune and his high Birth,
Yet was not Cotta void of Wit or Worth.
Slight his mistake: he held it for a Rule, That every man in want was Knave or Fool.
What tho (the use of barb'rous Spits forgot)
His Kitchen vy'd in Coolness with his Grott?
The Cresse the Nettle, Coverts & moats afford, He
Fit Soupe, and unbought Sallads for their Lord.

[Margin notes:]

Silly! — and yet ~~but still~~ I'll name a sillier.
Hark in your ear ———

Extremes in Nature equal ~~ends~~ Good produce
Extremes in Man ~~they join to some myste-rious~~ concur to Gen'ral use.

Riches like Insects when most shut close they lie
Wait but for Wings, & in due season fly.

His Court wth Nettles moats wth Cresses stor'd
Wth Soupes unbought & Sallads blest his board

a
"All this is Madness" cries ~~some~~ sober Sage.

and yet
Silly!—~~but still~~ I'll name a sillier
Hark in your ear-----

But who, my Friend, has Reason in his Rage?
Each ruling Passion, be it what it will,
That ruling Passion conquers Reason still: 165

we
Less mad the wildest Whimsy ~~that Man~~ ^ can frame,
Than ev'n the Passion, if it have no aim;

Tis true,
~~And if~~ such Motives folly you may call,

But tis
~~Tis~~ still ~~a~~ greater to have none at all.
sends
Hear then the truth. Tis Heav'n each Passion ^ 170
And diffrent men directs to diff'rent Ends:

Good
Extremes in Nature equal ~~ends~~ produce ^ ^
Extremes concur to Gen'ral
In man ~~they join to some myste-rious~~ use.

Ask we, what makes one keep, & one bestow?
That Pow'r, who bids the Ocean ebb & flow;
2 Thro' reconcild Extremes of Drought or Rain;
1 Bids Seed time, Harvest, still their course maintain, 175
Builds Life on Death; on Change Duration founds;

know
And gives th'Eternal Wheels to ~~run~~ their Rounds.

most
Riches like Insects w[n] shut close y[y] lie
Wait but for Wings, & in due season fly:
^

^ Who sees pale Mammon pining on his Store,
Sees but a backward Steward for the Poor;
This year, a Reservoir to keep & spare, 180
The next, a Fountain spouting thro his Heir,
In lavish Streams to quench a Country's thirst,

shall
And Men and Dogs ~~to~~ drink him till they burst.

his
Old Cotta sham'd his Fortune and high Birth,
Yet was not Cotta void of Wit or Worth. 185
Slight his mistake: he held it for a Rule That evry man in want was Knave or Fool.
What tho (the use of barb'rous Spits forgot)
His Kitchen vy'd in Coolness with his Grott?
The Cresse the nettle, Courts & moats afford, He
Fit soupe, and unbought sallads for their Lord

His Court wth nettles moats wth Cresses stord
W[th] soupes unbought & Sallads blest his board

166: Whimsy] originally *Thought.*

167: the] originally *this.*

Margin: Extremes in Nature . . . .] The unrevised version of this couplet is the form that was to appear in the *Essay on Man*, II. 205-206.

If Cotta liv'd on
He liv'd himself on Pulse, which it was no more
Than Bramins, Saints, & Sages did before:
~~Slight his Mistake; he held it for a Rule,~~
~~That ev'ry Man in want was Knave or Fool;~~
To cramm the Rich, was ~~seem'd~~ prodigal expence;
And who would take the Poor from Providence?
Like some lone Chartreuse stands the good old Hall,
Silence without, and Fasts within the Wall:
No rafter'd roofs with Dance & Tabor sound,
No noontide Bell invites the Country round.
But the gaunt Mastiff, growling at the Gate,
Affrights the ~~Frighten'd those~~ Beggar: whom he cou'd, wish he longs to eat:
Be-nighted Wanderers the Forest o'er
Curse the sav'd Candle, and un-opening Door:
Sighs The dry Squire ~~sighs, her~~ them Turrets to survey,
And turns ~~tuggs~~ th' unwilling Steed another way.

Her ancient Guests the smokeless Towrs survey

Not so, Curio ~~his Heir~~: he mark'd this Over-sight,
And then mistook Reverse of Wrong for Right.
(For what to shun, will no great knowledge ask,
But what to follow, is another task.)
Yet sure of Qualities deserving Praise More go to ruin Fortunes, yn to raise.
T'oblige the Wealthy, and the Poor to feed,
See! slaughter'd Hecatombs around him thee bleed;
No selfish ~~Yet no mean~~ Motives his thy Profusion stain,
'Tis ~~Twas~~ in his thy Country's Cause his thy Beeves are ~~were~~ slain.
'Tis ~~Twas~~ George & Liberty that crowns thy Cup,
And Zeal for his great House that eats thee up.

Go then, let Hecatombs around thee
T'oblige
No selfish
'Tis in thy
~~Yet George~~ unmov'd
Unmov'd

Un-

If Cotta livd on *it*
190 He livd himself on Pulse, which was no more
Than Bramins, Saints, & Sages did before:
~~Slight his Mistake; he held it for a Rule,~~ ∂
~~That ev'ry Man in want was Knave or Fool~~;

was
To cramm the Rich, ~~seem'd~~ prodigal expence;
195 And who would take the Poor from Providence?
Like some lone Chartreuse stands the good old Hall,
Silence without, and Fasts within the Wall:
No rafterd roofs with Dance & Tabor sound,
No noontide Bell invites the Country round.
200 But the gaunt Mastiff, growling at the Gate,

Affrights the *he could wish*
~~Frighten'd those~~ Beggar whom he longs to eat;
Be-nighted Wanderers the Forest o'er
Curse the sav'd Candle, and un-opening Door:

Sighs *the*
^The dry Squire| ~~sighs, her~~^ Turrets to survey, — Her ancient Guests the smoakeless Towrs survey

turns
205 And ~~luggs~~ th'unwilling Steed another way.

Curio
Not^so, ~~his Heir~~: he mark'd this Over-sight,
And then mistook Reverse of Wrong for Right.
(For what to shun, will no great knowledge ask,
But what to follow, is another task)
Yet sure of Qualities deserving Praise More go to ruin Fortunes *y^n to raise* — Go then, let Hecatombs around thee
210 T'oblige the Wealthy, and the Poor to feed, — T'oblige

him
See! slaughterd Hecatombs around thee bleed; — No selfish

No selfish *his*
~~Yet no mean~~ Motives thy Profusion stain, — Tis in thy

Tis *his* *his* *are* slain,
~~Twas~~ in thy Country's Cause thy Beeves ~~were~~^ — ~~Tis George~~ unmovd

Unmovd

Tis *s*
~~Twas~~ George & Liberty that crown~~d~~ thy Cup, ∂

s
215 And Zeal for his great House that eats thee up.

Un–

192: Rule] originally *rule*.
201: Beggar] originally *Beggars*.
202: Be-nighted] originally probably *Belated*.
204a: the] originally *those*.

Unmov'd he sees, around his naked Seat,
The Timber fall; no matter – for the Fleet:
~~Gone is~~ next goes his Wool, to cloathe our valiant Bands;
~~And~~ last for his Country's Love, he sells his Lands.
To Court he comes, compleats a Nations hope,
And heads the bold Train-bands, & burns a Pope.
Now grateful Albion! pay the Patriot's toils,
And let him share thy Buisness and thy Spoils.

Who next appears, & gladdens either all the Scene?
Now Providence once more shall shift the Scene?
~~And, Heavn'y Harley~~ Oh guard him Heavn, & show the Golden Mean!
Where one lean Herring furnish'd Cotta's Board,
And Nettles grew, ~~fit~~ meet Porridge for their Lord;
Where mad Good nature, Bounty mis-apply'd,
In lavish Curio blaz'd a while and dy'd;
There ~~generous~~ still may Lalius, Oxford, acting God's own part,
Ch–es and Ox–d
Relieve th' opprest, and ~~glad~~ glad chear the Orphan's heart;
There English Bounty yet a while may shall stand,
And Honour linger, ere they leave the Land.

Yet all our Incense why should Lords ingross?
Rise honest Muse! and sing the Man of Ross:
Pleas'd Vaga echoes thro her winding bounds
~~The Man, from Vaga to Sabrina known~~
And rapid Severn hoarse applause resounds
~~Good his sole joy, & Virtue all his own~~
~~Round the white Church, on yonder~~ Who hung wth woods ye mountains sultry Sunny Brow,
~~Who hung the Woods~~ from the dry rock who bid the Waters flow?
Not to the Skies in useless columns tost,
Or in proud Falls magnificently lost,
But clear & artless, pouring thro the Plain
Health to the Sick, & Solace to the Swain:
Who

Bankrupt at Court he ~~alas!~~ in vain he pleads his cause,
& thankless this Country leaves him to her Laws.
her Lover!

What & how great
To bear our Fortunes
Not meanly, nor ambitiously pursued;
Not sunk by Sloth, nor rais'd by Servitude
To wealth to sanctify by just expence
Join with Oeconomy
Splendor Charity, with Plenty
Oh teach us, Bathurst!

that safe mid-way a path between th' Extremes,
Of mad Goodnature, & of mean Self Love.
2. Whose wealth to merit, or to want is given?
Who emulate, or ease, the Care of Heavn
~~Oxford~~ & Ch–es & Ox–d
Relieve &c.

~~alas!~~ *in vain the*
Bankrupt, at Court^he

Bankrupt
~~vainly~~^pleads his cause,

thankless
~~& finds~~/ His^Country leaves
/ him / to her Laws.
her Lover/

~~Once more how Providence shall shift~~
~~Heavn guard ye next,~~ *a ~~blank~~*
~~& show ye Golden Mean~~ *here*
~~What losing, saving, B–d ner c^d hit~~
~~Nor G–'s goodness reach, nor Philip's Wit~~
St–'s

What & how great
To bear our fortunes
Not meanly, nor ambitiously pursud,
Not sunk by sloth, nor raisd by Servitude
How Wealth to sanctify by just expence
Join with Oeconomy
W^th Splendor Charity, with Plenty
Oh teach us, Bathurst!
~~Let gracious O–d, Ch–s,~~
~~Relieve~~ *That secret rare*
There *yet may*
~~Ah yet a while~~ ~~*There yet shall*~~
Which Wh– lost, and B– ner could find
~~*Englands ancient*~~
~~& Honor~~ ~~*Virtues stand*~~
Still mist by Vice & scarce by Virtue hit
By G–s Goodness or ⟷ by S–s Wit,
[~~Whose Wealth to Merit, or to Want is given~~?
~~Who emulate, or ease, ye Care of Heavn~~?
Oxfd ~~& Chandos, acting Gods own part~~
mid-way
That safe ^ ~~path~~ between th'Extremes
to move
Of mad Good nature, & of mean self Love.
2. Whose Wealth to merit, or to Want, is given?
Who emulate, or ease, the Care of Heavn?
~~Oxford &~~ Ch–os & Ox–d
Relieve &c.
~~Whose Wealth wth Arts improves y^e *British*~~
~~1. his native Soil~~ 200
~~W^th Works adorns, like H–x & B–~~
thine

Unmov'd he sees, around his naked Seat,
The Timber fall; no matter–for the Fleet:

Next, goes
~~Gone is~~ his Wool, to cloathe our valiant Bands;

Last,
~~And~~ for his Country's Love, he sells his Lands.
To Court he comes, compleats a Nations hope, 220
And heads the bold Train-bands, & burns a Pope.
Now grateful Albion! pay the Patriot's toils,
And let him share thy Buis'ness–and thy Spoils.

either
Who next appear~~s~~, & gladden~~s~~ all the Scene?
How Providence once more shall shift the Scene?

them
Oh! guard him Heav'n, &
~~And, showing^Harley~~, show the Golden Mean! 225
Where one lean Herring furnishd Cotta's Board,

meet
And Nettles grew, ~~fit~~^Porridge for their Lord;
Where mad Good nature, Bounty mis-apply'd,
In lavish Curio blaz'd a while and dy'd;

still may Laelius
There ~~gracious~~ Oxford, acting God's own part, 230
Ch–os and Ox–d

glad chear
Relieve~~s~~ th'opprest, and ~~glads~~ the Orphan's heart,

~~*there Charity*~~ ~~*may*~~
There English Bounty yet a while shall stand,
~~*takes her final stand*~~

And Honour linger, e're they leave the Land.
s *she* *s*

Yet all our Incense why should Lords ingross?
Rise honest Muse! and sing the Man of Ross: 235

Pleasd Vaga eccboes thro her winding bounds
~~The Man, from Vaga to Sabrina known~~,

and rapid Severn hoarse applause resounds
~~Good his sole joy, & Virtue all his own~~.

woods
Who hung w^th ~~shade~~ ye mountains sultry
~~Round the white Church~~, ~~on yonder~~ Sunny Brow,

From ⟷ ye dry Rock who
~~Who hung the Woods~~^& bid the Waters flow?
Not to the Skies in useless columns tost, 240
Or in proud Falls magnificently lost,
But clear & artless, pouring thro the Plain
Health to the Sick, & Solace to the Swain:

Who

Margin: How Wealth] *H* of *How* was originally *B*.

230a: Laelius] Pope is identifying Oxford with another great example of statesmanship and friendship, the companion of the satirist Lucilius and the major interlocutor in Cicero's *Laelius sive de Amicitia*. See the Twickenham edition of the *Essay on Man*, pp. 11, 129, where the name was applied to Bolingbroke.
230b: Ch–os] the Duke of Chandos.
Margin: G–'s] unidentified; Courthope's proposal, Granville, seems unlikely.
Margin: Philip's] Philip Stanhope, Earl of Chesterfield.
Margin: Wh–] Wharton.
Margin: B– ner could find] the Marquis of Blandford.
Margin: H–x] the Earl of Halifax.
Margin: B–] Richard Boyle, Earl of Burlington.
Margin: Whose Wealth wth Arts . . . H–x & B–] Pope added a variant of this couplet to the 1735 edition of the *Epistle to Burlington*, 177-78: "Who then shall grace, or who improve the Soil? / Who plants like Bathurst, or who builds like Boyle."

Who to the publick gives his
Whose Causeway parts the Vale in shady rows?
Whose Seats the weary Wanderer repose?
Who feeds yon' Almshouse, neat, but void of State,
Where Age & Want sit smiling at the gate?
Who taught yon' Heav'n-directed Spire to rise?
The Man of Ross, each lisping ~~Child~~ Babe replies.
Behold the Market place with Poor o'erspread,
The Man of Ross divides the weekly Bread:
Him portion'd Maids, apprentic'd Orphans blest,
The young who labour, and the Old who rest:
Is any sick? the Man of Ross relieves,
Prescribes, attends, the med'cine makes, & gives:
Is there a Variance? enter but his door,
~~The Courts, are eluded & the~~ Balk'd are ye Courts, and Contest ~~see~~ is no more:
Despairing Quacks with Curses ~~left~~ fled the place,
And vile Attorneys, ~~fled~~ now an useless Race.
'Thrice happy Man! enabled to pursue
'What all so wish, ~~but~~ but want ~~the~~ ye pow'r to do!
'O say what Sums ~~that~~ that gen'rous hand supply,
'What mine, to swell that boundless Charity?
Of ~~Taxes,~~ Debts, ~~and~~ of Taxes, wife, & children clear,
This Man possess'd —— five hundred p^{ds} a year.
Blush, Greatness! blush! false Pride withdraw thy Blaze!
Ye Little Stars! hide your diminish'd Rays.

† The Man of Ross, a name given by way of Eminence to a Gentleman of that Town in Herefordshire, who perform'd all the Good works here mentioned: His true name was John ~~Kairls~~ Kyrle, He dyed in the year 1724. aged ab^t 90 years. and was buried in ye Chancel of ye Church of Ross, with^t any Monum^t or Stone to distinguish his grave

Who to the publick gives his
Whose Causeway parts the Vale in shady rows?
245 Whose Seats the weary Wanderer repose?
Who feeds yon' Alms house, neat, but void of State,
Where Age & Want sit smiling at the gate?
Who taught yon' Heav'n-directed Spire to rise?

Babe
The Man of Ross, each lisping ~~Child~~ replies.
250 Behold the Market place with Poor o'erspread,
The Man of Ross divides the weekly Bread:
Him portion'd Maids, apprentic'd Orphans blest,
The young who labour, and the Old who rest:
Is any sick? the Man of Ross relieves,
255 Prescribes, attends, the Med'cine makes, & gives:
Is there a Variance? enter but his door,

Balkd are y.e Courts and is no more:
~~The Courts are~~‸~~eluded~~‸~~& the~~ Contest ~~oer~~,‸

fled
Despairing Quacks with Curses ~~left~~ the place,

now
And vile Attorneys, ~~fled~~, an useless Race.
260 'Thrice happy man! enabled to pursue

~~*all*~~ *ye*
'What all so wish, but‸want ~~the~~ pow'r to do!
'O say what Sums that gen'rous hand supply,
'What Mine, to swell that boundless Charity?

of Taxes,
Of ~~Taxes,~~ Debts, ~~and~~‸Wife, & Children clear,
265 This Man possess'd---five hundred pds a year.
Blush, Greatness! blush! false Pride withdraw thy Blaze!
Ye Little Stars! hide your diminishd Rays.

+ The Man of Ross, a name given by way of Eminence to a Gentleman of that Town in Herefordshire, who performd all the Good works here mentioned: His true name was *John* ~~*Kairls,*~~ *Kyrle,*
He dyed in the year 1724. aged‸*abt* 90 years. *and was buried in y.t Chancel of ye church of Ross, witht any Monum.t or Stone to distinguish his grave*

257: The Courts] Erasure over these words is *Balkd are.*
262: that] originally *thy.*
263: that] originally *thy.*

Such, only Such, to wealth give worth &

Such, Bathurst! alone, to wealth Such, alone, give Baches Grace,

Whose Measure full, o'erflows on human race;

Tis Death when aggregate, but Life 'tis Life

Such make it Virtue, Temperd diffus'd;

Tis Death, accumulated Life,

As Poyson heals, in due proportion us'd.

This, this is all ye blessings it can lend;

This all the Comfort it affords our End

What, and how great, the Virtue & the Art, You've seen

To bear our Fortunes in our Head, not Heart,

Large Wealth to sanctify, with by just Expence,

Join with Oeconomy, Magnificence,

And keep our Fame, our Reason, & our Health,

each Bound of Reason, Fame, and

with Splendor Charity, with Plenty Health:

Oh teach us, Bathurst! yet un-spoil'd by Wealth!

That Secret, rarely with full Affluence joind,

Which Villers lost, yet Cutler could not

Which Villers mist and W— x x ner shall find.

That only Blessing Wealth to Life can lend, That only Comfort it affords our End

[In the worst Inn's worst room, with Matt half hung,

The Floor of Plaister & the Walls of Dung,

On, once a Flockbed, but repaird with Straw,

With tape-ty'd Curtains, never meant to draw,

The George & Garter dangling from that Bed,

Where tawdry yellow strove with dirty red;

Great Villers lies! Alas, how chang'd from Him,

That Life of Pleasure, & that Soul of Whym,

Careless and gay Gay as he came from in Cliveden's proud Alcove,

The Bowr of wanton Shrewsbury & Love,

Or just as Careless at gay, from Britains the Council-board,

With mimick'd Statesmen & his merry Lord—

No Wit to flatter, left of all his store!

No Fool to laugh at, which he valu'd more.

There

Stet

This ye sole Blessing wealth to Life can lend

This, ye sole Comfort it affords our End

In ye worst Inn's &c

qu. to Leave out or preserve in this place

In heaps like ambergrise a stink it lyes

But well dispers'd is incense to the Skies.

[You've seen yt

That only Blessing Wealth to Man can lend:

In life, the only Comfort at his End.

See next wt. Comfort it affords our End.

Wealth
Such, only such, to give worth &
~~*only*~~ *Bathurst!* *alone, to wealth* ~~*alone use and*~~
Such, ~~Bathurst~~! such, ~~alone~~, give ~~Riches~~ Grace,
Whose Measure full, o'erflows on human race;
~~*Tis Death when aggregate, but Life*~~ *'tis Life*
~~Such make it Virtue, temper'd &~~ diffus'd; 270
Tis ~~*Death*~~*, accumulated* ~~*tis Life*~~*,*
As Poyson heals, in due proportion us'd.
~~*well temperd and right usd.*~~

Stet
Wealth
This, ye sole Blessing ~~it~~ to Life can lend,
~~*can give*~~
This, ye sole Comfort it affords our End
In ye worst Inn's &c

This, this is all ye blessing it can lend;
This all the Comfort it affords our End. *You've seen*
What, and how great, the Virtue ~~& the Art,~~
To bear our Fortunes in our Head, not Heart,

qu. to Leave out
or preserve in
this place

by
Large Wealth to sanctify, ~~with~~ just Expence,
Join with Oeconomy, Magnificence, 275
each Bound of Reason, Fame, and
And keep our Fame, our Reason, & our Health;
With Splendor Charity, with Plenty Health:

In heaps, like ambergrise
it
a ~~it~~ stink~~ing~~ lyes,
well dispers'd is Incense to
But ~~spread, is incence to ye Earth~~
the Skies.
or

Oh teach us, Bathurst! yet un-spoil'd by Wealth!
rarely
That Secret, rare~~ly~~ with ⟷ Affluece join'd,
lost, yet Cutler could not
Which Villers ~~mist~~ and ~~Wxx ner shall~~ find.

[*You've seen w^t^*
e
~~That only~~ Blessings Wealth ⟷ *to Life* ~~Man~~
can lend:
at
~~In Life, the only Comfort in his End.~~
See next, w^t^ Comfort it affords our End.
Youve

That only Blessing Wealth to Life can lend, That only Comfort it affords our End
^ [In the worst Inn's worst room, with matt half hung, 280
The Floor of Plaister & the Walls of Dung,
On, once a Flockbed, but repaird with straw,
With tape-ty'd Curtains, never meant to draw,
The George & Garter dangling from that Bed,
Where tawdry yellow strove with dirty red; 285
Great Villers lies! Alas, how changd from Him,
That Life of Pleasure, & that Soul of Whym,
Gay as he came from
~~Careless and gay~~ in Cliveden's proud Alcove,
The Bow'r of wanton Shrewsbury & Love,
gay, from Britains
Or just as ~~careless, at~~ the Council-board, 290
With mimick'd Statesmen & his merry Lord—
No Wit to flatter, left of all his store!
No Fool to laugh at, which he valu'd more.
There

278a: rarely] altered from *hardly*.
290a: from] originally *at*.
Margin: the Skies] *the* written over &.
Margin: affords] originally *can give*.

Margin: Erased passage in pencil after *Youve* reads:
seen w^t^ Blessings Wealth
to Life can lend
See next ~~w^t^~~ Comfort it can give
affords our End

279: Wxx] Wharton.

There, Victor of his Health, ~~his~~ of Fortune, Friends,
And Fame; this Lord of ~~glittring~~ useless thousands ends.

But say, did Cutler better yield the Ghost? ^ [Lo! sober Cutler of his Spirits possest; His life more wretched, was his ~~Death~~ more blest?
~~Cutler~~ What gain'd the Gainer, more than He who lost?
Whose want was greater, his who gain'd or lost
His Graces Errour well the Knight could see,
And well (he thought) advis'd him, Live like me.
As well his Grace reply'd, Like you Sir John?
That I can do, when all I have is gone.
Resolve me Reason, wch of these is worse,
Want with a Full, or with an empty Purse?
Cutler saw Tenants break, and Houses fall,
For very want; he could not build a Wall:
He ~~Saw~~ saw his ~~lov'd~~ Daughter in a Stranger's pow'r,
For very want; he could not pay a Dow'r: ^ A few grey Hairs his reverend temples crown'd;
What ev'n deny'd a Cordial at his End, ^ ^ 'Twas ~~For~~ very want, ~~he~~ that sold them for 2 pd
Banish'd the Doctor, and expell'd the Friend?
What but a Want, which you perhaps think mad,
Yet numbers feel; the Want of what he had.
Cutler and Brutus, dying both exclaim
"Virtue and Wealth! what are ye but a Name?

Say, for such ~~Pains~~ Worth, are other Worlds prepar'd?
Or are they both, in this, their own Reward?
~~A knotty Point! which shall I next discuss?~~ to which we now proceed [This knotty point, my Lord, shall I discuss,...
~~But you are tir'd – I'll tell a Tale –~~ agreed.
Or tell a Tale? — A Tale — It follows thus.

280

A

of
~~his~~
There, Victor of his Health, ~~Life~~, Fortune, Friends,
useless
295 And Fame; this Lord of ~~glittring~~ thousands ends.
But say, did Cutler better yield the Ghost?
What
~~Cutler~~ gain'd the Gainer, more than He who lost?
Whose want was greater, his who gaind or lost

[Lo! Sober Cutler of his Spoils possest:
His Life more wretched, was his Death more blest?

His Grace's Errour well the Knight could see,
And well (he thought) advisd him, Live like me.
300 As well his Grace reply'd, Like you Sir John?
That I can do, when all I have is gone.
Resolve me Reason, wch of these is worse,
Want with a full, or with an empty Purse?
Cutler saw Tenants break, and Houses fall,
305 For very want; he could not build a Wall:

He
Saw his ~~lov'd~~ Daughter in a Stranger's pow'r,
For very want; he could not pay a Dow'r:

A few grey Hairs his revrend temples crownd;
Twas very Want, that sold them for 2 pd

What ev'n deny'd a Cordial at his End,
Banish'd the Doctor, and expell'd the Friend?
310 What but a Want, which you perhaps think mad,
Yet numbers feel; the Want of what he had.
Cutler and Brutus, dying both exclaim
"Virtue and Wealth! what are ye by a Name?

Worth
Say, for such ~~Pains~~, are other Worlds prepar'd?
315 Or are they both, in this, their own Reward?

to which we now proceed
A knotty Point! ~~which shall I next discuss?~~
But you are tird—Ill tell a Tale—agreed.
Or tell a Tale?—A Tale—It follows thus.

[This knotty point, my Lord, shall I discuss,

280

A

303: Want with] *with* was originally *of*.
306: Saw] originally *He*.
309: Banish'd] originally *Deny'd*.
316: next] originally *now*.
Margin: Death] originally *End*.

A plain good Citizen of sober fame,
In Cheapside dwelt, and Balaam was his name.
Religious, punctual, frugal, and so forth:
His Word would pass for more than he was worth.
One solid Dish his each Day meal affords,
An added Pudding solemniz'd the Lord's.
Constant at Church, and Change: His Gains were sure,
His Givings rare, save Farthings to the Poor.

The Dev'l was piqu'd, such Saintship to behold,
And long'd to tempt him, like good Job of old;
~~But knew (for now the Dev'l was grown a Witch)~~
~~The way was not, to make him Poor, but Rich.~~

But, ~~times now changed~~ measures change, the
Dev'l is now grown a Witch,
& tempts no more by making
poor, but rich.

Rowz'd by the Prince of Air, the ~~Tempests~~ Whirlwinds sweep
The Surge, and plunge his Father in the Deep;
Then full against his Cornish Lands they roar,
And two rich Shipwrecks bless the lucky shore.

Sir Balaam now, he lives like other folks;
He takes his chirping Pint, he cracks his jokes:
"Live like yourself, was soon my Lady's word,
And lo! two Puddings smok'd upon the Board.

Asleep and naked as an Indian lay,
An honest Factor stole a Gem away:

He

measures change,
But, ~~Times now changd~~, the
now
Dev'l is grown a Witch,
& tempts no more by making
poor, but rich.
^

A plain good Citizen, of sober fame,
In Cheapside dwelt, and Balaam was his name.
Religious, punctual, frugal, and so forth: 320
His Word would pass for more than he was worth.
One solid Dish his each Day meal affords,
An added Pudding solemniz'd the Lord's.
Constant at Church, and Change: His Gains were sure,
His Givings rare, save Farthings to the Poor. 325
The Dev'l was piqu'd, such Saintship to behold,
And long'd to tempt him, like good Job of old;
But knew (for now the Dev'l was grown a Witch)
The way was not, to make him Poor, but Rich.

Whirlwinds
Rowz'd by the Prince of Air, the ~~Tempests~~ sweep 330
The Surge, and plunge his Father in the Deep;
Then full against his Cornish Lands they roar,
And two rich Shipwrecks bless the lucky shore.
Sir Balaam now, he lives like other folks;
He takes his chirping Pint, he cracks his jokes: 335
"Live like yourself, was soon my Lady's word,
And lo! two Puddings smok'd upon the Board.
Asleep and naked as an Indian lay,
An honest Factor stole a Gem away:

He

319: and] Pope first wrote *S*, probably intending *Sir* by mistake.

He pledg'd it to the Knight; the Knight had Wit,
So kept the Diamond, and the Rogue was bit.
So robb'd the Robber, and was rich as P—. +
Some Scruples past, but thus he calm'd his thought,
"I'll now give Sixpence where I gave a Groat,
"Where once I went to Church, I'll now go twice,
"And am so clear too, of all other Vice."

The Tempter saw his time: the Work he ply'd,
Stocks and Subscriptions pour on ev'ry side;
And all the Dæmon makes his full descent
In one abundant Show'r of Cent per cent.

Behold! Sir Balaam turns a Man of Spirit,
Ascribes his Gettings to his Parts and Merit,
What late he call'd a Blessing, now was Wit,
And God's good Providence, a lucky Hit.
Things chang'd their names, & took another turn;
His Counting-house employ'd the Sunday morn;
Seldom at Church, 'twas such a busy life,
But duely sent his Family and Wife.
~~Fitt~~ Where, so the Devil ordain'd, one Christmas-tide,
My good old Lady ~~there~~ catch'd a Cold, & dy'd.

A Nymph of Quality admires our Knight:
He marries, bows at Court, and grows polite:

Leaves

\+ P—tt, once Governour of Fort St. George, who there became Master of a Diamond wch he afterwds. sold to the K. of France for one hundred & twenty thous'd pounds.

340 He pledg'd it to the Knight; the Knight had Wit,

So kept the Diamond, and the Rogue was bit.
So robb'd the Robber, and was rich as P–.+
Some Scruples past, but thus he calm'd his thought,
"I'll now give Sixpence where I gave a Groat,
"Where once I went to Church, I'll now go twice,
345 "And am so clear too, of all other Vice."
The Tempter saw his time: the Work he ply'd,
Stocks and Subscriptions pour on ev'ry side;
And all the Dæmon makes his full descent
In one abundant Show'r of Cent per cent.
350 Behold! Sir Balaam turns a Man of Spirit,
Ascribes his Gettings to his Parts and Merit,
What late he call'd a Blessing, now was Wit,
And God's good Providence, a lucky Hit.
Things chang'd their names, & took another turn;
355 His Counting-house employd the Sunday morn;
Seldom at Church, 'twas such a busy life,
But duely sent his Family and Wife.

There
~~Till~~, so the Dev'l ordain'd, one Christmas-tide,

a
My good old Lady ~~there~~ catchd^Cold, & dy'd.
360 A Nymph of Quality admires our Knight:
He marries, bows at Court, and grows polite:

Leaves

\+ P–tt, once Governour of Fort St. George, who there became Master of a Diamond w[ch] he afterw[ds] sold to the K. of France for one hundred & twenty thous[d] pounds.

341a: Rogue] originally *thief.*

358: There] originally *Where.*

341: P–] Thomas Pitt.

Leaves the dull Cits, and joins (to please the Fair)
Your well-bred Cuckolds ~~of~~ in St James's ~~Square~~ air.
First, for his Son a gay Commission buys;
Who drinks, whores, fights, & in a Duel dies.
His Daughter ~~shines~~ flaunts a Vicount's tawdry Wife,
She bears a Coronet and P—x for life.
In Britain's Senate He a Seat obtains,
And one more Pensioner St. Stephen gains.
When lo! my Lady games — So bad her chance,
He must repair it, takes a Bribe from France:
The House impeaches, Coningsby harangues,
The Court forsakes him, and Sir Balaam hangs.
His Wife, Son, & Daughter, Satan! are thy ~~own~~ prize;
His Wealth, yet dearer, forfeit to the Crown;
The Devil and divide the prize,
And sad Sir Balaam curses God and dies.

the King

350.

Leaves the dull Cits, and joins (to please the Fair)

in *air.*
Your well-bred Cuckolds ~~of~~ St James's ~~Square:~~
First, for his Son a gay Commission buys;
Who drinks, whores, fights, & in a Duel dies. 365

flaunts
His Daughter ~~shines~~ a Vicount's taudry Wife,
She bears a Coronet and P–x for life.
In Britain's Senate He a Seat obtains,
And one more Pensioner St. Stephen gains.
When lo! my Lady games–So bad her chance, 370
He must repair it, takes a Bribe from France:
The House impeaches, Coningsby harangues,
The Court forsakes him, and Sir Balaam hangs.

& *prize*
His Wife, Son, Daughter, Satan! are thy own;
His Wealth, yet dearer, forfeit to the Crown; 375
The Devil and divide the prize,
And sad Sir Balaam curses God and dies.

350.

376: The words erased in the blank are *the King*.
The pencilled words, *the King*, at the bottom of the page are not in Pope's hand.

Of the
Use of Riches:
AN
EPISTLE
to the Rt. Honble
ALLEN Lord BATHURST.

Who shall decide, when Doctors disagree,
And soundest Casuists doubt, like you & me?
You hold the Word, from Jove to Momus givn,
That Man was made the standing Jest of Heavn;
And Gold but sent to keep the Fools in play,
For some to heap, & some to throw away.

But I, who think more highly of our Kind,
(And surely Heavn & I are of a mind)
Opine, that Nature (as in Duty bound)
Deep hid the shining Mischief under ground:

Invoke the Muse, to sing in loftier strain,
How deep great Nature hid this Curse for Man

But soon as Gold, by man's mad Labor won,
Came flaming forth, a Rival to the Sun;
Then, in plain Prose, God made 2 sorts of men
To squander some, & some to hide agen.

Like Doctors thus, when much dispute has past
We find our Tenets just the same at last.

Can We then follow the former Sect,
Think Wealth a sign of God's Elect?
But giv'n to plague the Evil,
To Wxd, to Wxxs, Chxrs, & the Devil.

What Nature needs, commodious Gold bestows,
We eat the Bread another sows.
But how unequal it bestows, observe;
'Tis thus we riot, while who sow it starve.
What Nature needs (a phrase I much distrust)
Extends to Luxury, extends to Lust;
And if we count among the Needs of Life
Another's Toil, why not another's Wife?

Both wisely leaning to the former Sect,
Wealth is no mark of God's Elect
But sent to shame ye Weak, & or plague ye Evil,
Nay given to W--rd, to W--s & ye Devil
The Lot of Bond, Blunt, Bladen,

of the

Use of Riches:

AN

EPISTLE ~~to~~

To the Rt Honble

ALLEN Lord BATHURST.

shall
Who ~~can~~ decide
~~clear~~
~~What can be judg'd~~, when Doctors disagree,

And soundest casuists
And the most Thoughtful ^ doubt, like you & me?
You hold the Word; from Jove to Momus giv'n,
That Man was made the standing Jest of Heav'n;

sent
but ~~meant~~
5 And Gold ~~bestowd,~~ ^ to keep the Fools in play,

That might might
~~For~~ half ~~to~~ heap, & half ~~to,~~ ^ throw away.
But I, who think more highly of our Kind,

While one half heaps what tother throws away.

surely
And ^ Heavn & I, ~~no doubt,~~ are of a mind)
Opine, that Nature (as in Duty bound),

8
Invoke the Muse, to sing in loftier strain,
How deep great Nature hid this Curse frō Man

the shining
10 Deep hid ~~from Man his~~ ^ Mischief under ground:
~~But when (observe!) the flaming Mine begun~~
~~To give a Rival to its Sire the Sun,~~
~~Then, must not Heav'n~~
~~See Providence two sorts of Men ordain,~~

~~when the mine~~
But soon as Gold, by Man's mad Labor won,
~~this~~
Came flaming forth, a Rival to the Sun,
God
Then, in plain Prose, ~~Heavn~~ made 2 sorts of men

some, some agen
To squander, ~~these~~, & ~~those~~ to hide ~~again~~ ^?

[Like thus,
~~Thus~~ Doctors ~~like,~~ when much dispute has past
~~our meaning~~ our Tenets
We find ~~the Matter,~~ ^ just ye same at last.
~~Both faithful and ←→~~
~~we hold the extremes of eith. we think ye~~ same
~~the thing~~
~~Both holding (my Lord, our Faith ye same~~
~~Both faithful ←→ to the first. both hate ye other Sect~~
Both holding Wealth no mark

~~We lean (my Bathurst) to~~
~~and~~ Shall then ~~judge this Gift no mark~~
15 Can We ^ brave Followrs of the former Sect,
Wealth & judge this Gift no
own Mark
Think ~~Gold~~ (my Lord) a ~~Sign~~ of God's Elect?
~~But sent to~~ shame ye weak ←→, & plague the evil,
see to what hands
~~Mark but to whom~~ he gives the precious Evil!

men, &
~~Declare this Gold~~ is sent ~~of~~ weak & ~~of~~
But ~~givn,~~ ^ to shame ye ~~foolish~~ plague ye Evil
~~weak men & punish evil~~
and givn to to
~~The Lot of~~ W rs. ~~of~~ W–rs, & ye devil
Taught by th' Extremes of either frantic Sect
~~That Gold was not ye~~ mark of Gods El
But givn sent to
The Lot of W–

~~Tis~~ givn to W–d to W–s, ~~to~~
To Wxd, to Wxxs, to Chxrs, & the Devil.

commodious
we ~~grant it can~~
"What Nature needs, (~~they tell us~~) Gold bestows,
Tis ~~and~~ thus ~~I eat~~ we eat ~~we~~ another
20 ~~Man eats by that~~ the Bread ~~he never~~ sows."

9: Duty] originally *duty.*
19: bestows] originally *bestow'd.*
20: sows] originally *sow'd.*
21: deserves] originally *deserved.*
22: starves] originally *starved.*

Margin: opposite line 1] in pencil, *and soundest Casuists.*
Margin: Doctors like] originally *Doctor-like.*
Margin: ~~faithful ←→ to~~] This may read *~~faithful follow'rs to.~~*

18: Wxd, to Wxxs, to Chxrs] Ward, Waters, Chartres.

~~Tis well, but~~ ⟷ *But how unequal it bestows, observe.*

we *you*

~~But eats he then not more than he deserves~~,

Nor ~~not it~~ *Tis thus we riot, while*

~~And is it just if he~~ who sow'd it, starves.

What Nature needs (a phrase I much distrust)

Extends to Luxury, extends to Lust;

we ~~you~~

25 And if ~~they~~ count among the Needs of Life

Another's Toil, why not another's Wife?

~~But~~

~~We own this Gift no mark~~

~~& lean a little to ye former Sect~~

—last: ~~& somewhat leaning to~~

~~Conclude this Gift no~~

But sent to Both

and rather Sect

—last ~~Nay givn~~ A little leaning to ye former

& owning Gold | is, we own, | no mark of God

~~& lean a little~~ Elect

~~& clear~~ yt Gold's

But sent

Nay givn

Both wisely leaning to ye former Sect

And owning

~~Both / Both / and sure, yt~~ Gold's no mark of Gods Elect

~~Useful~~ But sent to shame ye Weak, & or plague ye Evil,

Nay givn to W—rd, to W—s & ye Devl

of

The Lot of Bond, Blunt, Bladen,

22a: we] over *I*.

Margin: Bond, Blunt, Bladen] Denis Bond, Sir John Blunt, Martin Bladen.

Useful we grant, it serves what Life requires,
But, dreadful too, the dark assassin hires:
Trade it may help, Society extend;
22 But lures the Pyrate, & corrupts the Friend:
It raises Armies in a Nation's aid,
But bribes a Senate, & the Land's betray'd.

Oh! that such bulky Bribes as all might see
Still, as of Old, encumber'd Villany!
In vain may Heroes fight, & Patriots rave
If secret Gold saps on from Knave to Knave.
A Statesman's Quiet how this Speech wd spoil!
Sir, Spain has sent a thousand Jars of Oyl;
Of British Cloth, Sir, block up ye door;
A huge Blockade of broad cloth stops
An hundred Oxen at your Levee roar.

[Poor Avarice one Torment more wd find,
Nor could Profusion squander all, in kind.
Astride his Cheese Sir Morgan might we meet,
And Worldly crying Coals from street to street.
His Grace will game: To White's a Bull be led
With spurning heels & with a butting head:
To White's be carry'd, as to ancient Games,
Fair Coursers, Vases, & alluring Dames.
Shall then uxorio if ye stakes he sweep,
Bear home six Whores, & make his Lady weep;
Or soft Adonis, so perfum'd and fine,
Drive to St. James's a whole Herd of Swine:
Oh filthy Check for all industrious Skill,
To spoil the Nation's last great Trade, Quadrille!

Once

In modest Gold the Great, the Holy share,
But Bribes in kind nor men nor Gods could bear
A Statesman's Quiet &c.
Could France or Rome divert our brave designs,
With all their Brandies & with all their Wines?
What cd they more, than Knights & Squires confound,
all Clergy ten mile round?
Or water
Poor Avarice &c.
a Statesmans
Huge Bales

Could Moor tiny sell
were moor to sell
his hogs
Send in one year his fortune
to ye Dogs!

Useful, we grant, it serves
~~But grant it useful to~~ what Life requires,

But dreadful *dark assasin*
~~Destructive~~ too, the ~~Murderer it~~ hires:

~~*can*~~
Trade it may help, Society extend;
22 But lures the Pyrate, & corrupts the Friend: 30
It raises Armies in a Nation's aid,
But bribes a Senate, & the Land's betray'd.
Oh! that such bulky Bribes as all might see
Still, as of old, encumber'd Villany!

Heroes fight,
In vain may ~~Preachers sweat,~~ & Patriots rave 35
If secret Gold saps on from Knave to Knave.
~~*Much w^d it check sage F—'s deep Design*~~
~~To break a Trust were Peter brib'd wth Wine,~~
~~*dear Lepidus! like*~~
~~Peter! Twou'd pose a head as wise as~~ thine:
~~*Should France reward Ambassadors with wine*~~ ~~confound~~
~~What more could Wine, than Knights & Squires~~
~~*or & sprinkle*~~
~~And water all the Clergy ten mile round~~ 40

Quiet
A Statesman's ~~Visions~~ how this Speech w^d spoil!
has sent a thousand
"Sir, Spain ~~presents the hundred~~ Jars of Oyl:
Huge Bales of British ~~*English*~~ *ade*
"~~The Bales of broad~~ Cloth, ~~Sir~~, block up ye door;
A ~~The~~ huge Blockade of broad cloth stops
"An hundred Oxen at your Levee roar.

~~*Could France &c*~~
[Poor Avarice one Torment more w^d find, 45
Nor could Profusion squander all, in kind.

Morgan
Astride his Cheese Sir ~~Humphry~~ might we meet,
And Worldly crying Coals from Street to Street.
~~*Could Moore, were Moore to sell his Hops and*~~
~~Were Gx to sell his Cattle & his~~ Hogs,
~~*Send in one year*~~
~~Could Gx have sent~~ his fortune to the Dogs 50

His Grace
~~My Lord~~ will game: To White's a Bull be led
With spurning heels & with a butting head:
To White's be carry'd, as to ancient Games,
Fair Coursers, Vases, & alluring Dames.

Uxorio
~~And~~ Shall then ~~Bxx~~ if ye stakes he sweep, 55
Bear home six Whores, & make his Lady weep?

soft Adonis, so perfumd and
Or ~~thou sweet Vx so essenc'd & so~~ fine,
Drive to St. James's a whole Herd of Swine?

Oh *filthy* *on*
~~How vile a~~ Check ~~to~~ all industrious Skill,
~~Our last great Trade, in Burroughs, & Qua~~ 60
last
To spoil the Nation's ~~greatest~~ Trade, Quadrille!
Once

[Left margin:]

Gold
In modest ~~Gifts,~~ ~~well addrest~~
the
~~The Great~~ ⟷ the Great ~~&~~ Holy share,
But Bribes in Kind nor men nor Gods
could
~~can~~ bear. ~~*Much twould expose ye deepest*~~ *lay'd* ~~*Design*~~ *were France to pay her Pensioners in wine*
A Statesmans Quiet &c.

~~These~~
—Knave. Could France or Rome divert our brave Designs
~~after~~
their
With all ~~their~~ Brandies, & with all ~~their~~ their Wines?
~~*They*~~ ~~*at worst but*~~
What c^d they more, than Knights & Squires confound,
~~& sprinkle~~ all ye Clergy ten mile round?
Or water
~~In modest Gold the Great, the Holy share~~
Poor Avarice &c ~~but these~~
~~But Bribes in Kind not~~
A Statesmans ~~first~~

Could Moor himself, were Moor to sell his hogs
~~*What Could*~~ ~~*by selling*~~
~~No Could~~ Hampshire Heirs, whose ~~Wealth is Hops & Hogs,~~
in one year ~~*their*~~ *his*
~~Could~~ Send, ~~at once, his~~ fortune to ye Dogs?

48: Worldly] originally *Wxxy*.
55: Shall] originally *shall*.
57a: soft] originally *sw*, undoubtedly intended for *sweet*.

Margin: all their Brandies] *their* over *their* altered from *her*; *Brandies* originally *brandies*.
Margin: all their their] second *their* originally *her*.

37a: F—'s] Fleury.
37: Peter] Peter Waters.
49a: Moore] James Moore Smythe.
49: Gx] Joseph Gage.
55: Bxx] Lord Bristol.
57: Vx] Lord Hervey, Vice-Chamberlain.

'Tis true, that once beneath ye Patriot's
~~Once, when the Patriot bore beneath his cloak~~
From the hand full Bag
~~The Latent Bag~~ ^ the dropping Guinea spoke,
And, gingling down the Back-stairs, told the Crew
"Old Cato is as great a Rogue — as You.

Blest Paper-Credit! ~~that~~ advanc'd so high,
Now lends Corruption lighter Wings to fly!
[illegible]
Well then, since with the World we stand or fall,
Come, take it as we find it, Gold & all.

2 Gold, imp'd by this, shall compass hardest things!
~~[illegible]~~
Shall pocket States, shall fetch or carry Kings,
A single leaf shall waft an Army o'er,
Or send a Senate to some distant Shore,
~~[illegible]~~
A Leaf, like Sybil's, [illegible]
Scatters our Fates, & fortunes to or fro.

What Riches give us? let us first enquire:
"Meat, Fire, & Cloaths — What more?" Meat, Cloaths & Fire.
How? think we, this too little? Cooks we crave?
'Tis more, much more than Turner found they gave.
'Tis more, than (all his Dream of Pleasure past)
Unhappy Wh××n waking found at last. — waking
What can they give? not Vultur Breath, God knows,
Not Charters Vigour, Japhet Ears & nose:
Can they, in Gems, bid pallid Hippia glow?
In Fulvia's Buckle, ease the Throbs below?
~~Or [illegible]~~
Or heal, old Narses, thy obscener ail,
With all th' Embroid'ry plaister'd at thy Tail?
They might, were S××k not too wise to spend
Give S××k's self the Blessing of a Friend
~~[illegible]~~
~~Give such a Doctor as would save his life~~
But thousands dye, without or this or that;
~~And leave them to~~ Dye, and endow a College, or a +Catt.
To some, indeed, Heav'n grants the happier fate,
T'enrich a Bastard, or a Son they hate.

+ A famous, covetous Duchess left a considerable part of her Estate for ye maintenance of her Catts.

Why then the poor & needy Rich revile?
They claim our Pity, or at worst, our Smile.
The Wretch who gives not, n'er enjoys his self,
And does but hate his Neighbor as himself. ^

Damn'd to the mines, an equal fate betides
The Slave that digs it, & the Slave that hides.

Such Suff'rings lead my Charity to doubt,
They may have Reasons none of us find out;
Some War, some Plague, some Famine they foresee,
Some Revelation, hid from you & me.
Why starves the Peer his Son? the cause is found,
He thinks a Loaf will rise to fifty pd.
Why heaps lewd Lesbia that enormous Sum?
alas! she fears a Man may cost a Plum.

[Wise Peter sees the World's Respect for Gold,
& hopes in time these Kingdoms may be sold
Glorious Ambition! Peter swells his store
To be what Rome's great Didius was before

[illegible]

Tis true, that once beneath ye Patriot's
~~Once, when the Patriot bore beneath his~~ cloak

From the ~~hand~~ / full Bag
~~The latent Bag~~ the dropping Guinea spoke,
And, gingling down the Back-stairs, told the Crew

~~M–~~
"Old Cato is as great a Rogue – as You.

~~shall~~ ~~more~~
65 1 Blest Paper-Credit/ ~~that~~ advanc'd ~~so~~ high,
~~Shall Shall~~
Now lends Corruption lighter Wings to fly!

A as the wind shall blow
~~Whose~~ Leaf~~es~~ like Sybils, ~~pregnant with our fates~~
~~Bears Fates~~ ~~of Men & Empires~~ to or fro,
Scatters our Fates ~~& Lives & Fates~~ & Fortunes
Well then, since with the World we stand or fall,
Come, take it as we find it, Gold & all.
What Riches give us? let us first enquire:
70 "Meat, Fire, & Cloaths–What more? "Meat, Cloaths & Fire.

~~Is~~ ~~& looks Peter~~
How? think we this too little? look we grave?

much more, than ~~Coleby~~ / Turner
Tis more, than ~~Hxxe yet has~~ found they gave.
Tis more, than (all his Dream of Pleasure past)
Unhappy Whxxn waking found at last.
75 What can they give? not Vultur Breath, God knows,
Not Charters Vigour, Japhet Ears & nose:
Can they, in Gems, bid pallid Hippia glow?

ease
In Fulvia's Buckle '~~swage~~ the Throbs below?
~~Say could they heal old Narse's~~
~~Or~~ once Cxxxn~~'s ease~~ thy aukward Ail,

thy ~~his~~
80 With all th' Embroid'ry plaister'd at ~~thy~~ Tail?
They might, were Sxxk not too wise to spend
Give Sxxk's self the Blessing of a Friend

Or some
~~But~~ find a Doctor that w[d] save the Life
~~They might to Wxx (spite of Worldly's Wife)~~

Of wretched Worldly, spite of Worldly's Wife
~~Give such a Doctor as would save his life~~
85 But thousands dye, without or this or that;

Dye, and endow
~~And leave them to~~ a College, or a +Catt.
To some, indeed, Heav'n grants the happier fate/
T'enrich a Bastard, or a Son they hate.
Why then the poor & needy Rich revile?
90 They claim our Pity, or at worst, our Smile.
The Wretch who gives not, n'er enjoys his pelf,
And does but hate his Neighbor as himself.
Such Suff'rings lead my Charity to doubt,
They may have Reasons none of us find out;
95 Some War, some Plague, some Famine they foresee,
Some Revelation, hid from you & me.

[Right margin:]

2 *Gold, imp'd wth this, shall compass* *Stent* *~~dele~~*
~~When both unite~~,
~~Possest of both, how easy~~ hardest things!
Shall ~~They~~ pocket States, *shall* ~~they~~ fetch or carry Kings,
shall waft
~~Waft on~~ A single Leaf an Army o'er
~~hot Patriots~~ *~~a~~* *~~forein~~*
Or send a Senate to some distant shore,
~~These Sybil's Leaves all~~ *~~our~~* ~~oracles have given,~~
~~And silenc'd~~ *~~all~~* ~~the 'Ambassadors of Heav'n~~
~~A Leaf~~ ~~Leaves that~~ like Sybil's, ~~pregnat wth Fates~~ *~~our~~*
A Leaf,
~~whatere wind~~
~~Bears to or fro Lives, fortunes, and Fates~~
as the Winds shall blow,
~~Bear Fates, & Lives~~, & Fortunes to or fro.
~~Can~~ *Scatters our Fates*

– *waking*

Narses
Or heal, old ~~Gen'ral,~~ thy obscener ail,

covetuous
\+ A famous Duchess left a considerable part of her Estate for y[e] maintenance of her Catts.

Damn'd to the Mines, an equal fate betides
The Slave that digs it, & the Slave that hides.

66: Wings] originally *wings*.
67a: Whose] originally *Those*.
Leaf~~es~~] originally *Leaves*.
74: waking] originally *wakd &*.
76: Charters] originally *Chxxrs*.
83: Worldly's] originally *Wxx's*.
83a: Doctor] originally *doctor*.
Margin: A single Leaf] originally *a single leaf*.
Margin: opposite 74: in pencil, *waking*.

64a: M–] Sir Christopher Musgrave.
72a: Coleby] Sir Thomas Coleby, a rich miser (Elwin-Courthope, III. 136 n.).
Turner] Richard ("Plum") Turner.
72: Hxxe] Sir Gilbert Heathcote.
74: Whxxn] Wharton.
75: Vultur] John ("Vulture") Hopkins.
79: Cxxxn's] Cadogan.
81: Sxxk] Selkirk.
83: Wxx] Wortley Montagu.

Why starves the Peer his Son? the cause is found,
He thinks a Loaf will rise to fifty pd. ~~Why~~ ~~(fears)~~
Why heaps lewd Lesbia that enormous Sum?
100 Alas! she fears a Man may cost a Plum.

[Wise Peter sees the Worlds Respect for Gold,
& hopes in time these Kingdoms ~~will~~ *may* be sold
Glorious Ambition! Peter swells ~~his~~ *thy* store
~~To~~ *And* be what Rome's great †Didius was before

† A Lawyer so rich y[t] he Bought y[e] Roman Empire when it was set to Sale upon the death of Pertinax.

2 Why heaps Lord Lesbia that enormous Sum?
Alas! she fears a Man may cost a Plum.
Why steals the Soldiers Bread, why stole a Chief renown'd?
He thinks a Loaf will rise to fifty pound:
Why held no Chief, but Mordaunt, so in fault,
To save all Europe, & not save a Groat.
To just 3 Millions stinted modest Gage
Peter
from head to head, by Auction will be sold:
Glorious Ambition. See what Peter meant!
Didius was his Precedent.
The Polish Sceptre, venal twice an age,
To just three Millions stinted modest G—ge.
why bore
A Lawyer, so excessive rich
Roman Empire for
to Sale upon ye death of Pertinax.
The Crown of Poland, venal twice an age
To just 3 Millions stinted modest —

Stole His
Why steals the Soldiers Bread, why stole a Chief renown'd?
He thinks a Loaf will rise to fifty pound:
Lord Lesbia that enormous
Why heaps Nigrina what a monstrous Sum?
Alas! she fears a Man may cost a Plum.
He thinks a Loaf will rise to fifty pd.
bore
Why bears Sir John the Nations Curse & Hate
A Wizard told him in these words our Fate
"At length, Corruption like a gen'ral Flood,
"(By Statesmen, Churchmen, Patriots, long with stood)
"Shall deluge All! What shall not then be sold?
"When Bishops ... & Chancellors take Gold;
"When Dukes shall pick ye pockets of ye Town,
"And Duchesses pack Cards for half a Crown"!
What push'd, great Scriv'ner! thy bold aims so high?
Not City Gain, not Lordly Luxury;
No, 'twas thy gen'rous view, asham'd to see
Senates degenerate, & Patriots disagree,
And nobly wishing Party Rage to cease;
To buy both sides, & give thy Country Peace.

"All this is Madness" cries a sober Sage.
But who, my Friend, has Reason in his Rage?
The ruling Passion, be it what it will,
The ruling Passion conquers Reason still.
Less mad, the wildest Whymsy we can frame
Than ev'n that Passion, if it has no Aim;
For tho' such motives Folly you may call,
The Folly's greater to have none at all.

Strange as it is I'll name a Stranger
Hath in your ear —

Hear then the Truth: 'Tis Heav'n each Passion sends
And diff'rent men directs to diff'rent Ends:
Extremes in Nature equal Good produce;
Extremes in Man concur to gen'ral Use.
Ask we what makes one keep, & one bestow?
That Pow'r, who bids the Ocean ebb, & flow;
Bids Seedtime, Harvest, equal course maintain,
Thro' reconcil'd Extremes, of Drought or Rain;
Builds Life on Death, on Change Duration founds,
And gives th' Eternal Wheels to know their Rounds.

Why
~~a duke! and~~
~~steal a Groat?~~ 2 Why heaps lewd Lesbia that enormous Sum?
xx starves his Alas! she fears a Man may cost a Plum.
~~Sire~~ his son's
1 Why steals the His soldiers Bread why stole a Chief renownd?
Duke
Peer a Groat? ye A Loaf, he thought, w^d^ rise to 50 p^d^
cause is found, & held no Chief, but Mordaunt, so in fault,
He thinks a Loaf will *half*
rise to 50 p^d^ To save ~~all~~ Europe, & not save a Groat.

crown of Poland ~~*crown of Poland*~~
3 [~~The Polish sceptre~~, venal twice an age,
To just 3 millions stinted modest Gage. ~~*She fears, perhaps,*~~
~~*Weak*~~ ↔ ~~*thought*~~ ~~*our own*~~
~~*Mad*~~ Peter's ~~may think~~, ye Crown wch long had rolld
Mad *dreamd* ~~*hopes*~~
would
From head to head, by Auction ~~will~~ be sold:
2 Glorious ambition! see what Peter meant! x
~~*and The*~~ *frugal* *is* ~~*a*~~ *his*
1. ~~Attorney~~* Didius was ~~his~~ Precedent–
The Polish Sceptre, venal twice an age,
To just three millions stinted modest G–ge.
Why bore–

x
~~*Didius Julianus*~~ *A Lawyer, so excessive rich*
~~*by avarice*~~
* ~~A Lawyer so excessive rich~~ y^t^ he bought y^e^
for ~~*Bands*~~ *when it was set*
Roman Empire ~~of ye Praetorians upon ye death~~
*to Sale upon y^e^*
death of Pertinax. ~~who set it to sale~~

The Crown of Poland, venal twice an age
To just 3 Millions stinted modest –––

Strange as it is I'll name a stranger
Hark in y^r^ ear–

~~*stole*~~ *His* *why stole a*
~~Why steals the~~ Soldiers Bread, ~~our~~ Chief renown'd?
~~*he thought*~~, *would* ~~*and might would*~~
~~*A Loaf,*~~ ~~He thinks a Loaf will~~ rise to fifty pound;
lewd Lesbia that enormous
~~*Such*~~
Why heaps ~~Nigrina that a monstrous~~ Sum?

fears *may* ~~*might*~~
Alas! she ~~fears~~, a Man ~~may~~ cost a Plum.
The soldiers Bread why steals our Chief renownd

~~*enormous*~~
~~Why rais'd old Helluo that prodigious store~~? 105

He thinks a Loaf will rise to fifty pd.
~~He judg'd a Goose w^d^ rise to ten pence more.~~

bore
[Why bears Sir John the Nations Curse & Hate

A Wizard told him in these words our Fate

"At length, Corruption like a gen'ral Flood,
"(By Statesmen, Churchmen, Patriots, long with stood) 110

then
"Shall deluge all! What shall not be sold?

~~*Judges job,*~~ ~~*Bishops write for*~~
"When ~~Bishops job, & Chancellors take~~ Gold;
Friends inform, & ~~*Brothers*~~ *pimp for*
~~*Judges*~~

"When Dukes shall pick ye pockets of ye Town,
"And Duchesses pack Cards for half a Crown."

aims
What push'd, great Scriv'ner! thy bold ~~Views~~ so high? 115
Not City Gain, not Lordly Luxury;

View,
No, 'twas thy gen'rous ~~Aim,~~ asham'd to see
degen'rate,
Senates ~~so sunk, &~~ Patriots disagree,
And nobly wishing Party Rage to cease;
To buy both sides, & give thy Country Peace. 120

"All this is Madness" cries a sober Sage.
But
~~And~~ who, my Friend, has Reason in his Rage?
~~Ea~~*The* ruling Passion, be it what it will,
The
~~That~~ ruling Passion conquers Reason still.

we
Less mad, the wildest Whymsy ~~y^u^~~ can frame 125
Than ev'n that Passion, if it has no Aim;

For tho'
~~Tis true,~~ such Motives Folly y^u^ may call,
Tis *Folly*
~~But still 'tis~~ greater to have none at all.

103: heaps] originally *heap'd*.
104: fears] originally *fear'd*.
123: ~~Ea~~The] originally *Each*.
Margin: Why heaps] written over *Why*.
Margin: A Loaf, he thought] originally . . . *he thinks*.
Margin: wch long had rolld] originally . . . *has rolld*.
Margin: by Auction ~~will~~ be sold] *would* over *will* was originally *might*.
Margin: A Lawyer] originally *a Lawyer*.

101: Chief] Duke of Marlborough.
107: Sir John] Sir John Blunt.
Margin: Mordaunt] Charles Mordaunt, Earl of Peterborough, a famous general and close friend of Pope.

[sion sends
Hear then the Truth: 'Tis Heav'n each Pas-^
And diff'rent Men directs to diff'rent Ends: 130
Extremes in Nature equal Good produce;
Extremes in Man concur to gen'ral Use.
Ask we what makes one keep, & one bes-
tow?
That Pow'r, who bids the Ocean ebb, & flow;
Bids Seedtime, Harvest, equal course main- 135
-tain,
Thro' reconcil'd Extremes, of Drought or Rain;
Builds Life on Death, on Change Duration founds,
And gives th'Eternal Wheels to know their
Rounds.

[Riches, like Insects, when conceal'd they lie,
Wait but for wings, and in their season fly.
Who sees pale Mammon pine amidst his Store,
Sees but a backward Steward for the Poor;
This year, a Reservoir, to keep & spare;
The next, a Fountain spouting thro' his Heir;
In lavish Streams to quench a Country's thirst,
And Men & Dogs shall drink him till they burst.
Riches, like Insects, when conceal'd they lye,
Wait but for Wings, & in the Season fly.

Old Cotta sham'd his Fortune & his high Birth,
Yet was not Cotta void of Wit or Worth:
Slight his mistake; he held it for a Rule,
"That ev'ry Man in Want was Knave or Fool."
What tho (the Use of barb'rous Spits forgot)
His Kitchen vy'd in Coolness with his Grot?
His Court with Nettles, Moat with Cresses stor'd,
With Soupes unbought, & Sallads, blest his board.
If Cotta liv'd on Pulse, it was no more
Than Bramins, Saints, & Sages did before;
To cram the Rich, was prodigal expence;
And who would take the Poor from Providence?
Like some lone Chartreuse stands the good old Hall,
Silence without, & Fasts within the Wall:
No rafter'd Roofs with Dance & Tabor sound,
No Noontide Bell invites the Country round:
~~But the gaunt Mastiff growling at the Gate~~
~~Affrights the Beggar he could wish to eat.~~
Be-nighted Wanderers the Forest o'er
Curse the sav'd Candle & un-opening Door.
Tenants with Sighs the smoke-less Tow'rs survey
~~And turn th' unwilling Steed another way.~~

Not so his Son: he mark'd this Over-sight,
And then mistook Reverse of Wrong for Right;
For, what to shun will no great knowledge ask,
But what to follow is a harder task.
Yet sure of Qualities deserving praise
More go to ruin Fortunes, than to raise.

Tenants with sighs the smokeless Tow'rs survey,
And turn th' unwilling Steeds another way.
Benighted wanderers ye Forest o'er,
Curse ye sav'd Candle, & unopening door;
While the gaunt Mastiff, growling at ye Gate,
Affrights the Beggar whom he longs to eat.
On him who having sav'd the Tapers End:
High on his Tomb a wicked Statue stands
Belies his features, & extends his hands;
The very Wig that Gorgon's self might own
Eternal buckle takes in Parian Stone.
Well sees ye Son the Fathers Oversight
But then mistakes —
To will, the Son, who mark'd his Sire's Oversight,
& then mistook Reverse

[Riches like Insects, when conceald they lie,
Wait but for wings, and in their season fly.

Who sees pale Mammon pine ~~ng on~~ *amidst* his Store,
140 Sees but a backward Steward for the Poor;
This year, a Reservoir to keep & spare;
The next, a Fountain spouting thro' his Heir;
In lavish streams to quench a Country's thirst,
And Men & Dogs shall drink him till they burst.

145 Riches, like Insects, when *so* ~~they~~ ~~most~~ close~~st~~ *they* lye,
Wait but for Wings, & in the Season fly.

Old Cotta sham'd his Fortune & his Birth, *high*
Yet was not Cotta void of wit or worth:
Slight his mistake; he held it for a Rule,
150 "That ev'ry man in want was Knave or Fool."
What tho (the use of barb'rous Spits forgot)
His Kitchen vy'd in Coolness with his Grot?
His Court with Nettles, Moat with Cresses stor'd,
With Soupes unbought, & Sallads, blest his board.
155 If Cotta livd on Pulse, it was no more
Than Bramins, Saints, & Sages did before;
To cram the Rich, was prodigal expence;
And who would take the Poor from Providence?
Like some lone Chartreuse stands the good old Hall,
160 Silence without, & Fasts within ~~the~~ *ther* Wall:
No rafter'd Roofs with Dance & Tabor sound,
No Noontide Bell invites the Country round:
~~But the gaunt Mastiff, growling at the Gate~~
~~Affrights the Beggar he could wish to eat~~: / ~~*whom he longs to eat*~~
165 Be-nighted Wanderers the Forest o'er
Curse the sav'd Candle & un-opening Door.
~~*No smoking Tow'rs Her ancient Guests no smoking*~~ ~~*sunless*~~
Tenants with Sighs the smoke-less Tow'rs survey
~~*all*~~ ~~*But*~~
~~And turns th'unwilling Steed~~s ~~another way~~

Not ~~Curio so~~ *so* ~~*his*~~ *the Son*: he mark'd this Over-sight,
170 And then mistook Reverse of Wrong for Right;

For, what to shun will no great knowledge ask, / ~~*need*~~
But what to follow is ~~another~~ ~~*indeed*~~ *a harder* task. / ~~*indeed*~~
Yet sure of Qualities deserving praise
More go to ruin Fortunes, than to raise.

Tenants with sighs ther smokeless Towrs survey,
and turn th'unwilling Steeds another way.
~~By night poor Wanderers~~ *Benighted Wanderers* ye Forest o'er,
Curse y^e ~~Rush~~ sav'd ~~*quenchd*~~ Candle, & unopening door:
~~And~~ *While* the gaunt mastiff, growling at ye gate,
Affrights the Beggar whom he longs to eat.
~~He dies! and lo! a thous^d lights attend~~
On him who living savd ~~the~~ *a* Tapers End:
High on his Tomb a wicked Statue stands,
Belies his features, & extends his hands:
The very Wig that Gorgons self might own
Eternal buckle takes in Parian Stone.
[Well sees ye son the Fathers oversight
& then mistakes——
[So wills the Son, who mark'd
~~His oversight~~ his ~~the~~ Sire's O'ersight,
& ~~then mistook Reverse~~

139: Who] originally *who*.
pine] altered from *pining*.
149: Rule] originally *rule*.

160a: the] altered from *her*.
Margin: So wills] *wills* perhaps altered from *willed*.

Margin: He dies! . . . Parian Stone.] This passage, here assigned to the senior Cotta, is transferred in the margin of p. 124 to Hopkins.

T'oblige the wealthy & the Poor to feed,
See slaughter'd Hecatombs around him bleed.
Yet no vulgar Motives his Profession stain;
'Tis in his Country's cause his Beeves are slain;
Unmov'd he sees, around his naked seat,
The Timber fall — no matter — for the Fleet:
Next goes his Wool, to cloathe our valiant Bands;
Last, for his Country's Love, he sells his Lands.
Bankrupt, at Court in vain he pleads his cause;
His thankless Country leaves him to her Laws.

The golden Mean ...
What & how great, the Virtue & the Art,
To bear our Fortunes in the Head, not Heart,
Not meanly, nor ambitiously pursu'd,
Not sunk by Sloth, nor rais'd by Servitude;
Our Wealth to sanctify by just Expence;
Joyn with Oeconomy, Magnificence;
With Splendor, Charity; with Plenty, Health;
Oh teach us, Bathurst, yet un-spoil'd by Wealth!
That secret rare, wch affluence hardly join'd,
Which Wh—n lost, yet B—y ne'r cd. find;
Still mist by Vice, & scarce by Virtue hit;
By Unreach'd by Ox—'s Worth, or S—'s Wit;
That secret rare, between th' Extremes to move
Of mad Good nature, & of mean Self Love.

Whose Wealth, to Merit or to Want is given?
Who emulate, & ease, the Care of Heaven?
[2] Oxford & Chandos, acting God's own part,
Relieve th' opprest, & glad the Orphans heart.
There English Bounty yet a while shall stand,
And Honour linger, ere it leaves the Land.

But all our praises why shd Lords engross?
Rise honest Muse! & sing the† Man of Ross.
Pleas'd Vaga ecchoes thro' her winding bounds,
& rapid Severn hoarse applause resounds.

[The Sense to value Riches, with the Art
To enjoy them, & the Virtue to impart;

Affluence to sanctify by just expence, —

if thou know'st thy self

With, only such &c.
Increase to ye Skies.

† The Man of Ross, a name given by way of Eminence to a Gentleman of that Town in Herefordshire, who with a small Estate performed these good Works: His true name was John Kyrle; he died in ye year 1724, aged about 90, and was buried in ye chancel of ye church of Ross, without any Stone or Inscription.

T'oblige the Wealthy & the Poor to feed, 175
See slaughterd Hecatombs around him bleed.

vulgar
Yet no mean Motives his Profusion stain;

Tis *are*
'~~Twas~~ in his Country's cause his Beeves ~~were~~ *slain;*
~~*Tis Grand Liberty y^t crowns his cup & Zeal for that g^t House w^ch*~~ slain
~~*eats him up.*~~

Unmovd he sees, around his naked Seat,
The Timber fall~~,~~—no matter~~,~~—for the Fleet; 180
Next goes his Wool, to cloathe our valiant Bands;
Last, for his Country's Love, he sells his Lands.

cause;
Bankrupt, at Court in vain he pleads his ^
His thankless Country leaves him to her Laws.
~~Laws.~~

~~*How Riches to injoy & yet impart*~~

Wealth *well* ~~*with*~~
The golden Mean of ~~*Riches poisd*~~ *poizd with*
~~*wealth w^th*~~
~~*of*~~ ~~*wealth*~~ *with*

~~Of governd~~
~~of well poiz'd~~
~~the~~
~~qu:~~ [~~To govern Wealth, by Virtue~~

Riches, with ~~*& the art,*~~
[The Sense to value ~~Riches Wealth~~, ye art ^ ~~What, & how great, the Virtue & the~~ Art, 185
them, and ~~Keep~~—
~~Well~~ To'enjoy ^ the Virtue to impart; ~~ye greater art~~ *Kept in our eye, yet banishd fr^o our heart,*
~~Riches, ye great art~~ ~~T'enjoy the greatest~~ ~~To^bear our Fortunes in the Head, not Heart,~~
~~T'injoy, and greater Virtue to impart~~ ~~to thee he imparts~~
~~To value Wealth, enjoy & yet impart~~

Not meanly, nor ambitiously pursu'd,
Not sunk by Sloth, nor rais'd by Servitude;

Affluence to sanctify by just expence,—
~~*How Fortune vindicate*~~
~~But Wealth to sanctify~~ by just Expence;
~~*But wealth*~~ *affluence to sanctify*

Joyn with Oeconomy, Magnificence; 190
With Splendor, Charity; with Plenty, Health;
× if thou know'st thy self Oh teach us, Bathurst, yet un-spoild by Wealth!
That Secret rare, wth affluence hardly joind,
Which Wh—n lost, yet B—y ne'r c^d find;
Still mist by Vice, & scarce by Virtue hit, 195
~~By~~ Unreach'd by ~~Or—'s Worth, or S—'s~~ Wit;
That Secret rare, between th'Extremes to move
Of mad Good nature, & of mean Self Love.
Whose Wealth, to Merit or to Want is given?

&
Who emulate, ~~or~~ ease, the Care of Heaven? 200

[2]Oxford & [1]Chandos, acting God's own part,
Relieve th'opprest, & glad the Orphans heart.
stand,
There English Bounty yet a while shall ^

they
And Honour linger, e're ~~she~~ leave~~s~~ ye Land.

184: thankless] altered from *Count*, probably intended for *Country*.
186a: Kept] originally *Keep*.

204: she] originally *they*.
Margin: to value Riches] over *R* of *Riches*, *W*.
Margin: if thou know'st thy self] in pencil.

194: Wh—n] Wharton. B—y] Robert Benson, Baron Bingley.
196: Or—'s] possibly the Earl of Orkney, of whose "worth, conspicuous both in publick & private Life" Pope wrote Orkney on 4 October 1736 (Sherburn, IV. 35-36). Swift also held Orkney in high esteem.
S—'s] Philip Stanhope, Earl of Chesterfield.

Such, only such &c.

Incense to y^e^ Skies. But all our praises why sh^d^ Lords engross? 205
Rise honest Muse! & sing the +Man of Ross.

Pleasd
~~The Man from~~ ^ Vaga ecchoes thro' her winding [bounds,
~~*all the*~~
& rapid Severn hoarse applause
~~Good his sole Joy, & Bounty~~ resounds.
~~*sacred*~~

~~Round~~

+ The Man of Ross, a name given by way of Eminence to a Gentleman of that Town in Herefordshire, who ~~performed all~~ *with* the *Estate* ~~good works~~ here mentioned. *performd these good works.* ^ ~~His~~ *His true* name was *John Kyrle;* ~~K-rles,~~ he died in ye year 1724. aged ^ *about* 90, years in ye y^r^ 172 ^ *and was* ~~*of age*~~ *buried in ye Chancel of ye Church of* ~~church< >buried in~~ *Ross, with^t^ any Stone or Inscription.*

Who hung with Woods yon mountains sultry Brow?
From the dry Rock who bade the waters flow?
Not to the Skies in useless columns tost,
Or in proud Falls magnificently lost,
But clear & artless, pouring thro' the plain
Health to the Sick, & Solace to the Swain.
Whose Causeway parts ye Vale with shady Rows?
Whose Seats the weary Wanderer repose?
Who feeds yon Almshouse, (neat, but void of State)
Where Age and Want sit smiling at the Gate?
Who taught that Heav'n-directed Spire to rise?
The Man of Ross, each lisping Babe replies.
Behold the Marketplace with Poor o'erspread;
The Man of Ross divides the weekly bread:
Him portion'd maids, apprentic'd Orphans blest,
The Young who labour, & the Old who rest.
Is any sick? the Man of Ross relieves;
Prescribes, attends, the med'cine makes & gives.
Is there a Variance? enter but his door,
Balk'd are the Courts, & Contest is no more:
Despairing Quacks with Curses fled the place,
And vile Attornies, now an useless Race.
Thrice happy Man! enabled to pursue
What all so wish, but want the pow'r, to do!
Oh say, what Sums that gen'rous hand supply?
What mines to swell that boundless Charity?
Of Debts, of Taxes, Wife, and Children, clear,
This Man possest — five hundred pounds a year.
Blush, Grandeur! blush! false Pride withdraw thy Blaze!
Ye Little Stars! hide your diminish'd Rays.

Yet see'n no monument, no Bust, no Stone,
His Race, his form, his name almost unknown!

Such, only! such, to Wealth give Worth & Grace,
Whose measure full, o'erflows on human race:
'Tis Death, accumulate; its Life, diffus'd;
As Poyson heals, in just proportion us'd;
In Heaps, like Ambergrise, a Stink it lies,
But well dispers'd; is Incense to the Skies.

2 who builds a church to God & not to fame,
Will never mark ye marble with his name.

1 The Register enrolls him w. ye Poor,
2 Tells he was born & dy'd, & tells no more.

When H— dies, a thous^d^ Lights attend
The wretch &c. Parian Stone.

his Image
A wicked
Belyes his ... at God's altar stands,

& see w. content
& you've seen not.

yon'
Who hung with Woods ~~the~~ Mountains sultry Brow?
~~Round the white Church~~

From the dry Rock who bade the Waters flow?
210 ~~Who hung the Woods~~
Not to the Skies in useless Columns tost,

Not
~~Nor~~ in proud Falls magnificently lost,
But clear & artless, pouring thro' the plain
Health to the Sick, & Solace to the Swain.
215 Whose Causeway parts ye Vale with shady Rows?
Whose Seats the weary Wanderer repose?
Who feeds yon' Almshouse, (neat, but void of State)
Where Age and Want sit smiling at the Gate?

that
Who taught ~~yon'~~ Heav'n-directed Spire to rise?
220 The Man of Ross, each lisping Babe replies.
Behold the Marketplace with Poor o'erspread;
The Man of Ross divides the weekly bread:
Him portiond Maids, apprentic'd Orphans blest,
The Young who labour, & the Old who rest.
225 Is any sick? the Man of Ross relieves,
Prescribes, attends, the Med'cine makes & gives.
Is there a Variance? enter but his door,
Balkd are the Courts, & Contest is no more:

fled
Despairing Quacks with Curses ~~left~~ the place,
230 ✳ And vile Attornies, now an useless Race.
Thrice happy Man! enabled to pursue
What all so wish, but want the powr, to do!
Oh say, what Sums that gen'rous hand supply?
What mines to swell that boundless Charity?
235 Of Debts, of Taxes, Wife, and Children, clear,
This Man possest – five hundred pounds a year.

Blaze
Blush, Grandeur! blush! false Pride withdraw thy ~~rays~~!
Ye Little Stars! hide your diminishd Rays. ^
~~and yet no monum^t records his race, no stone his name no Bust,~~ ^

~~*only*~~
Such, ~~Bathurst~~! such, to Wealth give Worth & Grace,
only
240 Whose Measure full, o'erflows on human race:
'Tis Death, accumulate; tis Life, diffus'd;
As Poyson heals, in just proportion us'd;
In Heaps, like Ambergrise, a Stink it lies,
But ~~spread,~~ is Incense to the ~~Earth &~~ Skies.
well dispers'd,
~~*His*~~ *Image*
A wicked ~~Idol~~ at Gods altar stands
Belyes his

Monument,
Yet see! no ^ no Bust, no Stone.
~~*Race*~~
His ~~deeds~~, his form, his name
almost unknown!
~~not ev'n a~~
~~Monum^t of Parian~~
~~And yet no Stone~~
~~preserves his~~ ~~his name~~ ~~hides~~
~~good mans name~~
~~Face makes his virtue known~~

2 Who builds ~~y^e~~ *a* church to God
& not to fame,
Will never mark ye marble
wth his name.

1 (2) one The Register enrolls him w ~~y^e~~ Poor, ~~*& see*~~ *his*
tells
Tells he was born & dyd, & ~~told~~ no more
~~*Well as he could*~~
~~he filld his~~ ~~ye space between~~
∂ ~~*Just as he ought*~~
~~Then stole to rest unheard of & unseen~~
When H– dies, a thous^d Lights attend
The wretch &c. Parian Stone.

You've seen w^t
& see w^t comfort

Margin: Who builds] originally *Who built.*
Margin: & not to] originally *& not fo.*
Margin: Will never] originally *Would never.*

Margin: Register enrolls] originally *Register enrolld.*
Margin: Tells he was] originally *Told he was.*

Margin: H–] John Hopkins.

You see what Blessings Wealth to Life can lend;
See next, what Comfort it affords our End!

In the worst Inn's worst room, with Matt half-hung,
The Floor of Plaister, & ye Walls of Dung,
On, once a Flockbed, but repair'd wth Straw,
With Tape-ty'd Curtains, never meant to draw;
The George & Garter dangling from that Bed,
Where tawdry yellow strove with dirty Red;
Great Villers lyes! — Alas, how chang'd from him!
That Life of Pleasure & that Soul of Whym,
Gallant & gay, in Cliveden's proud Alcove
— The Bow'r of wanton Sh——y & Love;
Or just as gay, at Council, in a Ring
Of mimick'd Statesmen, & the merry King!
No Wit to flatter, left of all his store!
No Fool to laugh at, wch he valu'd more!
There, Victor of his Health, of Fortune, Friends,
And Fame; this Lord of useless thousands ends!

Lo! sober Cutler of his spoils possess'd:
His Life more wretched, was his Death more bless'd?
His Grace's Error well the Knight cd see.
And well (he thought) advis'd him, "Live like me!"
As well his Grace reply'd: "Like you, Sr John?
"That I can do, when all I have is gone."
Resolve me, Reason! which of these is worse,
Want with a full, or with an empty purse?
Cutler saw Tenants break, & Houses fall,
For very Want; he could not build a Wall.
His only Daughter in a Stranger's pow'r
For very Want; he could not pay a Dow'r.
A few gray hairs his rev'rend temples crown'd,
'Twas very Want, that sold them for 2 pd.
What ev'n deny'd a Cordial at his End,
— Banish'd the Doctor, & expell'd the Friend?

What

You've seen what Blessings Wealth to Life can lend.; 245
See next, what Comfort it affords our End?
In the worst Inn's worst room, with Matt half-hung,
The Floor of Plaister, & ye Walls of Dung,
On, once a Flockbed, but repaird wth Straw,
With Tape-ty'd Curtains, never meant to draw, 250
The George & Garter dangling from that Bed,
Where taudry Yellow strove with dirty Red;
Great Villers lyes!—Alas, how chang'd from Him!
That Life of Pleasure & that Soul of Whym,

Gallant & ~~Returning~~ *gay, in*
~~Gay as he came from~~ Cliveden's proud alcove 255

Sh---y
The Bow'r of wanton ~~Shrewsbury~~ & Love;

at Council, in a Ring
Or just as gay/ ~~from Britains Council board~~,

Of ~~*with his*~~ *the* *King*
~~With~~ mimick'd Statesmen, ~~& their~~^ Merry ~~Lord~~^!
No Wit to flatter, left of all his store!
No Fool to laugh at, wch he valu'd more! 260
There, Victor of his Health, of Fortune, Friends,
And Fame; this Lord of useless thousands ends!
Lo! sober Cutler of his spoils possess'd:

bless'd
His Life more wretched, was his Death more^
His Grace's Error well the Knight c^d see. 265
And well (he thought) advis'd him, "Live like me."
As well his Grace replyd, "Like you, Sr John?
"That I can do, when all I have is gone."
Resolve me, Reason! which of these is worse,
Want with a full, or with an empty purse? 270
Cutler saw Tenants break, & Houses fall,
For very Want; he could not build a Wall.

His only
~~He saw his~~^ Daughter in a Stranger's pow'r
For very Want; he could not pay a Dow'r.
A few gray hairs his rev'rend temples crown'd, 275

~~*What was't*~~ *Twas very*
~~For very~~ ^ ~~but~~^ Want, that sold them for 2 p^d
What ev'n deny'd a Cordial at his End,
Banishd the Doctor, & expelld the Friend?

What

253: Him] originally *him*.

What but a Want, wch you perhaps think mad,
Yet Numbers feel, the Want of what he had.
Cutler, and Brutus, dying both exclaim,
"Virtue! and Wealth! what are ye but a Name?

Say, for such Worth are other Worlds prepar'd,
Or are they, both, in this their own Reward?
That knotty Point, my Lord, shall I discuss;
Or tell a Tale? — A Tale — It follows thus.

A plain, good Citizen, of sober fame,
In Cheapside dwelt, and Balaam was his name.
Religious, punctual, frugal, & so forth;
His Word wd pass for more than he was worth.
One solid Dish his week-day meal affords;
An added Pudding solemniz'd the Lord's.
Constant at Church, & Change; his Gains were sure,
His Givings rare, save Farthings to the Poor.

When London's monument was rear'd so high
Like some tall Bully, to look big & lye
~~[illegible]~~
Where London's Column, pointing at the skies
Like some proud Bully, ye lifts ye head & lies:
There dwelt a Citizen of sober fame,
A plain good man, &c —

The Devil was piqu'd, such Saintship to behold,
And long'd to tempt him, like good Job of old:
~~But measures change, the Devil is grown, Satan, more a Witch,~~
~~And tempts not, by making poor, but making rich~~

But times are chang'd; measures change; and wiser. n of yore
But Satan now is wiser than of yore;
He tempts
& tempts by making rich, not making poor.

Rouz'd by the Prince of Air, the Whirlwinds sweep
The Surge, & plunge his Father in the Deep; —
Then full against his Cornish Lands they roar,
And two rich Shipwrecks bless the lucky Shore.

Sir Balaam now, he lives like other folks;
He takes his chirping Pint; he cracks his Jokes:
"Live like yourself" was soon my Lady's word;
And lo! two Puddings smok'd upon the Board.

Asleep, and naked, as an Indian lay,
An honest Factor stole a Gem away;
He pledg'd it to the Knight, the Knight had wit,
So ~~robb'd the Robber, & was rich as~~ — | So kept ye Diamond, & ye Rogue was bit.
Some Scruple past, but thus he eas'd his thought;
"I'll now give Sixpence where I gave a Groat,
"Where once I went to Church, I'll now go twice,
"And am so clear too, of all other Vice".

you
What but a Want, w^ch ~~we~~ perhaps think mad,
280 Yet numbers feel, the Want of what he <u>had</u>.
Cutler, and Brutus, dying both exclaim, X
"<u>Virtue</u>! and <u>Wealth</u>! what are ye but a <u>Name</u>?
Say, for such Worth are other worlds prepar'd,
Or are they, both, in this their own Reward?

That *my Lord,*
285 ^~~This~~ knotty Point, ~~which~~ shall I ~~next~~ discuss,
Or tell a Tale?—A Tale—It follows thus.
A plain, good Citizen, of sober fame,
In <u>Cheapside</u> dwelt, and <u>Balaam</u> was his name.
Religious, punctual, frugal, & so forth÷
290 His Word w^d pass for more than he was worth.

week
One solid Dish his ~~each~~ day Meal affords;
An added Pudding solemniz'd the Lord's.
Constant at Church, & Change; his Gains were sure,
His Givings rare, save Farthings to the Poor.
295 The Dev'l was piqu'd, such Saintship to behold,
And long'd to tempt him, like good Job of old:

~~*the Dev'l is grown*~~
~~But Measures change, &^Satan, more a Witch,~~
~~*And*~~ ~~*no more*~~
^~~Tempts not^by making poor, but making rich~~
Rouz'd by the Prince of Air, the Whirlwinds sweep
300 The Surge, & plunge his Father in the Deep;—
Then full against his <u>Cornish</u> Lands they roar,
And two rich Shipwrecks bless the lucky Shore.
<u>Sir</u> <u>Balaam</u> now, he lives likes other folks;
He takes his chirping <u>Pint</u>; he cracks his Jokes:
305 "Live like yourself" was soon my Lady's word;
And lo! two Puddings smok'd upon the Board.
Asleep, and naked, as an Indian lay,
An honest Factor stole a Gem away;
He pledg'd it to the Knight, the Knight had wit,
Rogue
310 ~~So robbd the Robber, & was rich as~~ — / *So kept ye Diamond, & y^e ~~Thief~~^ was bit.*
Some Scruple past, but thus he eas'd his thought;
"I'll now give Sixpence where I gave a Groat,

~~*For*~~
"Where once I went to Church, I'll now go twice,
"And ~~stand~~ so clear ~~of ev'ry~~ other Vice."
am *too, of all*

[Margin:]

was
Where London's Monum^t is rear'd so high
Like some tall Bully, to look big & lye
~~Edwyn reard ye Monum^t so high~~
towring to ye Skies
Where Londons Column towrs into y^e ^

lifts ye head and
Like some proud Bully, y^t looks tall, & lies;
to look *lye*

There dwelt a Citizen of sober fame,
A plain good man, & —

times are changd; and wiser y^n of yore
But measures change;

He tempts
But Satan now is wiser than of yore;
& tempts by making rich, not making poor.

285: This knotty Point,] originally *A knotty Point!*

298: Tempts] altered to *tempts*.

310: rich as —] i.e., Thomas Pitt.

Margin: Edwyn] See above, p. 47, note 117.

The Tempter saw his Time; the work he ply'd,
Stocks & Subscriptions pour on ev'ry side,
And all the Dæmon makes his full descent,
In one abundant Show'r of Cent per Cent.

Behold, Sir Balaam seems a Man of Spirit,
Ascribes his Gettings to his Parts & Merit,
What late he call'd a Blessing, now was Wit,
And God's good Providence, a Lucky Hit.
Things chang'd their names, & took another turn;
His Counting-house imploy'd the Sunday-morn;
Seldom at Church; 'twas such a busy Life,
But duely sent his Family and Wife:
There (so the Dev'l ordain'd) one Christmass-tide
My good old Lady catch'd a Cold, & dy'd.

A Nymph of Quality admires our Knight,
He marries, bows at Court, & grows polite:
Leaves the dull City, & joins (to please ye Fair)
The well-bred Cuckolds in St. James's air.
First, for his Son, a gay Commission buys,
Who drinks, whores, fights, & in a Duel dies.
His Daughter flaunts a Viscount's taudry Wife
She bears a Coronet & P-x for Life.
In Britain's Senate He a Seat obtains,
And one more Pensioner St. Stephen gains.
my Lady falls to play; so bad her chance,
He must repair it; takes a Bribe from France;
The House impeach him; Co— by harangues,
The Court forsakes him; & Sir Balaam hangs.
Wife, Son, & Daughter, Satan! are thy prize,
And sad Sir Balaam curses God & dies.

my Lady games ... plies the cards;

Finis.

The Tempter saw his Time; the work he ply'd, 315
Stocks & Subscriptions pour on ev'ry side,
And all the Dæmon makes his full descent,
In one abundant Show'r of Cent per Cent.
Behold, Sir Balaam turns a man of Spirit,
Ascribes his Gettings to his Parts & Merit, 320
What late he calld a Blessing, now was Wit
And God's good Providence, a lucky Hit.
Things chang'd their names, & took another turn;
His Counting-house imployd the Sunday-morn;
Seldom at Church, 'twas such a busy Life, 325

But
~~Yet~~ duely sent his Family and Wife:

There,
~~Till~~ (so the Dev'l ordain'd) one Christmass-tide

catchd a
My good old Lady ~~there, took~~ Cold, & dy'd.
A Nymph of Quality admires our Knight,
He marries, bows at Court, & grows polite: 330
Leaves the dull Cits, & joins (to please y[e] Fair)
The well-bred Cuckolds in St. James's Air.
First, for his Son, a gay Commission buys,
Who drinks, whores, fights, & in a Duel dies.
His Daughter flaunts a Viscount's taudry wife 335
She bears a Coronet & P-x for Life.
In Britain's Senate He a seat obtains,
And one more Pensioner St. Stephen gains.

~~My Lady games all day; so plies the Dice;~~ *Cards;*

My Lady ~~takes to~~ falls to Play ~~And~~ so bad
~~When lo! my Lady games — so vile~~ her chāce,
He must repair it; takes a Bribe frō France; 340

him,
The House impeach~~es~~, Co–by harangues;
The Court forsakes him; & Sir Balaam—hangs.
Wife, Son, & Daughter, Satan! are thy prize,
And sad Sir Balaam curses God & dies.

Finis.

327a: There] originally *Where*.

341: Co–by] Thomas, Earl Coningsby.

HM 6008

Gold but mean

most wisely
most sure that wealth's
Both wisely leaning to
Maintain. this Wealth no
But lent

Gold but mean

Most wisely

Most sure that Wealth's

Both wisely leaning to

Maintain this Wealth no

But sent

The recto of this leaf, which is conjugate with leaf "1" of Manuscript III (pages 104, 108), is blank.

◆ The Edition of 1732 ◆

OF THE

USE OF RICHES,

AN

EPISTLE

To the Right Honorable

ALLEN Lord BATHURST.

By Mr. POPE.

London:

Printed by J. Wright, for Lawton Gilliver

at Homer's Head against St. Dunstan's Church in

Fleetstreet, 1732.

AN

EPISTLE

To the Right Honorable

ALLEN Lord BATHURST

Who shall decide, when Doctors dis-agree,
And soundest Casuists doubt, like you and me?
You hold the word from Jove to Momus giv'n,
That Man was made the standing Jest of Heav'n,
(5) And Gold but sent to keep the Fools in play,
For half to heap, and half to throw away.

But I, who think more highly of our Kind,
(And surely Heav'n and I are of a mind)
Opine, that Nature, as in duty bound,
(10) Deep hid the shining Mischief under ground:
But when, by Man's audacious Labor won,
Flam'd forth this Rival to its Sire the Sun,
Then, in plain prose, were made two sorts of men,
To squander some, and some to hide agen.
(15) Like Doctors thus, when much Dispute has past,
We find our Tenets just the same at last:
Both fairly owning Riches in effect
No Grace of Heav'n, or Token of th'Elect;
Giv'n to the Fool, the Mad, the Vain, the Evil,
(20) To W—rd, to W—t—rs, Ch—rs, and the Devil.
What Nature wants, commodious Gold bestows,
'Tis thus we eat the bread another sows:
But how unequal it bestows, observe,
'Tis thus we riot, while who sow it, starve.
(25) What Nature wants (a phrase I much distrust)

Extends to Luxury, extends to Lust;
And if we count among the Needs of life
Another's Toil, why not another's Wife?
Useful, we grant, it serves what life requires,
(30) But dreadful too, the dark Assassin hires:
Trade it may help, Society extend;
But lures the Pyrate, and corrupts the Friend:
It raises Armies in a nation's aid,
But bribes a Senate, and the Land's betray'd.

(35) Oh! that such Bulky bribes as all might *see*
Still, as of old, encumber'd Villainy!
In vain may Heroes fight, and Patriots rave,
If secret Gold saps on from knave to knave.
Could France or Rome divert our brave designs,
(40) With all their brandies, or with all their wines?
What could they more than knights and squires confound,
Or water all the Quorum ten miles round?
A statesman's slumbers how this speech would spoil,
"Sir, Spain has sent a thousand jars of oyl;
(45) "Huge bales of British cloth blockade the door;
"A hundred Oxen at your levee roar.
Poor Avarice one torment more would find,
Nor could Profusion squander all, in kind.
Astride his Cheese Sir Morgan might we meet,
(50) And Worldly crying Coals from street to street,
Whom with a Wig so wild, and Mien so maz'd,
Pity mistakes for some poor Tradesman craz'd.
Had H—wl—y's fortune layn in Hops and Hogs,
Scarce H—wl—y's self had sent it to the dogs.
(55) His Grace will game: to White's a Bull be led,
With spurning heels and with a butting head;
To White's be carry'd, as to ancient Games,
Fair Coursers, Vases, and alluring Dames.
Shall then Uxorio, if the stakes he sweep,
(60) Bear home six Whores, and make his Lady weep?
Or soft Adonis, so perfum'd and fine,
Drive to St. James's a whole herd of Swine?
Oh filthy Check on all industrious skill,
To spoil the Nation's last great Trade, Quadrille!

(65) Once, we confess, beneath the Patriot's cloak,*
From the crack'd bagg the dropping Guinea spoke,
And gingling down the back-stairs, told the Crew,
"Old Cato is as great a Rogue as you."

* *Beneath the Patriot's Cloak.*] This is a true Story, which happen'd in the Reign of King William, to an eminent unsuspected old Patriot; who coming out at the Back-door from having been closeted by the King, where he had received a large Bag of Guineas, the Bursting of the Bag discover'd his Business there.

Blest Paper-credit! that advanc'd so high,
(70) Shall lend Corruption lighter wings to fly!
Gold, imp'd with this, may compass hardest things,
May pocket States, or fetch or carry Kings;
A single Leaf may waft an Army o'er,
Or ship off Senates to some distant shore;
(75) A Leaf like Sybil's, scatter to and fro
Our Fates and Fortunes, as the winds shall blow.
Well then, since with the world we stand or fall,
Come take it as we find it, Gold and all.
What Riches give us, let us first enquire:
(80) Meat, fire, and cloaths; what more? Meat, cloaths, and fire.
Is this too little? wou'd you more than live?
Alas 'tis more than Tu**r finds they give.
Alas 'tis more than (all his Visions past.)
Unhappy Wh**n waking found at last!
(85) What can they give? to dying † H*p*s, Heirs?
To Chartres, Vigour? Japhet, Nose and Ears?
Can they in Gems bid pallid Hippia glow?
In Fulvia's Buckle ease the Throbs below?
Or heal, old Narses, thy obscener ail,
(90) With all th'Embroid'ry plaister'd at thy Tail?
They might, (were Harpax not too wise to spend)
Give Harpax self the Blessing of a Friend;
Or find some Doctor, that wou'd save the Life
Of wretched Shylock, spite of Shylock's Wife.
(95) But thousands die, without or this, or that,
Die, and endow a College, or a * Cat:
To some indeed Heav'n grants the happier Fate
T'enrich a Bastard, or a Son they hate.

Perhaps you think the Poor might have their part?
(100) B*nd damns the Poor, and hates them from his heart:
The grave Sir G**t holds it for a Rule,
That every Man in want is Knave or Fool:
"God cannot love, (says Bl*t, with lifted eyes)
"The Wretch he starves"—and piously denies:
(105) But Rev'rend S**n with a softer Air,
Admits, and leaves them, Providence's Care.
Yet, to be just to these poor Men of Pelf,
Each does but hate his Neighbour as himself:

† A Citizen whose Rapacity obtain'd him the Name of Vultur. He dy'd worth three hundred thousand Pounds, and left it to no Person living, but to the first Son that should be born of the first Daughter of his next Relation. Being told by his Lawyer, that it would probably be thirty Years before his Money could be inherited, and it must all that time lie at Interest, he answer'd, He liked it the better, and so died.

Japhet, Nose and Ears.] Japhet Crook alias Sir Peter Stranger, was punish'd with the Loss of those Parts, for having forg'd a Conveyance of an Estate to himself, upon which he took up several Thousand Pounds. He was at the same time sued in Chancery on suggestion of having fraudulently obtain'd a Will, by which he possest another very considerable Estate, in wrong of the Brother of the Deceas'd.

* A famous Dutchess in her last Will left considerable Annuities and Legacies to her Cats.

Damn'd to the Mines, an equal Fate betides
(110) The Slave that digs it, and the Slave that hides.
Who suffer thus, meer Charity should own
Must act on Reasons pow'rful tho' unknown:
Some War, some Plague, some Famine they foresee,
Some Revelation, hid from you and me.
(115) Why S—l—k wants a Meal, the cause is found,
He thinks a Loaf will rise to fifty pound.
What made Directors cheat in South-Sea year?
To live on Ven'son when it sold so dear.*[1]
Ask you why Phryne the whole Auction buys?
(120) Phryne foresees a General Excise.
Why she and Lesbia raise that monstrous Sum?
Alas! they fear a Man will cost a Plum.

Wise Peter sees the World's respect for Gold,
And therefore hopes this Nation may be sold:
(125) Glorious Ambition! Peter, swell thy store,
And be what Rome's great *[2]Didius was before.
The Crown of Poland venal twice an Age
To just three Millions stinted modest——.
But nobler Scenes Maria's Dreams unfold,
(130) Hereditary Realms, and Worlds of Gold.
Congenial Souls! whose Life one Av'rice joins,
And one Fate buries in th' *[3]Asturian Mines.
Much-injur'd Bl—t! why bears he Britain's hate?
A Wizard told him in these words our fate.
(135) "At length Corruption, like a gen'ral Flood,
"(So long by watchful Ministers withstood)
"Shall deluge all; and Av'rice creeping on,
"Spread like a low-born Mist, and blot the Sun;
"Statesman and Patriot ply alike the Stocks,
(140) "Peeress and Butler share alike the Box,
"The Judge shall job, the Bishop bite the Town,
"And mighty Dukes pack Cards for half a crown.
"See Britain sunk in Lucre's sordid charms,
"And France reveng'd of Anne's and Edward's Arms!
(145) No poor Court-Badge, great Scriv'ner! fir'd thy brain,
No Lordly Luxury, no City Gain:
But 'twas thy righteous End, asham'd to see
Senates degen'rate, Patriots disagree,
And nobly wishing Party Rage to cease,
(150) To buy both Sides, and give thy Country Peace.

*[1] In the Extravagance and Luxury of the South-Sea Year, the Price of a Haunch of Venison was from three to five pounds.

*[2] A Roman Lawyer, so rich as to purchase the Empire, when it was set to Sale by the Prætorian Bands on the Death of Pertinax.

*[3] Two persons of distinction, each of whom in the time of the Mississipi despised to realize above three hundred thousand pound; the Gentleman with a view to the Crown of Poland, the Lady on a Vision of the like nature. They since retir'd together into Spain, where they are still in search of Gold in the Mines of the Asturies.

"All this is madness, cries a sober Sage,
But who, my Friend, has Reason in his Rage?
The ruling Passion, be it what it will,
The ruling Passion conquers Reason still.
(155) Less mad the wildest Whimsey we can frame,
Than ev'n that Passion, if it has no Aim;
For tho' such Motives Folly you may call,
The Folly's greater to have none at all.
Hear then the truth: 'Tis Heav'n each Passion sends,
(160) And diff'rent Men directs to diff'rent Ends.
"Extremes in Nature equal Good produce,
"Extremes in Man concur to general Use.
Ask we what makes one keep, and one bestow?
That Pow'r who bids the Ocean ebb and flow;
(165) Bids Seed-time, Harvest, equal course maintain,
Thro' reconcil'd Extremes of Drought and Rain;
Builds Life on Death; on Change Duration founds,
And gives th'eternal Wheels to know their rounds.
Riches, like Insects, when conceal'd they lie,
(170) Wait but for Wings, and in their Season, fly.
Who sees pale Mammon pine amidst his Store,
Sees but a backward Steward for the Poor;
This Year a Reservoir, to keep and spare,
The next, a Fountain spouting thro' his Heir,
(175) In lavish Streams to quench a Country's thirst,
And Men, and Dogs, shall drink him till they burst.

Old Cotta sham'd his fortune, and his birth,
Yet was not Cotta void of wit or worth:
What tho' (the use of barb'rous Spits forgot)
(180) His Kitchen vy'd in coolness with his Grot;
His Court with Nettles, Moat with Cresses stor'd,
With Soups unbought, and Sallads, blest his board.
If Cotta liv'd on Pulse, it was no more
Than Bramins, Saints, and Sages did before;
(185) To cram the Rich, was prodigal expence,
And who would take the Poor from Providence?
Like some lone Chartreuse stands the good old Hall,
Silence without, and Fasts within the wall;
No rafter'd Roofs with Dance and Tabor sound,
(190) No Noontide-bell invites the Country round;
Tenants with sighs the smoakless Tow'rs survey,
And turn th' unwilling Steeds another way,
Benighted wanderers, the Forest o'er,
Curse the sav'd Candle, and unopening Door:
(195) While the gaunt Mastiff, growling at the Gate,
Affrights the Begger whom he longs to eat.
Not so his Son, he mark'd this oversight,

And then mistook reverse of wrong for right:
For what to shun will no great knowledge need,
(200) But what to follow is a task indeed.
What slaughter'd Hecatombs, what floods of wine,
Fill the capacious Squire and deep Divine!
Yet no mean motive this profusion draws,
His Oxen perish in his Country's cause.
(205) 'Tis the dear Prince (Sir John) that crowns thy cup,
And Zeal for his great House that eats thee up.
The woods recede around the naked seat,
The sylvans groan—no matter—"for the Fleet."
Next goes his wool—"to clothe our valiant bands:"
(210) Last, for his country's love, he sells his lands.
Bankrupt, at Court in vain he pleads his cause,
His thankless Country leaves him to her Laws.

The Sense to value Riches, with the Art
T'enjoy them, and the Virtue to impart,
(215) Not meanly, nor ambitiously persu'd,
Not sunk by sloth, nor rais'd by servitude;
To balance Fortune by a just expence,
Joyn with Oeconomy, Magnificence;
With Splendor Charity, with Plenty Health;
(220) Oh teach us, BATHURST yet unspoil'd by wealth!
That secret rare, between th' extremes to move
Of mad Good nature, and of mean Self-love.
To want or worth, well-weigh'd, be bounty given,
And ease, or emulate, the care of Heaven.
(225) Whose measure full, o'erflows on human race,
Mends Fortune's fault, and justifies her grace.
Wealth in the gross is Death, but Life diffus'd;
As Poyson heals, in just proportion us'd:
In heaps, like Ambergrise, a stink it lies,
(230) But well dispers'd, is Incense to the skies.

Who starves by Nobles, or with Nobles eats?
The wretch that trusts them, and the rogue that cheats.
Is there a Lord, who knows a chearful noon
Without a Fidler, Flatt'rer, or Buffoon?
(235) Whose Table, Wit, or modest Merit share,
Un-elbow'd by a Gamester, Pimp, or Play'r?
Who copies Yours or OXFORD's better part,
To ease th' oppress'd, and raise the sinking heart?
Where-e'er he shines, oh Fortune gild the scene,
(240) And Angels guard him in the golden Mean!
There English Bounty yet a while may stand,
And Honor linger, e're it leaves the Land.
But all our praises why should Lords engross?

Rise honest Muse! and sing the Man of Ross:
(245) Pleas'd Vaga ecchoes thro' her winding bounds,
And rapid Severn hoarse applause resounds.
Who hung with woods yon mountains sultry brow?
From the dry rock who bade the waters flow?
Not to the skies in useless columns tost,
(250) Or in proud falls magnificently lost,
But clear and artless, pouring thro' the plain
Health to the sick, and solace to the swain.
Whose Cause-way parts the vale with shady rows?
Whose Seats the weary Traveller repose?
(255) Who feeds yon Alms-house, neat, but void of state,
Where Age and Want sit smiling at the gate?
Who taught that heav'n-directed Spire to rise?
The Man of Ross, each lisping babe replies.
Behold the market-place with poor o'erspread!
(260) The Man of Ross divides the weekly bread:
Him portion'd maids, apprentic'd orphans blest,
The young who labour, and the old who rest.
Is any sick? the Man of Ross relieves;
Prescribes, attends, the med'cine makes, and gives.
(265) Is there a variance? enter but his door,
Balk'd are the courts, and contest is no more.
Despairing Quacks with curses fled the place,
And vile Attornies, now an useless race.
"Thrice happy man! enabled to persue
(270) "What all so wish, but want the pow'r to do.
"Oh say, what sums that gen'rous hand supply?
"What mines to swell that boundless Charity?
Of debts and taxes, wife and children clear,
This man possest—five hundred pounds a year.† [1]
(275) Blush Grandeur, blush! proud Courts withdraw your blaze.
Ye little *Stars*! hide your diminish'd rays.

"And what? no Monument, Inscription, Stone?
"His Race, his Form, his Name almost unknown?
Who builds a Church to God, and not to Fame,
(280) Will never mark the marble with his name.
Go search it there † [2], where to be born and die,
Of Rich and Poor makes all the history:
Enough that Virtue fill'd the space between;
Prov'd, by the Ends of Being, to have been.
(285) When H * p * s dies, a thousand Lights attend
The Wretch, who living sav'd a Candle's end:
Should'ring God's altar a vile Image stands,

† [1] This Person, who with no greater Estate, perform'd all these good Works, and whose true Name was almost lost (partly by having the Title of the *Man of Ross* given him by way of Eminence, and partly by being buried without any Inscription) was called Mr. *John Kyrle*: He died in the Year 1724, aged near 90, and lies buried in the Chancel of the Church of Ross in Herefordshire.

† [2] The Parish-Register.

Belies his features, nay extends his hands;
That live-long Wig which Gorgon's self might own,
(290) Eternal buckle takes in Parian stone.
Behold! what blessings Wealth to Life can lend,
And see, what comfort it affords our End!

In the worst Inn's worst room, with matt half-hung,
The floors of plaister, and the walls of dung,
(295) On once a flockbed, but repair'd with straw,
With tape-ty'd curtains, never meant to draw,
The George and Garter dangling from that bed
Where tawdry yellow strove with dirty red,
Great Villers lies—alas! how chang'd from him,
(300) That Life of Pleasure, and that Soul of Whym,
Gallant and gay, in Cliveden's proud alcove
The Bow'r of wanton Sh***y and Love;
Or just as gay, at Council, in a ring
Of mimick'd Statesmen and the merry King.
(305) No Wit to flatter, left of all his store!
No Fool to laugh at, which he valued more.
There, Victor of his health, of fortune, friends,
And fame, this Lord of useless thousands ends!
His Grace's fate sage Cutler could foresee,
(310) And well (he thought) advis'd him, "Live like me."
As well his Grace reply'd, "Like you, Sir John?
"That I can do, when all I have is gone."
Resolve me Reason, which of these is worse?
Want with a full, or with an empty purse:
(315) Thy Life more wretched, Cutler, was confess'd;
Arise, and tell me, was thy Death more bless'd?
Cutler saw Tenants break, and houses fall,
For very want; he could not build a wall.
His only Daughter in a Stranger's Pow'r,
(320) For very want; he could not pay a Dow'r.
A few grey hairs his rev'rend temples crown'd,
'Twas very want that sold them for two pound.
What ev'n deny'd a cordial at his end,
Banish'd the Doctor, and expell'd the friend?
(325) What but a want, which you perhaps think mad,
Yet numbers feel; the want of what he had.
Cutler and Brutus, dying both exclaim,
"Virtue! and Wealth! what are ye but a Name?"

Say, for such worth are other worlds prepar'd?
(330) Or are they both, in this, their own reward?
That knotty point, my Lord, shall I discuss,
Or tell a Tale?—A Tale—it follows thus.

Where * London's Column pointing at the skies
Like a tall Bully, lifts the head, and lyes:
(335) There dwelt a Citizen of sober fame,
A plain good man, and Balaam was his name.
Religious, punctual, frugal, and so forth—
His word would pass for more than he was worth.
One solid dish his week-day meal affords,
(340) An added pudding solemniz'd the Lord's.
Constant at Church, and Change; his gains were sure,
His givings rare, save farthings to the poor.

The Dev'l was piqu'd, such saintship to behold,
And long'd to tempt him like good Job of old:
(345) But Satan now is wiser than of yore,
And tempts by making rich, not making poor.
Rouz'd by the Prince of Air, the whirlwinds sweep
The surge, and plunge his Father in the deep;
Then full against his Cornish lands they roar,
(350) And two rich Ship-wrecks bless the lucky shore.
Sir Balaam now, he lives like other folks,
He takes his chirping pint, he cracks his jokes:
"Live like your self," was soon my Lady's word;
And lo! two puddings smok'd upon the board.
(355) Asleep and naked as an Indian lay,
An honest Factor stole a Gem away:
He pledg'd it to the Knight; the Knight had wit,
So kept the Diamond, and the Rogue was bit:
Some Scruple rose, but thus he eas'd his thought,
(360) "I'll now give six-pence where I gave a groat,
"Where once I went to church, I'll now go twice,
"And am so clear too, of all other Vice."
The Tempter saw his time; the work he ply'd,
Stocks and Subscriptions pour on ev'ry side;
(365) And all the Dæmon makes his full descent,
In one abundant Show'r of *Cent. per Cent.*
Sinks deep within him and possesses whole,
Then dubs *Director* and secures his Soul.

Behold Sir Balaam now a man of spirit,
(370) Ascribes his gettings to his parts and merit,
What late he call'd a Blessing, now was Wit,
And God's good providence, a lucky Hit.
Things change their titles as our manners turn,
His Compting-house imploy'd the Sunday-morn;
(375) Seldom at church, ('twas such a busy life)

* The Monument built in Memory of the Fire of London, with an Inscription importing that City to have been burn'd by the Papists.

But duly sent his family and wife.
There (so the Dev'l ordain'd) one Christmas-tide,
My good old Lady catch'd a cold, and dy'd.
  A Nymph of Quality admires our Knight;
(380) He marries, bows at Court, and grows polite:
Leaves the dull Cits, and joins (to please the fair)
The well-bred Cuckolds in St. James's air:
First, for his son a gay commission buys,
Who drinks, whores, fights, and in a duel dies.
(385) His daughter flaunts a Viscount's tawdry wife,
She bears a Coronet and P—x for life.
In Britain's Senate he a seat obtains,
And one more Pensioner St. Stephen gains.
My Lady falls to Play: so bad her chance,
(390) He must repair it; takes a bribe from France;
The House impeach him; Co**by harangues,
The Court forsakes him, and Sir Balaam hangs:
Wife, son, and daughter, Satan! are thy prize,
And sad Sir Balaam curses God and dies.